BASEBALL'S
100

BASEBALL'S 100

A Personal Ranking
of the Best Players
in Baseball History

Maury Allen

A&W VISUAL LIBRARY
New York

Published by
A&W Publishers, Inc.
95 Madison Avenue
New York, New York 10016

Designed by RFS Graphic Design, Inc.
Credit for photographs that appear on pages 4, 26, 76, 180, 300: United Press
International (Photo)
Library of Congress Number: 80-70369
ISBN: 0-89104-200-8

Printed in the United States of America

For Jennifer
She made me a father and I've made her a fan.

Baseball's 100

1 Willie Mays
2 Hank Aaron
3 Babe Ruth
4 Ted Williams
5 Stan Musial
6 Joe DiMaggio
7 Ty Cobb
8 Lou Gehrig
9 Walter Johnson
10 Rogers Hornsby
11 Jackie Robinson
12 Roberto Clemente
13 Christy Mathewson
14 Tris Speaker
15 Mel Ott
16 George Sisler
17 Grover Cleveland
   Alexander
18 Lefty Grove
19 Bill Dickey
20 Mickey Mantle
21 Rod Carew
22 Reggie Jackson
23 Sandy Koufax
24 Bob Feller
25 Pete Rose
26 Dizzy Dean
27 Warren Spahn
28 Hank Greenberg
29 Yogi Berra
30 Mickey Cochrane
31 Whitey Ford
32 Jimmie Foxx
33 Al Kaline
34 Carl Hubbell
35 Tom Seaver
36 Eddie Collins
37 Frankie Frisch
38 Gaylord Perry
39 Al Simmons

40 Paul Waner
41 Joe Morgan
42 Charlie Gehringer
43 Johnny Bench
44 Lou Brock
45 Carl Yastrzemski
46 Ralph Kiner
47 Steve Garvey
48 Jim Palmer
49 Bob Gibson
50 Brooks Robinson
51 Chuck Klein
52 Gabby Hartnett
53 Ernie Banks
54 Burleigh Grimes
55 Roy Campanella
56 Rube Marquard
57 Richie Allen
58 Maury Wills
59 Bob Lemon
60 Joe Cronin
61 Bill Terry
62 Three Finger Brown
63 Frank Robinson
64 Sparky Lyle
65 Willie McCovey
66 Juan Marichal
67 Willie Stargell
68 Mel Harder
69 Robin Roberts
70 Harmon Killebrew
71 Lou Boudreau
72 George Foster
73 Babe Herman
74 Marty Marion
75 Dave Parker
76 Phil Rizzuto
77 Fred Lynn
78 Pee Wee Reese
79 Nolan Ryan

80 Jim Bunning
81 Don Drysdale
82 George Brett
83 Duke Snider
84 Red Ruffing
85 Luke Appling
86 Eddie Mathews
87 Pie Traynor
88 Dave Winfield
89 Phil Niekro
90 Catfish Hunter

91 Jim Kaat
92 Joe Gordon
93 Fergie Jenkins
94 Billy Williams
95 Tony Oliva
96 Johnny Mize
97 Mark Belanger
98 Jim Rice
99 Don Sutton
100 Roger Maris

10 Honorable Mentions
10 Best Left-handed Hitters
10 Best Left-handed Pitchers
10 Best Right-handed
  Pitchers
10 Best Right-handed Hitters
10 Best Managers
10 Best General Managers
10 Best Defensive Infielders
10 Best Defensive Outfielders
10 Best Baseball Parks

Photo Acknowledgments

All photos of current players and of players of the recent past were supplied by the public relations directors of the major-league clubs. I thank them for their kindness. All photos of deceased players and of those who played before 1950 were supplied by a famed Chicago photo historian, George Brace. I thank him for those precious old pictures.

Acknowledgments

This is a work that has given me much pleasure. It was a joy to watch baseball as a kid and gain so many vivid impressions. It continues to be a thrill as an adult to observe baseball professionally as a sportswriter. To sit in the sun in Florida, to sit with the bleacher bums at Wrigley Field, to eat ice cream at Shea and watch Willie Mays play, to lean forward at Yankee Stadium to catch the disappearance of another Mantle homer, all adds up to a sweet way of making a living.

All of the observations here are my own. All disagreements and poison-pen letters are to be addressed to me.

But so many of the numbers, the evidence in my decisions, the small facts I needed to help my case came from many sources.

I thank, first, all my colleagues in journalism for making their strong arguments and helping to clarify my own. I needed facts from *The Book of Baseball Records*, the *Official Baseball Register, The Baseball Encyclopedia*, the *Sporting News* Daguerreotypes, and Martin Appel's glorious *Baseball's Best, the Hall of Fame Gallery*.

Mostly, as always, I needed the love, patience, and understanding of my troops, Janet, Jennifer, and Teddy.

Baseball, gentlemen, baseball.

JIMMY CANNON

You could look it up.

CASEY STENGEL

The only real game in the world, I think, is baseball.

BABE RUTH

Baseball's 100

I have been watching baseball games for more than forty years. I have been writing about baseball professionally for nearly a quarter of a century. When I was eight years old, I brought a brown bag filled with salami sandwiches to more than thirty Brooklyn Dodgers games at Ebbets Field. When I was fifteen I slept on the sidewalk at Bedford Avenue and Sullivan Place before a World Series game against the Yankees. I cried bitterly and refused to eat dinner when Bobby Thomson homered off Ralph Branca. In 1955, when I was stationed in Japan with the Army, I listened on Armed Forces radio as Elston Howard rolled out to Pee Wee Reese for the first and only Brooklyn Dodger World Series triumph. In 1958 I cursed Walter O'Malley nightly for moving my Dodgers to Los Angeles.

I have met presidents, governors, senators, and congressmen. I know famous writers, artists, musicians, and industrialists. The most exciting man I ever met—my only hero—was Casey Stengel.

Baseball is my job and my hobby. The New York Public Library, where I spend hours reading old clippings of past games, and the Baseball Hall of Fame at Cooperstown, are my two favorite buildings.

As a kid I read the sports pages of a dozen daily New York newspapers. I subscribed to every baseball magazine. I have read almost every baseball book ever published. I have written more than twenty of my own. My mother looked at me strangely in the early 1940s and said, "That boy eats, sleeps, and breathes baseball." Now this man does.

In the 1930s growing up in New York, the names I heard and read about most often were Babe Ruth and Lou Gehrig. In the 1940s it was Joe DiMaggio and Ted Williams. In the 1950s, as I started covering sports myself, it was Mickey Mantle, Willie Mays, and Duke Snider. The 1960s belonged to Sandy Koufax. The 1970s were Hank Aaron and Lou Brock and Pete Rose and Maury Wills and Johnny Bench and Tom Seaver. In the first year of the 1980s it was George Brett and Reggie Jackson and Fred Lynn and Dave Winfield.

Then it struck me. Which of these men was best? Who was the best pitcher ever, a great of the 1920s like Walter Johnson or a commanding pitcher of the 1970s like Tom Seaver? Was Ruth really the best ever, as most observers always suggested, or was he the most publicized, the most adored, the most exciting for having hit 60 homers in one season (Roger Maris hit 61 and did that make him better?), 714 in a career (and Aaron had 755)—or for having eaten more hot dogs than any other player, hit more homers for dying kids, or caused more national furor over his antics? Did the Babe ever play a day game after a night doubleheader? How would Willie Mays have performed if he had Mondays and Thursdays off almost every week as the Babe did, never saw a hard-throwing relief pitcher in the eighth or ninth inning, never had to travel in an airplane across country, never had jet lag, never performed under the watchful eye of millions of people on television? Any modern player has performed before more people, courtesy of television, in any one game than saw Lou Gehrig in his lifetime. Was it a factor?

What about the impact of the black player on the game? If the Babe was best, he was the best among only the white segment of the population because the blacks, before Jackie Robinson in 1947, simply didn't exist for major-league baseball. How different would baseball be today if Jackie Robinson had hit the first player to call him a racial name and was banned for life, as all of his colored brethren before him were banned for their lives?

There was also the significant factor of salaries. A handful of players today are making more than a million dollars a year. Are they better than those who made three and four thousand dollars a half a century ago? Does big money make a player perform better or worse?

So I decided to take in all the changing conditions and rate baseball's best players from number 1 to number 100, not just hitters against hitters, but pitchers against hitters, batters against fielders, pitchers against relief pitchers. All of the factors were vital: day ball to night ball, cross-country flights to quiet railroad trips from New York to Boston, airplane food against dining-car food, television coverage against no coverage, small press coverage, and some radio coverage, pressures of modern baseball against the relaxed times of the past, huge salaries to meager salaries.

I arbitrarily set only one boundary in judging them. No player who performed in the nineteenth century was eligible. There have been more than ten thousand players in the major leagues from 1900 to the present. They were the only ones I examined.

I was influenced, most certainly, by those I saw over the last forty years. But I had studied, read about, and discussed the others, sometimes with teammates (Casey Stengel told me about every player, from 1910 on, whom he had played with or against), sometimes with old sportswriters, sometimes with retired officials of the game.

The major problem was not in crossing eras—having spanned six decades myself I could deal with those changes—but in comparing pitchers and hitters, fielders and pitchers, pitchers of the 1920s against pitchers of the 1980s.

The numbers in baseball are important. The .300 average is as significant a mark of excellence today as it was fifty years ago. So is a pitcher's twenty games won. But did he do it with a dead ball or a live ball? Did he do it in a big ball park or a small one? Did he do it with night games or only day games? Did he do it under the hot lights of television or in the calm, quiet days in St. Louis?

So now I come to *Baseball's 100*, the best of the best, some equally recognized by all, Hall of Famers, accepted stars, recognized heroes. Some are strange selections, included here because of the influence on the game, on the country, or simply on me.

When I was young and argued the relative merits of players with kids in the street, we often would wind up screaming, fighting, and cursing. Torn pants would be my medal of honor. Then, later, it would be a discussion with an old player or an old manager, and they might say, "Yep, you might be right on that one."

Now I have picked my 100. I might be right on all of them, some of them, none of them. It is for the reader to decide. Are these Baseball's 100 or only mine? Are they yours? Who shouldn't be here? Whom did I leave out? Let's hear your picks. Let's not fight about it or tear our pants. Let's just have fun.

That, my friends, is why I have been in love with baseball for so many years.

Willie Mays

(*1951–1973*)

On a bright, sunny Sunday afternoon, October 14, 1973, the greatness of Willie Mays was etched deep into the public mind.

It was the second game of the World Series, Charles O. Finley's bombastic Oakland A's against the New York Mets, managed by that lovable gnome, Yogi Berra.

Oakland's Deron Johnson was at the plate. Mays, much gray around the edges of his hair, extra girth around his middle, and his face lined with the ravages of twenty-two baseball seasons, was in center field for New York. He had started as a New York Giant in 1951 and was near the end now as a New York Met at age forty-two.

A high line drive sailed off Johnson's bat, cutting through the high sky, moving toward Mays as he flipped his sunglasses down and searched out the ball. His feet suddenly twisted under him. He groped for the baseball. He staggered under it like a Saturday night drunk. And then he fell.

There were 49,151 witnesses to that event in the stands and millions more on television. There was an almost universal gasp, cutting across the streets of San Francisco, racing across the Great Plains, driving past the Mississippi, ending on the sidewalks of New York.

Willie Mays had fallen. Is nothing sacred anymore? It was the end of an era.

In twenty-two seasons with the Giants in New York and San Francisco, and with the Mets in New York, Mays had conditioned baseball observers to his excellence and perfection. He simply did not make mistakes. Oh, sure,

1

there could be a strikeout here and there or an error once in a while or a missed cutoff man, but these were mechanical errors. Mays simply didn't make mental errors in the game.

His timing, his instincts, his reflexes were unmatched in baseball's history.

Mays hit 660 home runs, batted .302, lasted as a quality player twenty of his twenty-two seasons, knocked in 1,903 runs, was the best defensive outfielder the game has ever seen, and ran bases with a flair unmatched in the twentieth century.

He played in four World Series and starred in the All-Star Game from 1954 through 1973, winning a couple himself with key hits, fielding gems, or base running.

Mays was an entertainer. People paid to see him play and never felt cheated. On days he didn't hit, he caught the ball excitingly or ran the bases with verve or threw somebody out.

"My idea was to do everything better than anybody else ever had," he said. "I concentrated on every aspect of the game."

When he was elected to the Hall of Fame, he was asked who was the greatest player he'd ever seen. "I am," he answered honestly.

He did it when baseball was changing dramatically. He had to hit against some of the best pitchers the game ever saw and certainly the best relief pitchers—young, hard throwers or knuckleball pitchers or slider pitchers whose very professional lives depended on the one or two outs they got in tight spots, often against Mays.

He played when conditions were toughest: new huge baseball parks, increased travel, jet lag, night baseball, increased pressures from the press and television, late-night food, and bad airplane meals.

Willie Howard Mays, Jr., was born May 6, 1931, at Westfield, Alabama. He was turned on to baseball early by his father, who was a professional player in the old Negro Leagues. Young Willie made his first appearance in New York at the age of fifteen.

"I was with the Birmingham Black Barons," he said. "We bussed up from Alabama and got to the Holland Tunnel between New York and New Jersey. The bus stalled and the old guys on the bus ordered me out to push. I had the last laugh. The bus caught fire and they all had to race out."

After hitting .477 at Minneapolis in 35 games, Mays joined the Giants. He was twenty years old, a shy, unschooled southern boy in a profession that had only opened up to blacks four years earlier. He was hitless in his first 12 at bats. He cried in the clubhouse in Philadelphia.

Manager Leo Durocher came to him, put his arm around his shoulder, and said, "I don't care if you never get a hit, you're my center fielder."

The next day he was bouncy again before batting practice. He then homered in the game off future Hall of Famer Warren Spahn.

"If it wasn't for me," Spahn says, "nobody would have ever heard of Willie Mays."

Soon he was loosening up, a fan favorite, a favorite of his teammates and manager, the Say Hey Kid of the Giants. His play the rest of his rookie season helped the Giants catch the Dodgers for the pennant, an effort topped off by Bobby Thomson's homer.

"We pitched to Thomson with first base open," Dodger manager Charlie Dressen said, "because Willie Mays was the next hitter."

In five short months he had gained incredible respect. It was not lost on the league as Mays left for military service and missed most of the 1952 season and all of 1953.

"I wanted to entertain the troops when I was playing so I started the basket catch," he said. "I came back and asked Leo if I could use it. He said I could as long as I caught them."

The basket catch became his trademark. He used it on balls hit in front of him. Balls hit over him, as was the case with his famed catch of Vic Wertz's smash in the 1954 World Series against Cleveland, he simply ran down.

Mays played only five seasons before moving west to San Francisco, but he remained a New York hero, always in competition with other great New York center fielders such as Mickey Mantle of the Yankees and Duke Snider of the Dodgers. None of this attention ever seemed to affect Willie while he spent many late afternoons playing stickball with the kids on the streets of Harlem.

If not for those two years lost in service, Mays would have outdistanced Babe Ruth in career homers. He outdistanced him in fielding, running, and throwing.

Willie Mays was baseball's best, the most exciting player the game has ever seen, the number-one pick as the lead-off hitter among Baseball's 100.

Hank Aaron

(1954-1976)

The date was April 8, 1974. The place was Atlanta Stadium. The pitcher was a hard-throwing left-hander from Trenton, New Jersey, by the name of Al Downing. The man of the hour was the Hammer, Bad Henry, the greatest home-run hitter of all time—Henry Louis Aaron.

In the fourth inning of a game against the Dodgers, Aaron caught one of Downing's pitches on the fat part of his thirty-three ounce bat and drove it over the small fence in left field into the Atlanta bullpen. Relief pitcher Tom House caught it on the fly as he leaned against the fence.

It was number 715 and it passed the Babe. The lights flashed on the scoreboard at Atlanta Stadium: 715. That was all it had to say. Baseball fans knew the rest.

The number 714 had been a figure all baseball fans could recall in an instant. It was the number of homers Babe Ruth had hit in his glorious career. Now this lithe, trim forty-year-old black man from Mobile, Alabama, had passed the Babe.

Hank Aaron hit that dramatic record-breaking homer under the most intensive glare of media coverage in baseball history. When Babe Ruth hit 714 in Pittsburgh, he had been the home-run record holder for years. When Aaron hit 714 in Cincinnati and 715 in Atlanta he was breaking the mark of a baseball god. Aaron was relieved when it happened.

"Thank God it's over," he said, "now I can get some rest. And thank God I hit it in Atlanta."

Aaron had entertained his home fans with the historic homer as he had entertained all baseball in his twenty-three season career. He wound up hitting .305. He had 3771 hits, second on the all-time list behind Ty Cobb. He played more games, had more at bats, had more home runs, more RBIs, more sacrifice flies, and more intentional walks than anyone in the history of the game.

He did all these things under the pressures of a watching press, in the era of night ball, against the best relief pitching the game ever saw, under the stress of baseball's first franchise shift in more than fifty years, and with the problems of jet lag, cross-country air flights, and changing conditions.

Henry Louis Aaron was born February 5, 1934, in Mobile, Alabama. He was soon a baseball hero in the black school leagues around home. He was signed to play baseball in the dying days of the old Negro League and was soon purchased by the Boston Braves. He was a cross-handed-hitting skinny second baseman.

"I weighed about 140 pounds in those days," Aaron remembered, "but I always had those wrists."

He had learned how to snap a bat at a baseball with incredible speed, on the strength and reflexes of his marvelous wrists.

He hit .336 and .362 in his two minor-league seasons. His fielding average was about as high.

"I really couldn't field very well, and when I threw the ball to first base it usually wound up in the stands," Aaron said.

He joined the Braves in spring training in 1954 for a look. He was no great shakes as a fielder and wasn't hitting very much until an outfielder named Bobby Thomson, the same man who had beaten the Dodgers with his homer in the 1951 playoff, broke his ankle.

Charlie Grimm, the famous banjo-playing first baseman of the Cubs, was the Milwaukee manager. He liked the quick bat of the skinny kid from Mobile. "Let's try him in the outfield in Thomson's spot," Grimm said.

Soon Aaron had found his niche as the right fielder on the marvelous Milwaukee teams of the 1950s along with two other future Hall of Famers, Ed Mathews and Warren Spahn. The Braves won pennants in 1957 and 1958. Aaron hit .322 in 1957 and .326 in 1958. He wore uniform number 44 and ironically hit 44 homers in four separate seasons. His home run high was 47 in 1971. He was thirty-seven years old that season.

Aaron was one of the game's complete players, the game's greatest home-run hitter and RBI man, of course, a line-drive hitter of such skills no pitcher could contain him for more than a game, an incredible fielder, a marvelous base runner, and the perfect team man.

"I played with the Hammer for a long time," said Mathews. "I never saw him ever put his own records above the good of the team."

A quiet, dignified, respected gentleman throughout his career, Aaron may have put on his finest performance in 1969 in the play-off against the Mets. While the rest of his team seemed petrified by the pressures, Aaron collected three homers among his five hits, knocked in seven runs, batted .357, and kept the Braves in contention all three games.

6

After hitting number 714 and number 715, he finished out that season with 20 homers for the Braves and then was traded back to Milwaukee, now in the American League, as the DH. He added 22 American League homers to his total in two seasons. He finished with 755 career home runs.

Fans may argue that it was Willie May's flamboyance on the field that made him seem better than Aaron. They may argue that it was an easy home-run park in Atlanta that made him a greater home-run hitter than the Babe.

In this list of Baseball's 100, Hank Aaron has to be number two. He always tried harder.

Babe Ruth

(1914–1935)

That small cap tilted on his head, that round, bulbous nose on that fleshy face, those spindly legs supporting that huge torso, those massive shoulders and arms, and a bubbling bellow of "Hiya, kid," that echoed across a field. That was as much the Babe of Baseball, the Sultan of Swat, the King of Swing, as those monstrous home runs in the upper deck of Yankee Stadium.

"I remember the first time I saw Babe Ruth," said Hank Greenberg. "It was in 1933 and I was a rookie with the Tigers. I was taking batting practice and I heard that greeting across the field. The Babe was coming out of the dugout for batting practice and the entire field suddenly seemed electrified."

That was the effect Babe Ruth had on his own teammates, opposing players, fans, and press. Babe was unlike any other athlete of his time or any time. He was loud, coarse, flamboyant, enthusiastic. He dominated every ball park he ever played in, every room he ever walked into, every town he ever visited.

He was credited, rightfully so, with saving the game of baseball in 1920 with his 54 homers in his first Yankee season after the public had soured on baseball after the White Sox scandal of 1919. With his ebullient style, Babe made the game clean, healthy, and fun again.

If Babe's listing in a third-place position here is shocking to many fans, it is only because he never played a night game, he never hit against fireball relief pitching (relief pitchers in his day were worn-out old starters), he never traveled cross-country for a night game and played a day game the next day, he never performed before millions of television viewers, he never had to run on artificial turf. It is the changes in the game, the modern factors that have made the game more difficult, that bring Babe in here as number three, behind Mays and Aaron. His feats were heroic. So were theirs. They simply did them under tougher conditions.

Babe was one of the game's greatest pitchers in his Boston days. He was one of the all-time finest hitters, certainly the most dramatic home-run hitter ever, a wonderful fielder, an impressive base runner. After he reached eminence as a slugger, his attention to fielding, throwing, and running diminished. He often moved from right field to left field on sunny days because, as he explained to sportswriter John Drebinger of the *Times,* "The Babe doesn't like the sun field."

George Herman "Babe" Ruth was born February 6, 1895, in Baltimore, Maryland. By the time he was eight he was living in a home for orphaned children, even though both his parents were still alive. They simply couldn't or wouldn't, care for him. His mother died when he was sixteen; and his father, who was the Babe's look-alike, died when the Babe was twenty-four, shot to death after a barroom brawl.

George played baseball as a left-handed-throwing catcher for St. Mary's under the coaching of Brother Matthias. At nineteen he was signed by the Baltimore Orioles. The team was owned by a man named Jack Dunn, and young George soon became known as Jack's Babe.

Baltimore sold the Babe to Boston. The Red Sox optioned him to their Providence farm club in 1914, and brought him back at the end of that season, and he was soon in their regular pitching rotation with his blazing fastball and good curve. He was 23–12 and 24–13 with the Red Sox in 1916 and 1917. In 1916 he beat the Brooklyn Dodgers in the World Series with a player named Casey Stengel on the bench.

"I was left-handed and the Babe was left-handed, so they sat me down the same as they do now," Casey once said. "It didn't take no genius to see he was a great pitcher."

It didn't take no genius, as Casey might say, to see that he was also a great hitter. On January 3, 1920, the financially troubled Boston Red Sox sold him to the Yankees for $125,000—a fortune in those days. Boston had won six pennants in nineteen years before they traded him. They went twenty-six years after trading the Babe before winning another in 1946. The Yankees, meanwhile, had never won until the Babe keyed their first triumph in 1921. They were to win seven pennants in Babe's time with the club.

His impact on baseball, on New York, on the country was enormous. He was a folk hero bigger than almost anyone. He was paid eighty thousand dollars in 1928 after his 60-homer season, and when asked if he didn't feel embarrassed that he was making more money than the President of the United States he said, "I had a better year than he did."

In the decade known as the Roaring Twenties, Babe Ruth, Red Grange, and Charles Lindbergh were America's greatest heroes.

10

In 1924 the Babe hit .378. In 1927 he hit 60 homers, breaking his own mark of 59 set in 1921. He hit 40 or more homers in eleven separate seasons.

The Babe played with the Yankees through the 1934 season and then was traded to the Boston Braves. He hit three homers in one game for Boston on May 25, 1935, and retired on June first after a squabble with the Boston ownership.

He wanted to manage the Yankees, but owner Jacob Ruppert felt Babe couldn't manage himself because he was a night owl who enjoyed the proverbial wine, women, and song. His only official baseball job after his playing days was as a showpiece Brooklyn Dodger coach at first base in 1938.

Unlike that of most players, Babe's importance grew after his retirement. He was a most beloved national figure who continued to work closely with kids, make appearances, lend his name to charity efforts.

Babe Ruth Day was held at Yankee Stadium on June 13, 1948, and as a cancer-ridden man of only fifty-three he could just barely whisper to the kids of America, "The only real game in the world, I think, is baseball." He died on August 16, of that same year a legend of the Great American Pastime.

Babe Ruth wore number 3. In Baseball's 100, that's where he belongs.

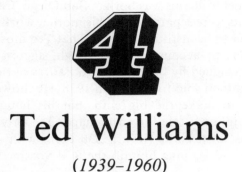

Ted Williams

(*1939–1960*)

"I want to walk down the street when I'm an old man," Ted Williams once said, "and have people look at me and point me out and say, 'There goes the game's greatest hitter.'"

The Splendid Splinter, the Thumper, Ted the Kid, is about right. He was the game's greatest hitter. But he paid less attention to the other aspects of the game: fielding, running, throwing, and winning. The Red Sox won only one pennant in the twenty-one years Williams played for them.

A rangy left-handed hitter with long arms and legs, Williams hit from an open stance that drove the ball a huge distance. He could pull any ball pitched to him and defied the Boudreau shift (all infielders on the right side, all outfielders on the right side) by lining baseballs through and over it.

Williams was one of the game's most outspoken players. Often in bitter public feuds with the Boston press, he fought too, with fans, angered his own teammates, sometimes was jealous of the attention heaped on his opposing rival, Joe DiMaggio, the New York Yankee star. When the government, in 1952, called him back to service as a Marine pilot after he had finished his tour in World War II, he was openly upset.

Because he was a great hitter but was not perfect, fans in Boston often booed their hero. He grew more and more antagonistic toward them, on one occasion spitting at the fans and making an obscene gesture toward them. This wasn't quite in keeping with the image of the Great American Pastime so Williams was fined five thousand dollars for that performance.

His hitting performances could hardly be questioned. In 1941, at the age of twenty-three he batted .406 for the season. No player has been able to hit .400 since. He won six batting titles and ended his career with a lifetime mark of .344. He hit .388 in 1957 at the age of thirty-nine and hit .316 at the age of forty-two. He hit 521 homers, the last one coming in the final Boston home game of the 1960 season off young Baltimore right-hander Jack Fisher. Williams was one of the few players to play in four different decades.

Theodore Samuel Williams was born in San Diego, California, on August 30, 1918. His parents were separated and his mother worked for the Salvation Army. She was later to be institutionalized. That Ted mostly raised himself in his early days helps to account for his tough, aggressive, often abrasive personality. He was signed by the San Diego Padres of the old Pacific Coast League in 1936 and then sold to Boston in 1938. He showed enough at spring training that year to make the big club, but his haughty manner, sharp tongue, and undisciplined style forced manager Joe Cronin to send him out to the Minneapolis farm club. He hit .336 there with 43 homers and 142 RBI's, so there was no keeping him off the Red Sox in 1939. He was soon a Boston hero.

Williams won the RBI title with 145 as a rookie, hit .327, and lifted his average to .344 during the second season. Then he hit .406 in 1941.

"I asked him if he wanted to sit out the last day and settle for .400," said manager Cronin. "He wanted to play."

He played and got six hits in a doubleheader to finish at .406. Even that triumph was overshadowed by DiMaggio, who hit in 56 straight games, led the Yankees to the pennant, and won the league's MVP award. DiMaggio always seemed to be getting in Ted's way.

He hit .356 the next season and then left for three years of service as a Marine pilot in World War II. He retained his reserve rank and was recalled in 1952 for combat action in Korea.

Williams returned to baseball in 1946 with another wonderful season and a .342 average but put a dent in his reputation by hitting only .200 in the World Series with only five singles. The Red Sox lost to the Cardinals when Enos Slaughter scored from first base on a single while shortstop Johnny Pesky held the ball on a relay.

Williams won the Most Valuable Player Award in 1946 and 1949 but lost out to DiMaggio in 1941 when he hit .406 and in 1947 when he hit .343. Williams also won four home-run titles to go along with his six batting titles.

Even though he was universally considered the greatest hitter of his time—and I think of all time—Williams had one failing as a hitter: he would not offer at a pitch outside the strike zone. Since Williams was taking walks with men on base, other Boston hitters were forced to drive in the runs.

Other aspects of his game were only average. He was not an aggressive base runner, and he was only an average fielder—though he did learn to master the tricky wall at Fenway Park.

He retired after the 1960 season to fish in Florida, work some for the Red Sox, help raise funds for the Jimmy Fund for crippled children, and engage in battles over baseball and politics with newsmen. He bowed out with a dramatic flourish, hitting a huge home run in his final Boston at bat and then retiring.

In 1969 he was named manager of the Washington Senators, became a big pal of President Richard Nixon, kept a huge photo of the president in his office, enthusiastically worked with young players. He managed there and in Texas for a year when the franchise moved. Then he retired again to hunt and fish.

Ted Williams was the game's greatest hitter. They ultimately did invent a position perfectly suited for him, the designated hitter. It came after he quit. No man ever born was better fit to be a DH. Hitting wasn't everything to Ted Williams, it was the only thing.

Stan Musial

(1941–1963)

Stan Musial, a man with a perpetual smile on his face, was once asked why he always seemed so happy.

"Heck," he said, "if you hit .331 all your life you'd be happy, too."

Batting out of a crazy corkscrew stance, this left-handed slugger from the coal-mining town of Donora, Pennsylvania, dominated National League hitters for more than twenty years.

His favorite place to hit seemed to be the small ball park in Brooklyn called Ebbets Field. He would smash a double off that wall, a home run over that screen, a triple down the line or a single past the pitcher's ear. A Dodger fan was so shocked at Musial's constant peppering of the Dodger staff that he said, "That man . . . that man. . . ." He stammered and stuttered. He could say no more. Musial simply became The Man after that. His hitting skill was so incredible a legend grew up that he was so careful he hit only the top half of the baseball.

"That was just a joke I made up," Musial said. "I told that to a reporter when I was in the Navy. He wrote it and it stuck."

Whether he was hitting the top half of the ball or the bottom, or the entire baseball, he seemed always to be hitting it hard and often. He won seven batting titles, his last in 1957 at the age of thirty-seven.

Stanley Frank "The Man" Musial was born in Donora on November 21, 1920. He was a pitcher-outfielder-first baseman in school, left-handed all the way, and signed with the Cardinals in 1938 as a pitcher and outfielder.

While pitching and playing the outfield for manager Dickie Kerr at

Daytona Beach, Florida, in 1940, Musial fell on his left shoulder. He was ready to quit baseball before he'd begun.

"Let's stay with it," said Kerr. "I think you can become a pretty good outfielder. You're already a good hitter."

He batted .379 at Springfield in 1941 and .326 in 54 games with Rochester later the same year. Then he was promoted to the Cardinals, hit .426 in a dozen games, and stayed in the St. Louis outfield for twenty-two seasons.

In 1942 the Cardinals stole a pennant for St. Louis from the Brooklyn Dodgers with the rookie hitting .315. The next season he batted .357 for his first batting title. He hit .347 in 1944, missed 1945 in the Navy, and returned for another pennant winner in 1946 with a .365 mark and a batting title.

By the late 1940s Musial had established himself as the best hitter in the National League and a constant competitor with Ted Williams as the best in the game. He was, unlike Williams, a gregarious, friendly, ebullient man who was always getting a good press from sportswriters. Even on those rare days when he didn't hit, he was always friendly.

"Why should I get upset if I go oh-for-four one day," he said. "I know I'll get three hits the next day."

Batting from that coiled stance, Musial said the secret of high batting averages was his third, fourth, and sometimes fifth time up in a game.

"Some hitters relax after their first hit. I bear down more. If I get two hits, I want three, if I get three I want four, and I try for five if I get up again after I have four."

Musial was a marvelous outfielder with excellent speed and a strong enough throwing arm despite his injury as a young player. He was always an excellent base runner, an accomplished first baseman, and a great team player. "The man who doesn't like Stan Musial hasn't been born yet," said teammate Ken Boyer.

At the age of forty-one he batted .330 but slumped to .255, only his fourth under-.300 season in twenty-two years, in his last season of 1963. By then he had slowed down in the field and manager Johnny Keane didn't want to play him every day.

The next year the Cardinals won the pennant after they obtained a fleet young left fielder from the Cubs by the name of Lou Brock.

"If I didn't quit," Musial kidded, "the Cardinals never would have won in 1964."

Musial continued to stay close to the Cardinals organization, worked out in spring training with young players, and went into his patented batting stance at the drop of a hat. A statue of Stan sits outside Busch Stadium in St. Louis, and a kid baseball league is named after him. Great man. Great player.

18

Joe DiMaggio

(1936–1951)

There never was a more stylish-looking, self-disciplined, and controlled baseball player than the Yankee Clipper, Joe DiMaggio.

He roamed center field at Yankee Stadium with the grace of a deer. He hit line drives with the coordination of a computer. He ran bases with the ease and grace of a ballet dancer. He was a leader among men.

"When he walked into the clubhouse," said his feisty friend and teammate, Billy Martin, "it was like some senator or president walking in there."

DiMaggio dominated baseball for the thirteen seasons he played and would have rated higher on the list in *Baseball's 100* were it not for injuries, illness, and a military service that curtailed his career.

He owns baseball's one unreachable record, the 56-game hitting streak compiled from May 15, 1941, through July 17, 1941, with a .408 mark. He was stopped in Cleveland on the strength of two brilliant fielding plays by third baseman Ken Keltner.

Perhaps his excellence and leadership can best be measured by the fact that he played in ten Yankee pennant winners in his thirteen seasons, including his first four in a row.

DiMaggio was once asked what his greatest thrill in baseball was, and he answered simply, "Putting the Yankee uniform on every day."

Joseph Paul DiMaggio, Jr., was born November 25, 1914, in Martinez, California. He was the son of an Italian fisherman and spoke no English at home. He was self-conscious of his inability to handle his country's language

19

throughout his school years, a fact which accounted for much of his later shyness.

His older brother, Vince, played with the San Francisco Seals, and Joe signed with them in 1932. In 1933 he hit safely in 61 straight games for the Pacific Coast League team. The Yankees purchased his contract after the 1934 season and sent him back to San Francisco after a knee injury suffered when he was getting out of a car in 1935. He batted .323 as a New York rookie in 1936.

Babe Ruth had just left the Yankees a year and a half earlier. Lou Gehrig was still at his peak before illness would rob him of his skills. But DiMaggio made an enormous splash on the public mind with his skills, his grace, his class under stress. Restauranteur Toots Shor befriended him and DiMaggio could be shielded from the public in Shor's place.

"If the Yankees won he'd come in and have a good time and eat dinner," Shor said. "If they lost he'd stand outside and I'd come out and we'd walk around the block without a word until he calmed down from the defeat. Then he'd go home and eat alone."

He would soon marry actress Dorothy Arnold. They had one son, Joe junior. They divorced after DiMaggio's World War II service, and in 1954 he married actress Marilyn Monroe. The marriage lasted only 274 days but DiMaggio always stayed close to Marilyn and handled the funeral arrangements in 1962.

DiMaggio became a national hero after a great performance in Boston in 1949. The Yankees were struggling to hold their first-place lead against the charging Red Sox. Because of a slow-healing heel injury, DiMaggio had not yet played a game for new manager Casey Stengel. Now, in mid-June, he was ready. He unloaded four homers in a three-game sweep as the Yankees pushed the Red Sox back. Then they hung on to catch and pass Boston in the final two games of that season.

DiMaggio seemed somehow to transcend just being a player. He was a hero to all. Alan Courtney and Ben Homer wrote a song about him called "Joltin' Joe DiMaggio," and he has been the subject of several books, including this author's *Where Have You Gone, Joe DiMaggio?* a line first used in Paul Simon's celebrated song, "Mrs. Robinson."

Micky Mantle joined the Yankees in 1951 and DiMaggio retired after that year, turning center field over to the Oklahoma kid. He had batted .325, hit 361 homers, knocked in 1,537 runs, and scored 1,390. The Yankees still wanted him to play and offered him a hundred-thousand-dollar contract for 1952. He refused it. His older brother, Tom, who ran the family restaurant on San Francisco's Fisherman's Wharf, later explained, "He quit because he wasn't Joe DiMaggio anymore."

He could settle for nothing less than excellence. Baseball recognized this when they elected him the game's greatest living player in a 1969 centennial poll.

Joe played much golf in his retirement, tried a Yankee postgame television show for a while, soon became identified to younger fans more for his coffee and bank commercials than for his baseball.

But for those of us who were privileged to see the graceful DiMaggio glide across a field to catch a fly ball, he was simply the best. Only a relatively short career keeps him from a higher ranking here.

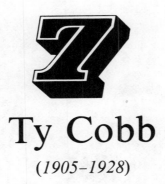

Ty Cobb

(1905–1928)

The Georgia Peach, Ty Cobb, a nasty, aggressive, self-centered, foul-mouthed man, was the only player in history to record more than 4000 hits, with a total of 4,191 in his twenty-four seasons with Detroit and Philadelphia. His lifetime average is the game's highest—a .367 mark—and when he quit he also led in runs scored and stolen bases. His stolen-base mark was later passed by Lou Brock.

Cobb was a slashing left-handed hitter who hit most of his balls through the infield or over the shortstop's head. He was not a home-run hitter, with two seasons at 12 his power high. His averages were always impressive, with marks of .420, .410, and .401 in three separate seasons. From 1909 through 1919 he never hit lower than .368. He won nine batting titles in a row and twelve overall.

Defensively he was better than average but not equal to Tris Speaker, the finest defensive outfielder of Cobb's time, or Joe DiMaggio, the finest defensive outfielder of any time in his league. Willie Mays rates as the finest defensive outfielder of all time among Baseball's 100.

Tyrus Raymond Cobb was born December 18, 1886, in Narrows, Georgia. His father was a schoolteacher and a politician. His mother was a wealthy local beauty. The marriage was stormy and in 1905 Mrs. Cobb shot her husband dead with a gun as he attempted to come through a bedroom window of the home. He was supposedly attempting to gather evidence that Mrs. Cobb was having an affair with another man. Mrs. Cobb told police she

23

accidently killed her husband, mistaking him for a burgler, a story Cobb himself never accepted.

Cobb was destroyed by the act. He never forgave his mother and had a bitter relationship with her until her own death. That murder never left him, and he seethed with anger all of his life. It drove him to incredible heights in baseball, but the heights were almost always tempered with nastiness.

When he was sixty years old and long retired from the game, he played in an old-timer's event in Yankee Stadium. He was at bat and told the old catcher to move back. He was afraid, he said, he might slip his bat at his advanced age and hit the catcher. When the catcher obligingly did, Cobb bunted on the next pitch for a hit.

He always went out of his way to embarrass his opponents and thought nothing of sliding high and hard to cut a second baseman on his steals.

"I'm there to get the base," he once said, "and anybody in my way better know that."

He may well have been one of the greatest players of all time—some say he should be number one among Baseball's 100—but he was also probably the most disliked superstar ever. He was cruel, nasty, vicious, on the edge of neurotic behavior throughout his career. He would be an awful example of a baseball hero.

Some of Cobb's records, his 96 stolen bases in a season have been surpassed by Rickey Henderson, Maury Wills, and Lou Brock; and 892 in a lifetime by Brock but the .367 lifetime mark, the 4,191 hits, and the 2,244 runs will probably stand forever.

It can also be noted that after Cobb left baseball he became a very wealthy man through shrewd business investments. It can also be noted that he may have been one of the cheapest men around. He ate canned food to save money, almost never ate in a restaurant if he had to pay, and spent a week on the cuff as a guest of the Yankees at one old-timers' day when others spent one night. He also charged the Yankees with a five-thousand-dollar fur coat that he bought for his second wife.

Ty Cobb died July 17, 1961, in Atlanta, Georgia, a bitter, unhappy old man. When asked to do his obituary one writer wrote, "The only difference now is that he is a bad guy who is dead."

Lou Gehrig

(1923–1939)

Who among us has not cried when Gary Cooper, playing the role of Lou Gehrig in the movie *Pride of the Yankees*, stands at the microphone and says, "Today, I consider myself the luckiest man on the face of the earth"?

Less than two years after the real Gehrig had spoken those words at Yankee Stadium, he was gone. He died June 2, 1941.

But the legend lives on in one of the game's greatest players. Certainly he was the most durable, with an unreachable record of 2,130 consecutive games played. And certainly he was one of the most decent, dedicated men the game has ever seen.

Although it was unfortunate that in his career Lou Gehrig was to be overshadowed by the bombastic Babe Ruth, baseball observers were quick to recognize the incredible skills in this huge, hulking New York first baseman.

While Babe Ruth hit some of the highest, longest drives in baseball's history, Gehrig hit some of the hardest.

"No man could ever hit a ball off the right-field or left-field wall harder than Lou did," said teammate Bill Dickey. "He was a left-handed hitter but he hit line drives off the left center-field wall no right-hander could accomplish."

Gehrig's incredible strength and stamina had much to do with his success. He simply overpowered the baseball on many occasions. That is why it was such a cruel stroke of fate that he should be struck down by amyotrophic lateral sclerosis, a debilitating muscle and spinal disease, now commonly known as Lou Gehrig Disease.

27

Henry Louis Gehrig, the Iron Horse of the Yankees and Larrupin' Lou, was born in Manhattan on June 19, 1903, the only child of German immigrant parents. His father worked as a janitor; his mother washed floors in the homes of wealthy women. While attending Commerce High in Manhattan, he won a baseball and football scholarship to Columbia. He was soon offered a professional baseball contract and signed with the Yankees in 1923. He had played a dozen games in 1921 at Hartford under the name of Henry Lewis. He played part of the 1923 and 1924 seasons at Hartford. He became the Yankee regular in 1925 when first baseman Wally Pipp came down with a headache and Gehrig substituted for him. His substitution lasted fifteen seasons.

Gehrig led the league in home runs twice and tied for the lead with Ruth once in 1931. He led the league in batting average once and in RBI's four times. He had the incredible total of 184 RBI's in 1931, the league record— surpassed only by Hack Wilson's National League mark of 190. He had 493 homers in seventeen seasons and had a lifetime average of .340.

When he started playing first base he was unsure and awkward in the position and fans called him "tanglefoot" for mixing up his legs. He worked hard, straightened out his play, and became a marvelous first baseman who could stretch the full length of his six-foot-one-inch, 212-pound frame to help an infielder's throw.

On June 3, 1932, he hit four consecutive home runs, but it didn't get much attention in the New York papers. John McGraw, the famed Giants manager, retired that day.

Gehrig was a soft-spoken, shy man who was thirty years old when he married a Chicago girl named Eleanor Twitchell. His mother, jealous of her only son's happiness, bitterly opposed the marriage and was never friendly to her daughter-in-law. After Gehrig's death, Mrs. Gehrig was a constant visitor to Yankee Stadium.

On May 2, 1939, Gehrig was congratulated by his teammates for a fielding play that was no more than routine. It was clear to him that they knew something was wrong. Soon he was being examined at Mayo Clinic. Told his life was ebbing, he accepted it with his normal stoic grace.

His death in June of 1941 was as emotionally heartrending as any public death in this country's history. He was the epitome of a national hero and people lined up for blocks to view his casket.

The Yankees retired his uniform number 4, created a monument to his memory at Yankee Stadium, and have kept his name alive all the years since.

There has been only one other Yankee captain since. His name was Thurman Munson, and he also died tragically young, in a plane crash on August 2, 1979, at the age of thirty-two. It is unlikely there will be another Yankee captain for a generation. There may never be another player or man like Lou Gehrig again.

Walter Johnson

(*1907–1927*)

      The story goes that Walter Johnson, the Big Train, whose fast ball whistled like a locomotive roaring through a small town, was on the mound against a young hitter. The first pitch whooshed by the batter and the umpire yelled, "Strike one." The next pitch came over the heart of the plate at over a hundred miles an hour and the umpire yelled, "Strike two." The batter gently dropped his bat at home plate, turned toward the dugout, and marched away. "Hey," the umpire yelled, "that's only strike two. You got another swing left." The batter turned toward the umpire. "Good," he said, "you take it. It won't do me any good."

      Whether or not hitters actually gave up against Johnson after two strikes, they sure considered him as unhittable as any man who ever toed the mound. Johnson struck out 3,508 hitters in his twenty-one years with the Washington Senators, including twelve seasons as the league's strikeout leader.

      Johnson won 416 games and lost 279 for one of baseball's worst teams, had a lifetime ERA of 2.17, started over 40 times in eleven seasons, led the league in wins six times, and dominated pitching for nearly two decades. He had a dozen seasons with 20 or more wins, ten of them in a row, and was 20–7 at the age of thirty-seven in 1925.

      When baseball established its Hall of Fame in 1936, Johnson was one of the first five elected along with Christy Mathewson, the only other pitcher, and Babe Ruth, Ty Cobb, and Honus Wagner.

      Because he so dominated pitching, because he has more wins than any man save Cy Young, because he has always been the standard of excellence

other pitchers are measured against, Walter Perry Johnson breaks the domination of hitters in Baseball's 100 and is hereby elected number 9.

Walter Johnson was born of Swedish descent in Humboldt, Kansas, a community of wheat and corn farms, on November 6, 1887. He moved west to California in 1901 with his family in search of oil. These hardworking people never found any oil but they did produce a solidly built young son with fine moral character who was soon blazing his fastball past young hitters in California and the northwest. He subsequently moved to Idaho with the promise of a job with the newly established telephone company and a chance to pitch in a fast semipro league. He had no problems with the hitters, only with his own catchers, who had more than enough trouble trying to hold on to his whooshing fast ball.

"I can't see the darn thing," one of his catchers complained. "I just put my glove up about where I hear the wind."

A traveling liquor salesman saw Johnson in a semipro game, recommended him to his hometown Washington team, and soon the gangling nineteen-year-old youth was signed to a Washington contract. He made his debut with the Washington Senators in August of 1907. The Senators were a last-place club and would soon be identified by the catchphrase about Washington, "First in war, first in peace, and last in the American League."

Johnson alone couldn't make the Senators into a winning team but he could make opposing hitters ill every fourth day when he pitched. More players came up with colds, pulled muscles, and sore knees when Johnson was scheduled than had ever ducked games before.

What was most interesting about this great pitcher's fast ball was the fact that it was usually thrown down the middle of the plate. Johnson never attempted to intimidate a batter. "I wouldn't think of hitting a man," he once said. "I know I'm capable of killing him if I do."

In twenty-one seasons in the big leagues, this flamethrowing right-hander walked more than a hundred batters only once, when he passed 132 in 1916. He never had a season with more walks than strikeouts. He won 32 games in 1912 and 36 in 1913. In 1916, with a terrible Washington team, he was 25–20 with a 1.89 ERA. When he was 36–7 in 1913, his ERA was 1.09.

Johnson finally made it to the World Series with Washington in 1924 and repeated again in 1925. Johnson was named manager of the Newark club in 1928, managed the Senators from 1929 to 1932, and later managed the Cleveland Indians.

Johnson was a gentleman farmer after his retirement from the game, ran unsuccessfully for Congress in 1940, tried broadcasting, and died on December 10, 1946, at the age of fifty-nine.

The Big Train belongs in the top ten. No other pitcher does. No other pitcher could get hitters to strike out on two pitches.

Rogers Hornsby

(1915–1937)

In the spring of 1962 Rogers Hornsby, a grizzled, snarling, sarcastic, nasty sixty-five-year-old man, was a special batting coach for the New York Mets.

He had been hired by manager Casey Stengel to impart some of his batting wisdom to the fledgling Mets. He was not asked to infect them with his combative personality.

One day a photographer asked Hornsby to pose with newly crowned home-run champion Roger Maris of the Yankees. Hornsby, standing next to the batting cage, looked over at the Yankee dugout and said, "If he wants to come over here, I'll pose with the busher."

Naturally, Maris, a proud man who had just hit more home runs, 61, in one season than any player in the history of the game, refused to march to Hornsby's orders. No picture was taken. The real picture still remains of Hornsby, arrogant, abrasive, abusive, and the best hitter the National League probably has ever seen.

In 1924 Hornsby batted .424, the highest average ever recorded in the league. From 1920 through 1925 his averages were ridiculous: .370, .397, .401, .384, .424, and .403. He won another batting title in 1928 at Boston with a .387 mark.

Rogers Hornsby—his first name was his mother's maiden name and was often written as Roger—was born at Winters, Texas, on April 27, 1896.

As a skinny, glib, brash young man, he was dedicated to baseball and his mother, who was a big ball fan and encouraged him, and he didn't pay much attention to his school studies. He was not a naturally gifted athlete and by the time he was eighteen he seemed an unlikely professional player. But he was signed to a contract by the Hugo, Oklahoma, club in the Texas-Oklahoma league and impressed his superiors with his dedication to the game.

The St. Louis Cardinals purchased his contract for five-hundred dollars in 1915 and he would dominate that team as a player and personality—and serve as its manager, too, in 1925 and 1926—during the height of the Cardinals' Gashouse Gang era; one of a collection of wild-living, free-swinging men who brought fame and fortune to St. Louis and gold and glory to themselves.

Hornsby, who had started out as a shortstop and third baseman, soon became the second baseman on the Cardinals, a position he played with skill and verve. He was unafraid at bat and equally tenacious in the field, thinking nothing of aiming a throw at the top of the head of a sliding runner. He was respected by all players, disliked by most. He was the nearest approach to Ty Cobb, considered the meanest man ever in the game, as the National League would see.

In nineteen of his twenty-three seasons Hornsby would record averages over .300. His lifetime mark of .358 is second only to Cobb's .361 and in his last full season as a player in 1931 he batted .331 for the Cubs. He played for the Cards, the Giants, the Braves, and St. Louis Browns, as well as the Cubs. He managed the Cards, Braves, Cubs, Browns, and Reds in a baseball career that lasted nearly fifty years.

Hornsby was never a good teacher of hitting even though his skills were enormous. He could not get the dedication out of most players that he was able to get out of himself. In his advancing years young players snickered at his most-often-quoted piece of advice. "Never got to a movie picture show. It's bad for your eyes."

Hornsby would never attend a movie, never watch television, never read a newspaper, always protecting his eyes even in later life.

It was ironic that he would be hospitalized late in 1962, after his one season with the Mets, for eye problems. He was recovering from cataract surgery when he suffered a heart attack and died in a Chicago Hospital on January 5, 1963.

Unlike Cobb, Hornsby not only was a high-average hitter, but a power hitter as well. He belted 302 homers in the dead-ball era and hit as many as 42 homers in 1922.

Known as the Rajah because of his great skill with the bat, Hornsby probably could hit a line drive as hard as any man who ever played the game.

Then he would sit around a hotel lobby and tell anybody who would listen what a great hitter he was. And he was a great hitter. He just wasn't a man you felt you wanted to invite over for a couple of beers.

Jackie Robinson

(1947–1956)

The numbers hardly begin to tell the story. In one of the great ironies of baseball, there is not one word on the Hall of Fame plaque for Jackie Robinson that attests to the real pressures he faced as the man who broke baseball's color line.

As the first black in organized baseball in 1946, and the first in the big leagues in 1947, Robinson played under the most enormous tensions any athlete has ever seen. On many days when he took the field his very life was in jeopardy from the lunatic fringe who did not want to see a Negro take part with whites in the Great American Pastime.

He dealt with those pressures, first turning the other cheek, as Brooklyn owner Branch Rickey had instructed him, and later fighting back with heart and body and soul. Robinson was still fighting for the rights of his people when an early death struck him down on October 24, 1972, at the age of fifty-three as a result of diabetes, a heart condition, and failing sight.

Only weeks before, he had stood on the field at Cincinnati's Riverfront Stadium at the World Series against Oakland and implored baseball to give blacks a chance as managers and general managers.

"I will not be satisfied until I look over at a dugout and see a black face leading his team."

Robinson did not live long enough to see Frank Robinson—no relation—Larry Doby, or Maury Wills manage in the big leagues.

It was only baseball's racial prejudice and color line that prevented Jackie

35

Robinson from making it to Brooklyn earlier and compiling records that would have moved him higher on the list of Baseball's 100.

Jack Roosevelt Robinson was born in Cairo, Georgia, on January 31, 1919. His mother, who supported five children by doing domestic work, then transported her brood to Pasadena, California. Jackie Robinson quickly became an electrifying athletic name in California, starring as a baseball and football player, breaking high school records in track and basketball, recording good grades, and developing a strong character as a teenager. UCLA offered Jackie a scholarship and he was soon a nationally known four-sport star.

He left UCLA short of his degree to play professional football with the Los Angeles Bulldogs and subsequently saw his career halted by World War II. He enlisted in the service, was discharged as a lieutenant, and soon signed with the Negro League Kansas City Monarchs.

Branch Rickey—who had held a black schoolmate's hand publicly at college a half century before—wanted a Negro to break the color line. And he wanted at the same time to produce new sources of revenue and talent. He was quickly led to Robinson, admired his skills, and believed in his courage.

Robinson was Montreal's MVP in his first pro season, and then began ten marvelous years with the Brooklyn Dodgers, the team made famous by author Roger Kahn as the "Boys of Summer."

Robinson may have been the most exciting player of all time; he was a deadly batter, a great clutch hitter, a marvelous second baseman, and the most thrilling base runner the game has ever seen. Robinson could make a rundown play into an Agatha Christie mystery—will he or won't he? He would dash around until he escaped the rundown or allowed his base-running mates to move up. His steals of home were breathtaking and his fake steals, as he charged down the line at third base, would electrify the gang of faithful fans at Brooklyn's Ebbets Field.

Robinson batted .311 in ten seasons, won the batting title in 1949 with a .342 mark, hit .300 in six of his ten seasons, played on six pennant winners and one world-championship team, and anchored the Dodger infield. He saved the Dodgers' chances for a pennant on the last day of the regular season in 1951 with a miraculous catch and a home run (Bobby Thomson later won the playoff for the Giants), and was the only man to have the poise to watch the base runner in his excitement touch all bases after the crushing blow.

He was traded to the hated Giants in 1956 but decided to retire instead. He worked for a coffee company, worked for a bank, did public relations work for New York Governor Nelson Rockefeller, continued to speak out for his people.

A great player, a great man, a thrilling performer. Jackie Robinson brought glory to himself, his people, and all baseball, and has clearly earned a high place among Baseball's 100.

Roberto Clemente

(1955–1972)

He was that kind of man. When Roberto Clemente heard that earthquake victims in Managua, Nicaragua, were without food, medical supplies, and clothing, he organized an emergency airlift from his home in San Juan to fly aid to the victims. The plane crashed into the sea shortly after takeoff and Clemente was killed, his body never recovered, his countrymen standing for days along the shores praying for a miracle that never was to happen.

The shock to baseball, to the Pittsburgh Pirates, and mostly to Clemente's devoted wife and children came so soon after he had finally begun to receive the recognition he had long deserved and only recently received. He had starred in the 1971 World Series, leading the Pirates back from a two-game deficit to a thrilling victory over the Orioles, and had registered his three-thousandth career hit with a line double off left-hander Jon Matlack at Shea Stadium, only the eleventh player to reach that exalted baseball goal.

"I am proud," he said, "to be the first player from Puerto Rico to have three thousand hits."

Clemente was always proud of his heritage and conscious of his color and background. People in baseball often reminded him of it, accusing him at times of being lazy, of being a hypochondriac, of carrying a chip on his shoulder.

All of this seemed to end in a warm glow for the multitalented right fielder of the Pirates when he personally took charge of the 1971 Series, batting .414 and leading his teammates to a glorious victory. He was named the Series MVP and was gracious in sharing the accolades of the prize with his teammates.

"Roberto was the leader of our club," said manager Danny Murtaugh. "He carried us when were down and he drove us when we were up."

Roberto Walker Clemente had every baseball skill in abundance. He was a marvelous line-drive hitter, with his ringing shots scattered throughout National League parks. He won four batting titles and his career ended with a lifetime .317 mark for eighteen seasons, thirteen years over .300, a high of .357 in 1967, and those 3,000 hits.

Clemente was also a daring right fielder whose trademark was a lunging, sliding catch on his backside with his glove reaching out to snare the baseball before it hit the grass. He was a sensational base runner, as adept at taking the extra base as any player who ever played the game. Perhaps it was his incredible throwing arm that separated him completely from the others. In an era of baseball when throwing and defense seemed to disappear in place of the long ball, Clemente was an astonishing thrower, unafraid to gamble on throwing out a runner from four hundred feet away in the deepest reaches of Forbes Field.

Clemente's career began in school back in San Juan. The youngest of seven children—his father was a sugar field worker—Clemente soon became a popular player at home. The Brooklyn Dodgers heard about the smooth-skinned, handsome, hard-throwing right-hander and soon offered him ten thousand dollars to sign, a huge bonus for a Latin player in those days.

Roberto went to Montreal in the Dodger system, batted .257, and was drafted by the Pirates at the end of the year while the Dodgers—not ready to bring him up—tried to hide him in their system.

In his second season as a Buc, he batted .311. He stayed under .300 for the next three seasons but hit .314 for the 1960 World Champion Pirates. Bill Mazeroski got most of the attention for hitting the homer that won the Series in the seventh game, but Clemente led his team in hits with nine and batted .310.

During the middle sixties Clemente continued to be a dominant player, but there always seemed to be somebody else—Willie Mays, Hank Aaron, later Johnny Bench—who captured most of the hitting attention. That all changed after Clemente starred in the 1971 postseason classic. His three thousandth hit the following season was a major sports event.

Then came his shocking death at the age of thirty-eight. All of his teammates attended his funeral and he was elected to baseball's Hall of Fame in a special election shortly afterwards.

Clemente could run, hit, field, and throw and he was a leader of one of the dominant teams of the 1960s. He certainly has earned his way into Baseball's 100.

Christy Mathewson

(1900–1916)

In some magical, mystical way Tom Seaver, then with the New York Mets, once mused that he could almost feel as if he knew Christy Mathewson. Mathewson died in 1925 and Seaver was not born until 1944. Their careers, appearance, and personalities were similar.

A pitcher rarely works more than once in four days if he is a starter and he must have made an overwhelming contribution to be considered worthy of inclusion with hitters who win games day after day after day for their teams.

Walter Johnson was the only pitcher we deemed worthy of a spot among the first ten of *Baseball's 100*, and Christy Mathewson is the first pitcher in the next ten.

Mathewson won 373 games in seventeen seasons for the New York Giants and Cincinnati Reds, won 20 games as a rookie in 1901, had four seasons with more than 30 wins, and won more than 20 games in thirteen of his seventeen seasons. He pitched in an incredible 56 games and started 44 in his best season of 1908 when he was 37–11. He led the league in strikeouts six times and he is credited with inventing a pitch now known as the screwball and then called a fadeaway.

Mathewson was a handsome youngster, born August 12, 1880, and brought up comfortably in his hometown of Factoryville, Pennsylvania, where his parents were both independently wealthy from old family money. He attended a private school and soon matriculated at Bucknell University where he excelled as a scholar and a gentleman as well as an athlete.

When Mathewson was offered a big-league contract his parents frowned on the idea. Baseball was a game then for rowdies and uncouth farmers while Mathewson was a gentleman—soft-spoken, well-educated, a literate man and a man with a chance for much success in business. He convinced his parents he must pursue his goals and they soon backed him, attending many games and watching him pitch at the Polo Grounds in New York.

Other players often made fun of Mathewson for being a college man but his quiet dignity, and his toughness and excellence on the mound soon won universal respect. It was hard to make fun of a pitcher who had gone to college, when he was making you look foolish with his fadeaway.

Unlike many pitchers of his day, especially those who played for Giants manager John McGraw (called Muggsy for his toughness), Mathewson refused to throw at hitters. He felt he was good enough to get them out without threatening their lives with his fast ball.

The Giants won the pennant four times during Mathewson's career, including three straight in 1911, 1912, and 1913. Casey Stengel was a rookie with the 1912 Brooklyn Dodgers and remembered hitting against Mathewson many times.

"He would throw that fast ball by you, whoosh," Stengel said, "and then when you moved back a little to get a better look, he fired that fadeaway and made you look like a damn fool. I faced [Walter] Johnson and [Babe] Ruth and all of them but if Mathewson wasn't the best they was," he said.

In Stengelese, that simply meant that Stengel rated Johnson, Mathewson, and the young Ruth as the three best pitchers he had ever seen.

Mathewson was traded to Cincinnati in 1916 to manage that club, stayed there through August 28, 1918, and then enlisted in the Army at the age of thirty-eight. He was soon overseas with the famed Rainbow Division and suffered a lung problem after inhaling poison gas.

He returned home a hero, quickly returned to New York to become a Giants coach, and served as president of the Boston Braves through 1925.

Mathewson—called Big Six throughout his career due to his over-six-foot height and streamlined 195-pound frame—developed tuberculosis as a result of the gassing and his health disintegrated rapidly. By 1925 he was rasping and coughing constantly. He entered an upstate New York sanitarium at Saranac Lake where he died on October 7, 1925, as the World Series was opening in Pittsburgh.

His legend grew larger through the years as a marvelous pitcher, a gentleman, a scholar, a college man, and as an idol for millions of young men, including his current look-alike, Tom Seaver.

Christy Mathewson was one of the first five players elected to baseball's Hall of Fame in 1936 along with Ty Cobb, Ruth, Johnson, and Honus Wagner. He was the only scholar among them.

Tris Speaker

(1907–1928)

It was Tris Speaker's misfortune to have a career that ran almost concurrent with Ty Cobb's, spreading some twenty-two years from 1907 through the 1928 season with Philadelphia. Cobb almost always won the batting title and Speaker could collect only one crown in that time with his .386 mark in 1916. He had eighteen seasons over .300—Cobb had twenty-three—and collected 3,515 hits for fourth on the all-time list. Speaker averaged .344 for his career, the seventh highest lifetime mark ever, but is probably better known for catching the ball than hitting it.

Tris Speaker was the man who turned outfield defense into an aggressive weapon. Before his time outfielders played deep against the walls, more concerned with trying to catch a ball before it went over their heads than catching anything in front of them.

"The idea when I broke in," Speaker once said, "was to keep a hit from being a double. I decided I would try to keep a batted ball from being a single."

His fielding soon caught the attention of all baseball and he proudly carried the nickname of the Gray Eagle for his ability to swoop down on a sinking fly ball and, like some great bird, catch it before it hit the ground.

On defense he could catch a fly ball behind second, back up the infielders, sneak in behind unsuspecting runners for a pick-off play, and even turn a double play at second when the second baseman was out of position.

Tristram Speaker was born April 4, 1888, at Hubbard City, Texas. By the turn of the century he was growing to his full height of five eleven, spending much of his time riding horses and playing ball in the fields, and paying little attention to school. He was a natural right-hander but broke his arm riding horseback as a teenager and soon switched over to throwing and batting left-handed.

His mother, left with seven children after her husband died of consumption, wanted Tris to stay in school near home and work on a nearby ranch. He liked horses but he liked baseball even more. He soon convinced his mother to let him play baseball, at least for a while, and signed his first contract at the age of seventeen. He was assigned to Cleburne in the North Texas League.

His contract was sold to the Boston Red Sox and he batted .309 as a rookie in 1909. He stayed with the Red Sox through 1915, where he was a teammate of a youngster named Babe Ruth, a hard-throwing left-handed pitcher.

In 1916, after a bitter contract dispute, Speaker was traded to Cleveland for the astonishing sum of fifty-thousand dollars. He had ten seasons over .300 for the Indians as his career flourished. His fielding skills were considered the standard of excellence in the game and young outfielders began duplicating his style of play.

On July 19, 1919, Tris Speaker was named the playing manager of the Indians and led his team to the flag in 1920. Speaker batted .320 in the Series as Cleveland defeated the Brooklyn Dodgers.

After the 1926 season Speaker resigned as manager of the Indians. Newspapers speculated about his sudden resignation and things became clearer when a story broke that named Speaker and Ty Cobb as possible game-fixers. The dumping of the 1919 World Series by the White Sox (forever afterwards known as the Black Sox) to Cincinnati was not considered unique. Rumors that many players were involved with gamblers sullied the game. Speaker thought it was better to quit than fight.

He did return the next season, after charges were dropped, to play for Washington. He finished his playing career at Philadelphia and played and managed in the International League at Newark at the age of forty-two.

Speaker made some poor business investments in retirement and was helped by baseball, and helped the game in his turn by serving on various committees. He died December 8, 1958, at the age of seventy.

Tris Speaker was one of the game's greatest hitters, a marvelous all-around player whose impact is probably measured by how few Texas League fly balls now fall in for hits. Good outfielders now play Little League depth on many hitters, a tribute to the innovative outfield play of the Gray Eagle.

Mel Ott

(1926–1947)

When I was a kid growing up in Brooklyn, we hated the New York Giants. It was a ritual to argue violently with Giants fans and demean their players. The discussions would be loud and noisy until someone would mention one name: Master Melvin Ott.

"Now that's different," I would say, "Ottie doesn't count."

The skills, style, dignity, excitement engendered by Mel Ott in lifting his right front foot at the plate and lining a drive over the 257-foot wall in the rightfield stands at the Polo Grounds, seemed to transcend the fact he wore an enemy uniform.

All kids in New York in the 1930s and 1940s knew the legend of Mel Ott, how he came to the Giants in 1925 as a baby-faced sixteen-year-old with that crazy swing, how he sat next to Mr. John McGraw (hence the nickname Master Melvin), and how McGraw nursed him along for a couple of seasons as a kid before he became a Giant's regular at nineteen and played right field nearly every day for New York until he was thirty-six.

Ott was one of the finest left-handed sluggers the game has ever seen, the first man in league history to hit 500 home runs, and a slugger of such repute he was walked several times with runners on first and second to avoid a three-run homer.

Ottie, as he was known to all baseball fans, was born Melvin Thomas Ott in Gretna, Louisiana, on March 2, 1909. He was a small youngster but enjoyed hunting quail, walked through the woods with his father, played

some basketball and football, and excelled as a left-handed-hitting and -throwing catcher.

Since left-handed throwers can not be big-league catchers—more because of tradition than mechanics—Ott switched to the outfield. He still felt most comfortable as a catcher and when a scout sent him up to New York for a Giants tryout, he told McGraw that's what he was.

"You, a catcher?" McGraw said, as he looked at the five-foot-nine-inch 150-pounder. "You're not a catcher."

"Yes, sir," he said, "Yes, sir, Mr. McGraw, I am."

McGraw sent Ott into the batting cage and after he'd lifted that front leg and driven those baseballs into the seats, McGraw said, "You sure are a catcher."

What the manager meant really was that Ott was a hitter. A defensive position would come later.

McGraw kept Ott on the bench next to him the rest of 1925 and played him in 35 games in 1926 and 82 in 1927. Across the river a slugger named Babe Ruth was making most of the baseball noise with his record-breaking 60 homers, so hardly anyone noticed that the eighteen-year-old sweet-talking southerner was developing as a player without minor league experience. At nineteen, he smashed 18 homers and could no longer be ignored.

In 1932 Bill Terry succeeded McGraw as Giants manager. Ott was becoming one of the finest players in the game. He had hit 42 homers in 1929, and continued to hit 20 or more homers in fourteen of the sixteen seasons that followed.

Ott led the league in home runs twice and tied for the lead on three other occasions. All the while he was keeping his average at or near .300; his play helped the Giants to pennants in 1933, 1936, and 1937.

In 1942 Terry resigned and Ott became the player-manager of the Giants. He lasted until 1948, when he was fired in one of the most painful moves owner Horace Stoneham ever had to make and replaced by Leo Durocher of the hated Dodgers.

It was to Ott that Durocher had referred in his famed remark "Nice guys finish last." Ott's Giants had finished last the previous season. Ott was a nice guy and would remain so until his death.

After he was let go by the Giants as manager, he stayed around as a scout and broadcaster. He was not suited to either profession because he wasn't tough enough to hurt anybody's feelings.

On November 21, 1958, Master Melvin Ott died after an automobile accident.

No one who was around baseball in the 1930s or 1940s could ever forget the graceful style, on and off the field, of Mel Ott, a man who hit 511 homers, had a lifetime mark of .304, knocked in 1,860 runs, and played the outfield with a marvelous arm and incredible grace. Even Brooklyn Dodger fans wept at his death.

George Sisler

(1915–1930)

There are some hitters who have such style, such poise, such coordination as they swing a baseball bat, that their efforts remind observers of stars in dance, gymnastics, or other artistic endeavors.

Such a hitter was George Sisler, who swung a baseball bat with such beauty he was considered the stylist of his time.

Sisler played for the lowly St. Louis Browns most of his career and was always in direct public competition with the crosstown rival and slugger, Rogers Hornsby. Hornsby was a self-promoter, a braggart, a man who would buttonhole newspapermen who did not write favorably of him. Sisler was self-effacing, a shy man who stayed clear of controversy, sometimes avoided newspapermen by hiding in his hotel room, and hardly ever bragged about his deeds. He figured it was out there for everybody to see.

What any observer of Sisler's career could see was a lifetime .340 average over fifteen seasons, two batting titles, and two seasons over .400 (at .407 in 1920 and .420 in 1922). At the peak of his career at the age of twenty-nine, Sisler came down with a mysterious eye infection. It forced him to remain inactive all of 1923. When he returned in 1924, he batted only .305 and was never the same hitter again.

Sisler was able to record six seasons over .300 after the eye problems but .345 was his highest average after that.

His hitting may have slumped off a bit but he certainly lost nothing in the field. He was the class first baseman in all baseball, a marvelous left-handed throwing first sacker whose moves were so quick he was considered as good as a shortstop in fielding grounders.

George Harold Sisler was born March 24, 1893, in Manchester, Ohio. Both parents were graduates of Hiram College (which later turned out baseball player and broadcaster Bill White and American League vice-president Bob Fishel) and young George was brought up in an intellectual atmosphere. He was a fine high school player but a university degree was still considered essential for his successful later life.

Sisler entered the University of Michigan, where he came into contact with coach Branch Rickey. He was to remain close to Rickey throughout his life. A dispute soon arose between the Pirates and St. Louis Browns over Sisler's signing as an underaged youngster. The dispute was resolved in St. Louis' favor and Sisler soon joined his ex-coach, Rickey, now the manager, without a day in the minors.

He was twenty-two years old and was the regular St. Louis first baseman inside of a year. He then proceeded to hit over .300 nine times in a row as he became the most celebrated player on one of the worst teams in the game.

In 1922 he set a mark for hitting in 41 consecutive games, a mark that was to last until 1941 when Joe DiMaggio, another smooth, stylish hitter, was to hit in 56 straight games for the Yankees.

Sisler had his last big year for the Browns in 1927 and was sold to Washington for the start of the 1928 season.

He had always been an all-around athlete and had actually joined the Browns originally as a pitcher. His hitting was so impressive he was soon switched and wound up pitching 22 games in six different seasons.

Sisler managed the Browns for three seasons; later he scouted and served as a batting instructor many years.

Sisler and his wife, Kathleen, had three sons and one daughter. Each of the sons became a professional player. George became president of the International League, Dick became a player with a famous 1950 homer for the Phillies. Later he served as a Big League manager and a coach for the New York Mets. And Dave, graduated from Princeton into the big leagues as a pitcher.

George Sisler had a nice, even lifetime average of .340. He was one of the finest hitters the game had ever seen and a lot of young players, including his own three sons, benefited from his teaching.

When George Harold Sisler died in St. Louis on March 26, 1973, at the age of eighty, some fans were certain he could still lash out a line drive to right with his dying breath.

Grover Cleveland Alexander

(1911–1930)

It has been said of many players, Grover Cleveland Alexander not being the first or the last, that fans could only wonder how good they would be if they didn't drink.

Alexander drank. Plenty. And often. He was to live sixty-three years, but a good part of his life was made unpleasant by illness and alcoholism, one possibly brought on by the other.

His face looked like a piece of raw meat in the later stages of his career and his managers often had to check with his teammates to see if they thought Old Pete could make it that day. His most famous public drinking bout occurred after the sixth game of the 1926 World Series between the Cardinals and the Yankees, on October ninth.

Alexander, then in the final seasons of his career, pitched for the Cards that game and beat the Yankees 10–2, holding Babe Ruth hitless and Lou Gehrig to a puny single. Alexander, then thirty-nine years old, celebrated his victory at some all-night taverns. He came to Yankee Stadium to sleep off his painful night. No manager in his right mind would call on a thirty-nine-year-old veteran in relief after he had pitched nine innings the day before. On the other hand, no one ever accused St. Louis manager Rogers Hornsby of doing the expected.

In the seventh game the Yankees loaded the bases. They were trailing 3–2. Veteran Jesse Haines seemed to be losing his stuff, and with a dangerous right-handed hitter, Tony Lazzeri, up for the Yankees, Hornsby wanted Alexander.

53

Alex had been fast asleep on the bullpen bench in the late afternoon sun. He was awakened, then threw a couple of pitches and sauntered in across the field.

Lazzeri hit the second pitch a ton down the left-field foul line. It was foul by several feet and Alexander later explained, "Do you think I would have thrown him the same pitch if I thought he could hit it fair?"

The current president of the Cleveland Indians, Gabe Paul, was a young fan at that game more than fifty-five years ago, and recalls the pitch clearly.

"I was sitting in the bullpen area. I had hitched all the way down from my home in Rochester, New York. I saw them shake Alexander awake and I saw that the pitch was easily foul. I never knew what the fuss was all about. It was a good pitch," Paul said.

Then Alexander threw a ball, fired another strike, and Lazzeri was out. Alexander retired the Yankees in order in the eighth, got two hitters in the ninth, walked Babe Ruth, and watched as Ruth was thrown out stealing to end the Series.

Grover Cleveland Alexander won 373 games in twenty big-league seasons, lost only 208, had nine seasons with 20 or more wins and three with 30 or more. He won 31, 33, and 30 for the Phillies in 1915, 1916, 1917.

Alexander served in the infantry in 1918 in France during World War I, developed epilepsy, and also began drinking heavily.

Alexander was born February 26, 1887, at Elba, Nebraska, one of thirteen children, twelve of them boys. He was named after the President of the United States.

He played semipro baseball until signed at the advanced age of twenty-three, by the Phillies. He led the league with 28 wins in 1911, his first big-league season. He won Philadelphia's first World Series game ever (they next won a pennant in 1950 and were beaten four games to none by the Yankees) in 1915 and was traded to the Cubs after the 1917 season. The Phillies finally won four games in a Series and the title by beating Kansas City in 1980.

He then went to the Cardinals in June of 1926, pitched for them until 1929, and finished up his career at forty-three with the Phillies again.

Alexander had a struggle with the bottle for the remainder of his life. He died of epilepsy and alcoholism back in his home state in St. Paul, Nebraska, on November 4, 1950.

He had a blazing fast ball, a fiery temper, and a competitive spirit. He was a great pitcher, a winner of 373 big-league games, but he could not conquer his own conscience. Big Pete died alone, a broken, diseased man, in a cheap hotel room.

Lefty Grove

(1925-1941)

Modern baseball fans, those who got into the game after World War II, think of only one name when they discuss blazing left-handed speed: Sandy Koufax.

For those who go a little further back, to the 1930s and late 1920s, there was a left-hander who was the Sandy Koufax of his time.

Lefty Grove was the hardest thrower of his era and one of the most successful all-around pitchers with a fast ball that probably would have registered over one hundred miles per hour if the currently used radar gun had been in existence then.

Grove was the pitcher all hitters tried to avoid and he had just enough comfortable control trouble to intimidate most batters. He was a fiery competitor who would think nothing of berating himself, or of doing the same to a teammate, an umpire, or a manager if he thought he was wronged.

One afternoon, shortly before his seventieth birthday, he was sitting quietly in a lounge chair at the Otesaga Inn at the Hall of Fame in Cooperstown. I approached him and began asking about the great hitters he'd faced.

"Damn it," he suddenly exploded, "there isn't a man playing the game I can't strike out."

"But Mr. Grove," I gently reminded him, "you are nearly seventy years old."

"That don't matter," he said. "The hitters know my reputation."

Every hitter knew Grove's reputation. Even Ted Williams, who played with Grove in Boston as a young kid outfielder, was saying some forty years later that Grove was the hardest thrower he had ever seen.

"I only caught him at the end," Williams said, "but nobody could throw a baseball any harder."

Grove used that fast ball, a crackling curve, and his later-acquired control to win 300 games on the button, lose only 140, and strike out 2,266 hitters in seventeen seasons. He had a legendary season of 32–4 with a league-leading 2.06 ERA in 1931. He had eight seasons with 20 or more wins and led the league in ERA nine times. He was the league's strikeout leader his first seven seasons, a feat never matched in baseball.

Robert Moses "Lefty" Grove was born March 6, 1900, at Lonaconing, Maryland, outside of Baltimore. He left school early, worked in the coal mines as a day laborer, worked in the railroads and as a glass blower. His flaming personality caused many squabbles and he lost several jobs over it. He played baseball on weekends and in the late afternoons during the summer and was soon recognized as one of the best pitchers around.

He was signed by the local professional club in 1920 and soon was playing for the Baltimore Orioles, the famed farm team near his home. He won 27 games twice and 25 games once for the Orioles.

Major-league teams panted after his services and the Philadelphia A's quickly purchased him from Baltimore for more than one hundred thousand dollars.

He had a couple of slow seasons at the beginning with a 10–12 rookie year and a 13–13 sophomore season. Then he hit his stride with Connie Mack's A's, winning 20 games in 1927 in a season dominated by Babe Ruth's 60 homers.

With his curve ball and control improving, Grove then recorded six straight and ultimately seven out of eight 20-game seasons. After his first season he would never again lose more games than he won, ending with a 7–7 mark in 1941 for Boston at the age of forty-one.

In 1933 Mack decided to break up his great Philadelphia teams, which had won pennants in 1929, 1930, and 1931, by selling off the key stars for profit. Grove was shipped to Boston in a five-player deal. The Red Sox gave the A's two players and $125,000 for Grove and two others. The four traded players were dealt even up with the money being obtained by the A's in exchange for Grove.

His fast ball no longer scared years off hitters' lives but was still plenty effective in Fenway. Grove won 20 games for the Red Sox in 1935 and then won 17, 17, 14, and 15 in the next four seasons.

After his 1941 season he retired on December seventh, as the Japanese were bombing Pearl Harbor. He lived a comfortable, quiet retirement and was named baseball's greatest living left-handed pitcher in 1969. He died at the home of one of his children in Norwalk, Ohio, in 1975.

Long after he was gone, the legend of Lefty Grove remained. Smoke.

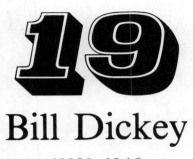

Bill Dickey

(1928–1946)

Yogi Berra was once asked how he got to be such a good defensive catcher.

"Bill Dickey learned me all his experiences," Yogi said.

Dickey was a coach on the Yankees when Berra was a young catcher. Whether or not he could "learn" Yogi all his experiences, he certainly had the credentials after a brilliant seventeen-year career.

The toughest position to play in baseball is catcher, not just for the squatting, kneeling, pounding it takes but for the handling of pitchers, the planning, the thinking, the overall responsibilities that fall to the only man on the field facing all of his teammates.

It is enough when catchers just catch and throw well, call a good game, and keep their pitchers winning. Whatever they hit is a bonus. Bill Dickey always hit, with eleven seasons over .300 and one year as high as .362.

Dickey was a devastating left-handed line-drive hitter with power who hit 202 homers in his career and had 133 RBIs in 1937.

Perhaps the most significant statistic next to Dickey's name is the eight World Series teams he played on. The Yanks lost only one of three championships—the 1942 series against the surprising St. Louis Cardinals.

Dickey may have gained as much fame for his relationship with Lou Gehrig as he did for his playing. After Dickey joined the Yankees in 1928, three years after Gehrig became a regular and began his incredible streak of 2,130 consecutive games played, they were inseparable friends. Gehrig and Dickey played cards together on road trips, socialized at home together,

sympathized with each other after a rare bad day. Dickey was the first Yankee to know that Gehrig was suffering from a fatal illness.

The tall, thin, soft-spoken southern gentleman from Bastrop, Louisiana, was born June 6, 1907. His family soon moved to Arkansas, where his father became a railroader, and Bill made his home in Little Rock from that day on.

He starred for his local high school team and began playing semipro baseball as a left-handed-hitting, strong-throwing catcher in 1924. He soon signed a professional contract and was moved to the New York Yankees in 1928. There he joined a club that had demolished all of baseball in 1927 and was generally conceded to be the best team of all time. Their only weakness was at catcher and the ramrod-straight, slugging left-handed-hitting kid soon filled that position on a team dominated by Gehrig, Babe Ruth, and a marvelous pitching staff.

"He was a young kid but in his quiet way he took right over," said Waite Hoyt, one of the pitchers on those great Yankee teams. "He was a no-nonsense guy and you did what he said or he wanted to know why."

Dickey soon established himself as one of the finest defensive players in the game, a wonderful hitter and, most importantly, a terrific clutch batter.

"I enjoyed hitting with men on base," Dickey once said. "It was more of a challenge. It helped me concentrate more on the pitch."

Dickey had four straight seasons with 100 or more RBIs and caught more than 100 games thirteen straight years, an incredible feat of stamina.

Dickey spanned two of the great Yankee eras, the Ruth-Gehrig teams from 1928, when he joined them, through 1934 when the Babe moved on to Boston; and the Gehrig-Joe DiMaggio years from 1936, when Joe D became a Yankee, until 1946 when Dickey quit as a player.

He was named the Yankee manager that season after Joe McCarthy resigned but wasn't particularly comfortable in the position. He gave it up at the end of the year and went home.

Dickey returned to coach under manager Casey Stengel and his first prize pupil was young Berra. Dickey stayed with the Yankees as a coach and scout through 1960.

Tall, handsome, and still as thin as ever, Dickey lives in Little Rock and still enjoys good health and success in the investment business as he nears his seventy-fifth birthday.

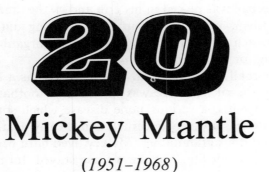

Mickey Mantle

(1951–1968)

If ever a man was born to be a great baseball player, it was Mickey Mantle, the blond, superstrong slugger from Oklahoma.

His short, colorful name, his blond good looks, his impressive power, his vulnerability as a country kid all combined to help the legend build.

The same guy the public now sees on beer commercials was once so shy that he couldn't lift his head up to talk or look someone in the eye. He didn't have to. Everybody looked at him.

"I remember when he first joined us that spring of nineteen fifty-one," said Ralph Houk, a teammate, friend, and manager, "and started hitting home runs left-handed and right-handed. He would stop batting practice or stop all the moving around in the stands when he came up."

Casey Stengel had seen Joe DiMaggio losing his skills as the Yankee center fielder due to injuries, illness, and age, and began grooming the nineteen-year-old kid from Commerce.

When he first saw Mantle boom a few over the wall, Stengel announced, "He's got it in his body to be great."

He sure did. And he sure was.

At a shade under six feet, Mantle began his career at less than 170 pounds but soon filled out to nearly 200 pounds as he became a distinct threat to become the only man to hit a fair ball out of Yankee Stadium. He came as close as any man ever has when he unloaded a six-hundred-foot drive off Kansas City relief pitcher Bill Fischer in 1962.

"That was the hardest ball I ever hit," Mantle said.

Mantle had always seemed to be hitting baseballs that caused long measuring sessions. He once hit a homer off Chuck Stobbs in Washington that went 565 feet. He also hit many balls on a liner off the center-field wall at Yankee Stadium over four hundred fifty feet away.

Born in Spavinaw, Oklahoma, on October 20, 1931, Mickey Charles Mantle was named after his father's baseball hero, Detroit catcher Mickey Cochrane. A baseball was placed in his crib and by the time he was two years old his father, Elvin, known as Mutt, was working out with him in the backyard as a switch hitter. He played on his first organized team at seven and was traveling for ball games at nine.

He was a football and basketball player as well as a baseball player in high school and a local hero. He was kicked in a football game and soon developed osteomyelitis, a serious bone disease which sometimes becomes malignant. Mantle was always concerned about early death. His father died at thirty-nine, as did his grandfather. Mickey lived hard because he assumed he would not live a full life. But the disease stayed dormant, and Mantle enjoyed good health as he passed forty and the legend disappeared.

Scout Tom Greenwade of the Yankees drove to see Mantle in a neighborhood sandlot game and offered him a contract. After the game, with the rain pouring down around them, Mantle signed the Yankee pact in the back of Greenwade's car.

He was a scatter-armed shortstop at Independence and Joplin before joining the Yankees in the spring of 1951 while they were training in Phoenix. It was DiMaggio's last season and when manager Casey Stengel saw Mantle throw, he moved him to the outfield.

Stengel took Mantle under his wing. He worked closely with the youngster and at one Brooklyn exhibition he walked him out to the tricky right-field wall at Ebbets Field.

"Did you ever play here?" Mantle asked.

"Sure," said Stengel, "did you think I was born old?"

Mantle started slowly as a Yankee, had to be farmed out to Kansas City, and was recalled in midseason to finish up with a .267 mark and 13 homers in 96 games. Hitting huge homers left-handed and right-handed, covering acres of turf in Yankee Stadium, throwing bullets from the outfield, and running the bases with abandon, Mantle soon became a crowd favorite.

Mickey won the Triple Crown in 1956 with 52 homers, 130 RBIs, and a .353 average. The next year he hit .365 with 34 homers. His best home-run season was 1961, when he hit 54. It didn't help him win the home-run title because teammate Roger Maris broke Babe Ruth's record that year with 61 homers.

Mantle hit 536 homers in his eighteen years, averaged .298, and knocked in 1,509 runs. He played some first base in the later part of his career but was mostly a center fielder.

Mantle played on twelve Yankee pennant winners from 1951, when he suffered a knee injury (and shared a hospital room with his dying father) through 1964. He hit a record 18 World Series homers.

Mantle became one of the game's most popular players toward the end of his career, as he battled numerous injuries to hang on. A hard player, he broke nearly every bone in his body in the course of his career. He had a flaming temper, which he manifested mostly against himself or against sportswriters, and he was liked and admired by teammates and opponents alike.

He seemed to mature and grow better looking in his later days and he made a comfortable adjustment to retirement after 1968 with many baseball banquet appearances, golf tournaments, and old-timers' days.

"I have this recurring dream," he says. "I'm in a car trying to get into Yankee Stadium. Casey is calling my name and I hear it announced on the public address. I can't get out the cab. Something is holding me back."

On October 20, 1981, Mickey Mantle will be fifty years old. That is what is holding him back. He wants back into the game, and anyone who ever saw him drive a ball four hundred feet, left-handed or right-handed, wants the same thing.

The memories are reward enough.

Rod Carew

(1967–present)

The first active player to make Baseball's 100, Rod Carew is number twenty-one and moving up. He may make the top ten if he keeps going the way he has been for nearly fifteen years.

Carew is the finest pure hitter in the game, a seven-time batting champion (only Ty Cobb has more) and such a skilled hitter that there is simply no way to pitch him.

"You just throw the ball down the middle of the plate," Baltimore's Jim Palmer says, "and hope he hits it at somebody."

A left-handed hitter with incredible bat control, Carew has proven to be the best hitter in the game over the last fourteen years with a lifetime mark of .333 through the 1980 season and twelve straight seasons over .300. He hit .388 in 1977, the first serious threat to Ted Williams's last American League .400 season in 1941, and missed out mostly due to injuries. George Brett's .390 in 1980 was even a bit closer.

In an era when batters concentrated on hitting home runs, Carew stood out because he thought hitting .300 or .350 would help his team more than hitting .250 with 25 homers.

"There's just no way to pitch him," said ex-Yankee ex-Detroit and now Boston manager Ralph Houk. "If you throw it three feet outside he throws the bat at the ball and dunks a single."

Carew's achievements are even more incredible when it is realized that he didn't play any organized baseball until he was fifteen.

Rodney Cline Carew was born October 1, 1945, on a railroad train between his family's home in Gatun and Panama City in Panama. A doctor happened to be aboard as Mrs. Carew started to give birth. Rodney Cline was the doctor's name and the offspring gathered both his doctor's name and his mother's appreciation.

The family moved to New York City when Carew was a teenager and he soon was playing baseball around his Washington Heights neighborhood in Manhattan.

"He must have been fifteen when I first saw him," said scout Herb Stein, a former New York City police officer. "He was skinny and not very tall but he had that wonderful swing. I watched him hit three or four line drives and I realized right off I had a kid who was a big leaguer."

Stein was a part-time scout for the Minnesota Twins and he signed Carew to a bonus contract in 1964. The youngster from Panama was sent to the Twins farm club in Melbourne, Florida. He hit .325, .303, and .292 as a minor leaguer before joining the Twins in 1967. Two years later he won his first of seven batting titles as the Twins won the American League west race under manager Billy Martin.

Carew was moody, quiet, withdrawn around his teammates. He spent most of his time by himself preparing for the next game.

"I wasn't unfriendly," he says. "I just had to put so much time and concentration into preparing myself I was better off alone."

His outstanding hitting soon drew much public attention. He was also gaining fame as a base stealer, stealing home seven times in 1969. He was a smooth-fielding second baseman with a weak arm as his only fielding drawback.

Soon the Twins were shifting him to first base to minimize that factor.

In 1970 he broke his ankle and recovered to play more than 140 games in the next eight seasons. He was an example of durability as well as skill.

For each of the last twelve seasons, including 1980, Carew has kept his average over .300 and at the age of thirty-five shows no signs of slowing down. He was driving on 2,500 hits as the 1981 season opened and should be able to record the exalted 3,000-hit mark sometime in 1983.

Then he can set his sights on lasting a half dozen more years and catching Ty Cobb's magical total of 4,191 career hits.

Reggie Jackson

(1967–present)

Mr. October, the man who excels during the pressures of play-off and World Series, has been the best home-run hitter and the best strikeout hitter in the last two decades.

Reggie Jackson has been able to hit 20 or more homers for thirteen seasons and has also been able to strike out more than 100 times in each of those seasons. It is part of what makes Jackson Mr. Excitement as well as Mr. October.

Whatever Jackson does in the game of baseball, from hitting a homer, to striking out, he has done it with exceptional flair. He has commandeered the attention of the press, almost since he arrived on the big-league scene, with his homers, his strikeouts, and his actions and reactions to everything said for or against him.

Baseball players have long considered him the ultimate hot dog—baseballese for showoff—as his career moved from Kansas City to Oakland to New York.

"There isn't enough mustard in all America," said Oakland teammate Darold Knowles, "to cover that hot dog."

Hot dog or not, Jackson has proven beyond a doubt that only the end of his career and the five-year waiting period can keep him from the Hall of Fame at Cooperstown.

He hit his first big-league homer in 1967, his four hundredth in 1980, and will probably hit his last the last day he plays somewhere around 1985.

When he hit his four hundredth, he was asked if he thought he could get close to Hank Aaron's leading total of 755.

"Aaron is an entire career away," he said.

Reginald Martinez Jackson was born May 18, 1946, in Wyncote, Pennsylvania, a suburb of Philadelphia. His father was a tailor, and young Reggie—named after the family doctor who delivered him—was one of six children. His parents divorced and Reggie lived with his father, helping him on the dry-cleaning route, working at home to keep the house going, picking up odd jobs, and playing baseball.

"Every time we needed him around the house for something," his dad, Martinez Jackson, still the owner of a Philadelphia tailor shop, once said, "he was at the ball field."

Reggie starred in four sports at Cheltenham High outside of Philadelphia and won a scholarship to Arizona State University. There he broke all the home-run records, starred on the football team, and left after his sophomore year with an eighty-five-thousand-dollar bonus from Charlie Finley in his pocket.

In 1967 Jackson joined the A's and subsequently led the team to five straight Western Division titles, three pennants, and three straight World Series titles—the only team other than the Yankees of 1936–1939 and 1949–53 to achieve that mark.

That great team included Catfish Hunter, Ken Holtzman, Rollie Fingers, Joe Rudi, Bert Campaneris, Dick Green, Gene Tenace, and Sal Bando, but it was Jackson who was the anchor. He was the league MVP in 1973 with 32 homers, 117 RBIs, and a .293 average.

In 1976, after a contract dispute, he was traded to Baltimore. He reported late but had another fine season with 27 homers, 91 RBIs, and a .277 mark.

Then he became a free agent and signed a $2.85 million contract with the Yankees.

The 1977 season was filled with turmoil between Jackson and manager Billy Martin—fanned by owner George Steinbrenner—but Jackson continued to excel. The Yankees won, beat Kansas City in the play-offs, and went into the Series against the Dodgers.

Jackson became the first player to hit five homers in a Series, including three on three swings in the final game. The only other player ever to hit three in one game? Babe Ruth. The Babe did it twice.

"The Babe was great," said Jackson. "I was only lucky."

Lucky or not, it marked Jackson as a very special player. Three more fine seasons followed and as Jackson drives on 500 homers, he is certainly one of the best all-around players of his time and worthy of inclusion among the top 25 of Baseball's 100.

Sandy Koufax

(1955–1966)

Sandy Koufax was thirty years old when he stood on a platform in 1966 at a Los Angeles hotel and announced, "I'm quitting. I'm leaving before I do permanent damage to my arm."

It was that early retirement after only twelve years as a big leaguer—six struggling seasons and six overwhelming ones—that keeps Koufax from finishing higher on the list of Baseball's 100. Given normal pitching health and another six or eight years of productive pitching, Koufax may have well begun to rival Walter Johnson, Christy Mathewson, and Lefty Grove.

"Trying to hit Sandy Koufax," says Pittsburgh's Willie Stargell, "was like trying to drink coffee with a fork."

It simply couldn't be done.

Koufax registered four no-hitters in his career. Only Nolan Ryan has as many. Koufax had one perfect game and led the league in wins three separate times. He led in ERA five straight times and he led in strikeouts four different times.

Koufax was so overwhelming that the first time the New York Mets beat him—with Tug McGraw getting the win in relief—a celebration was held. Koufax was as close to being invincible as a pitcher from 1961 through 1966 as any pitcher who ever put on a toe plate.

Sanford Koufax was born in Brooklyn, New York, on December 30, 1935. He grew up wild about his hometown Dodgers and often imitated the players on that team in street games. As a youngster at Lafayette High School his best sport was basketball with his left-handed jump shots leading his team to many victories.

He played some sandlot ball but won most of his fame as a basketball player. It earned him a scholarship to the University of Cincinnati.

Koufax played summer baseball after his freshman year at Cincinnati. He was considered by a Dodger scout as a hard-throwing pitcher and weak-hitting first baseman. He was later to prove both scouting reports correct, becoming a great pitcher and remaining a nonhitter who set a record by striking out twelve times in a row.

Dodger scout Al Campanis watched Koufax work out in the rain at Ebbets Field and immediately offered to sign him. Koufax had promised the Pittsburgh Pirates he would work out there and flew to Pittsburgh while the Dodgers fretted. Koufax did not know his father had already given the Dodgers his word that Sandy would sign with them. Even though the Pirates' offer was much larger—thirty thousand dollars to Brooklyn's fourteen thousand dollars—Sandy went with his hometown team. A bonus rule kept him on the Dodger roster. He never played a day in the minors. After he finally made it, manager Walter Alston was asked why Koufax was never farmed out.

"Because every day I expected him to become a great pitcher," he said.

Blessed with enormous hands and fingers, Sandy wrapped a baseball tightly and threw a blazing fast ball, a wicked curve, and an occasional change-up. It was his speed, overpowering and intimidating, that finally made him a winner after he conquered control trouble.

He struggled for five seasons until catcher Norm Sherry suggested he throw easier instead of harder.

"We were just talking on a bus going to an exhibition game. Sandy was depressed. I suggested he might do just as well throwing easier. It seemed like something to try," Sherry said.

Soon Sandy was throwing easier and the ball was in the strike zone. After six mediocre seasons he pitched six brilliant ones, 18–13 in 1961 with 269 strikeouts, followed by seasons of 14–7 (that 1962 season was cut short by a finger injury, but he lead the league with a 2.54 ERA), 25–5, 19–5, 26–8, and 27–9 in 1966, his final season. He had a 1.73 ERA that season, led the league with 317 K's (he had a record 382 in 1965 since broken by Nolan Ryan) and then the retirement.

Koufax was a soft-spoken young man who enjoyed theater and art, listened for hours to records, enjoyed golf, and tried broadcasting unsuccessfully after his retirement. He came back to the Dodgers in 1979 as a minor-league pitching instructor. He no longer was the brutish 215-pound left-hander with the wicked fast ball. He stood six two but weighed only 180. He lived quietly in southern California, with his wife, the former Ann Widmark, daughter of the movie villian, Richard Widmark.

It was nice to have Koufax back in the game, even without his fast ball. That speed was worthy of the best the game ever saw.

Bob Feller

(1936–1956)

No man ever threw a baseball harder than Rapid Robert Feller the big, high-kicking right-hander for the Cleveland Indians.

Feller was probably the greatest pitching draw of all time, with fans turning out in record numbers to see his strikeout performances. His man-to-man challenges against Joe DiMaggio and Ted Williams, the two premier hitters of his time, were thrilling episodes.

"I used to get real high when I went against Williams or DiMaggio," Feller said. "I would stand out there on the mound and think it was just me against them, alone, in some quiet place, man to man, forgetting that there might be fifty or sixty or seventy thousand people watching us."

In eighteen seasons with the Indians, Feller won 266 games, lost only 162, pitched 3 no-hitters and 12 one-hitters, and finished with an ERA of 3.25.

As impressive as his statistics are, the most incredible fact of Feller's career is that he lost nearly four years of baseball time while serving in the Navy in World War II. Feller was twenty-four when he left and nearly twenty-eight when he returned, certainly the peak pitching years for any hard thrower.

This flamethrowing right-hander had a huge curve and a good change to go with his mighty fast-ball. His motion, a full pump with arms moving in synch, then a huge kick, helped him hide the baseball until it was on the hitter.

Robert William Andrew Feller was born November 3, 1918, at Van Meter, Iowa, deep in the Midwest corn country. He was a farm boy who put

in a full day of summer chores on his father's farm before playing baseball at twilight. He was playing with older teenagers and grown men on local teams when he was just past thirteen.

When he was sixteen, the Cleveland Indians signed him and kept him hidden on a minor-league roster while he continued pitching locally. At seventeen he joined the Indians and made his debut pitching an exhibition against the Cardinals. Manager Frank Frisch, taking one look at Feller's fast ball in warmups, quickly scratched himself from the lineup.

"Face that kid? Are you crazy? The old Flash may be dumb, but he ain't that dumb," Frisch said.

Cleveland manager Steve O'Neill, who had been a catcher, worked with the youngster. He assigned veteran catcher Rollie Hemsley as his roommate and the two spent many late nights together on the road talking baseball.

Feller was 17–11 in 1938 and 24–9 in 1939, before he was twenty-one years old. In every city in the league, when the Indians came to town, fans wanted to know if Feller was pitching. His appearance was worth ten thousand fans at the gate.

In 1940 on opening day he pitched a no-hitter against the White Sox. He would later pitch one against the Yankees and his third against the Tigers. In one of the most ironic baseball accidents ever, Feller's mother, watching her son pitch for the first time, was injured when a foul ball struck her in the stands behind first base.

Feller led the league in wins, five times, tied one other time, led in innings pitched five times, led in strikeouts seven times, and was considered to throw harder than any other pitcher of his era.

The Indians won two pennants in Feller's time, in 1948 and 1954. He lost his two Series starts in 1948 and did not pitch in 1954.

He pitched two more years as a spot starter for the Indians and retired after the 1956 season. He went into private business in Cleveland, did some scouting for the Indians, worked at a hotel chain as a public relations representative, and now spends a good part of his summer traveling the country for organized baseball giving clinics to kids and working with minor-league organizations.

Feller can still excite an old-timer when he walks out to the mound in some small park in a minor-league town, lifts that left leg in the air, and throws a pitch to the plate. There isn't a lot of speed left in that famed right arm but just seeing the old Cleveland pitcher in his familiar number 19 is a warm enough memory for many people.

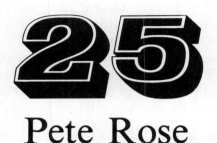

Pete Rose

(*1963–present*)

When the New York Yankees played an exhibition game against the Cincinnati Reds in Tampa in 1963, Yankee left-hander Whitey Ford sat in the sun watching the game.

Suddenly, a short, skinny Cincinnati infielder with a hard face and a crew cut drew a walk. He raced to first base as fast as his legs would carry him.

"Hey, Charley Hustle," Ford yelled from the bench, "take it easy."

Charley Hustle—Pete Rose—could never slow down. It wasn't in his game plan. Pete Rose knows only one way to play the game, full out, as hard as he can, never quitting, never failing to try, always proving that sheer talent isn't the only thing that counts.

The stocky two-hundred-pound first baseman of the Philadelphia Phillies has proven that great hitters are made, not born. Rose had average baseball talents. With determination, hustle, effort, courage, and an aggressive switch-hitting style he has moved close to Stan Musial's National League hit record and has an outside chance of catching Ty Cobb as the most prolific hitter of all time.

Rose has put together fourteen seasons over .300 and established a record for most seasons over 200 hits with ten. Only once in his entire career has Rose failed to play in over 145 games. He has been a National League all-star at five different positions, first, second, third, left field, and right field.

Rose has won three batting titles and finished in the top ten of the batting race every year but one since he became a regular.

Peter Edward Rose was born in Cincinnati on April 14, 1941. He played football as a youngster on the same semiprofessional team as his father. His first love was always baseball, and an uncle, who was a scout for the Cincinnati Reds, helped get him a tryout.

The Reds were unimpressed by the skinny, crew-cut kid who was a switch hitter with little power and awkward in the field.

But they took a chance on him and signed him to a class D contract. He hit .277 at Geneva, moved up to Tampa, and played a third minor-league season at Macon, Georgia. Ticketed for the Reds' Triple-A club, Rose came to camp in 1963 under manager Fred Hutchinson.

"Play me, play me," he kept badgering the Cincinnati manager.

Wanting to get the kid off his back and away from the bench, Hutchinson started Rose in several exhibition games. He was soon starting all of them at second base and was to become a regular on his way to the Rookie of the Year Award.

He hit .273 that first season and slipped back to .269 the second season. He was worried about his career.

"I had some doubts about whether I could hit big-league pitching," Rose said. "I had fallen off the second season and I was concerned."

Then he worked hard all spring, improved his batting stroke, and hit .312. There were no doubts after that as Rose put together nine .300 seasons in a row.

The Reds won four pennants and two World Series in Rose's time with the team. He was always considered an underpaid player behind slugger Johnny Bench and speedster Joe Morgan, and after a free-agency year he signed with the Philadelphia Phillies for five years at four million dollars.

He continued to excel with the Phillies, hitting .331 there his first year with the club and .282 his second season. He was a vital factor in Philadelphia's 1980 World Series win.

At thirty-nine Rose showed no signs of slowing down and if he could average 175 hits for the next four seasons he might wind up the leading hit man of all time.

If he fails in that goal he earns his spot among Baseball's 100 for another reason. Some seventeen years after Whitey Ford first saw him, Pete Rose is still Charley Hustle.

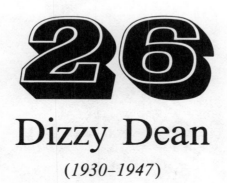

Dizzy Dean

(*1930–1947*)

"A lot of people who ain't saying ain't, ain't eating."

Dizzy Dean said that in answer to a letter from a teacher criticizing his misuse of the language while broadcasting baseball games.

Even in retirement Dizzy Dean wouldn't take nothin' from nobody.

As colorful a character as ever played the game, this Muhammad Ali of his day could brag loud and deliver. Once his pitching brother Paul pitched a no-hitter in the second game of a doubleheader against the woeful Brooklyn Dodgers.

"If I'da know'd Daffy was settin' out to pitch a no-hitter," Dean said, "I'd a done one myself." He had only pitched a one-hitter.

Dean pitched only twelve years in the big leagues and won only 150 games. Like those of Sandy Koufax, his numbers are unimpressive in their entirety but an injury dramatically shortened his career. In the 1937 All-Star Game, Dean was struck on the big toe by a line drive off the bat of Earl Averill. He tried pitching with his toe in a splint, soon hurt his arm, and could never throw hard again. He hung around for another half dozen years—including a token appearance as a gate attraction for the St. Louis Browns in 1947—but was never much of a pitcher after the injury.

From his rookie year of 1932 through 1937, before he was injured, Dean was a hard thrower with a good curve ball and excellent control. He seemed to pitch only as hard as he had to to win, often keeping up a constant chatter from the mound with fans, teammates, and opponents.

After a 26–10 minor-league season at Houston in 1931, he was 18–15 for

the Cardinals and then won 20, 30, 28, 24, and 13. He fell off to 7–1 for the Cards in 1937 and was traded to the Cubs.

His 30 victories in 1934 came against 7 losses in 50 games for a marvelous .811 pitching percentage. He also led the league in strikeouts with 195. He could only win 28 the next year for the Gashouse Gang but was generally regarded as the best pitcher in baseball during those two seasons.

Jay Hanna Dean—he sometimes told interviewers his given name was Jerome Herman—was born January 16, 1911, in Lucas, Arkansas. His father was a poor dirt farmer and the family moved through the south looking for seasonal work. Young Jay helped on the farms, drove horse-carrying wagons, did odd jobs, and enlisted in the Army during the Depression. He pitched in the Army and also acquired the name of Dizzy—a nickname he would be known by the rest of his life—while in service.

In 1930 he got out of the Army and soon signed with the St. Louis Cardinals. He pitched in St. Joseph and Houston before being called up to the big club.

A big kid who stood six three and weighed nearly 205 pounds, Dean could intimidate hitters with his close fast ball. He was amusing and entertaining off the mound—mostly because of his storytelling in cornpone English—but tough and aggressive on the mound. When he was in a close game he was all business, but when he was ahead he thought nothing of telling the batter where the next pitch was coming from and challenging him to hit it. When it was his number-one heater, that explosive fast ball, few could do it.

All his teammates were amused by him even though Dean drove his skipper, Frankie Frisch, a little wild with his antics. He was often late for games and seemed unconcerned about his manager's problems.

His brother Paul, who was called Daffy but wasn't, was a teammate from 1934 through 1937.

Old Diz, as he liked to be called as he aged, won only 16 games for the Cubs after being traded by the Cards.

Dean retired after the 1941 season—except for a brief last-day fling with the Browns in 1947—and became a broadcaster. He mangled the English language but was a beloved figure for his down-home humor, his singing on the air ("The Wabash Cannonball" was his favorite), and his enormous girth, which reached well over three hundred pounds.

He died July 17, 1974 in Reno, Nevada, and his body was shipped back in a huge casket to Wiggins, Mississippi, where he had made his home for years.

A short career but a wonderful one. Old Diz belongs among Baseball's 100.

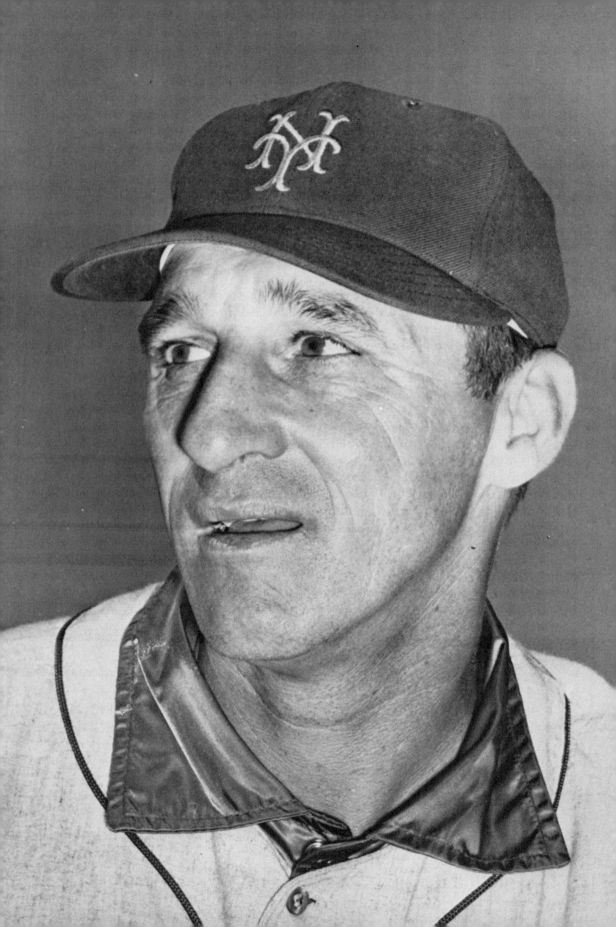

Warren Spahn

(1942-1965)

Casey Stengel was around baseball sixty-five years as a player, manager, coach, and scout. He managed the Boston Braves in 1942 and sent out a young, skinny left-hander after a short stay in Boston.

"It was the worst mistake I ever made in baseball," Stengel said.

The kid pitcher was named Warren Spahn. He did not get back to the big leagues until four years later in 1946, winning his first game at the age of twenty-five and then continuing on to win 363 games, more than any other left-hander in the history of the game and behind only Cy Young, Walter Johnson, Christy Mathewson, and Grover Cleveland Alexander.

Spahn might have started late but he was still going strong in 1965 at the age of forty-four when he was fired as a pitcher-coach of the New York Mets because he wanted to pitch more and coach less and they wanted it the other way around. The name of the man who fired him? Casey Stengel.

"I played for Casey Stengel before and after he was a genius," says Spahn.

Warren Spahn was always a pitching genius, using some speed and lots of smarts to win 20 games thirteen times, leading the league in wins eight times, pitching his first no-hitter at the age of forty and leading the league in ERA.

A tall, skinny, high-kicking left-hander with an outrageous nose and long face, Spahn was an all-around athlete. He was an excellent hitter, a fine fielder, and could run. He was also a humorous man who bounced lines off the Braves' midget traveling secretary, Donald Davidson, and was not above hanging the tiny man up on a clubhouse hook by his boy-sized jacket. Davidson led out a stream of obscenities as Spahn howled.

Hitters were never afraid to face Spahn and often walked out of the game with what they called "a comfortable oh for four." That meant two long-fly-ball outs, one hard line drive caught by an infielder, and one hard ground ball at the shortstop. No pitcher ever better knew how to set up a hitter to hit the ball a fraction of an inch away from his true power.

Warren Edward Spahn was born in Buffalo, New York, on April 23, 1921. Spahn's father had played some baseball and encouraged his hawk-nosed son to take up the game. Young Warren started as a left-handed first baseman, but when he saw he could not generate much power out of that rangy body he switched to pitching.

He was signed by the Braves in 1940 and brought to spring training under Stengel in 1942. He started two games, relieved in two others, and spent most of the season in the minors. He had an 0–0 record when he was drafted into the Army in 1943. He saw combat action in Europe and returned with a Purple Heart.

This time he made the Braves in 1946, won his first game and seven others, and was a 21-game winner the next season.

He was 15–12 in 1948 as the Braves won the pennant. He teamed with Johnny Sain as the key starter on the team, giving rise to a famous Boston phrase, "Spahn and Sain and pray for rain."

He had three more 20-game seasons in a row before a 14–19 record in 1952. He was thirty-one years old, a wounded war veteran, and most observers figured his career was ending. It was just beginning.

With the Braves now rejuvenated in Milwaukee, Spahn won 23, 21, 17, 20, 21, 22, 21, 21, 21, 18, and then 23 games at the age of forty-two in 1963. He slumped to 6–13 the next year and was traded to the New York Mets.

There he helped develop a young left-handed relief pitcher by the name of Tug McGraw.

Spahn and Stengel disagreed about how often he should pitch in 1965, so he was dropped at the All-Star break. Stengel soon had an accident, breaking his hip in a fall, and both their active careers ended at the same time.

Spahn managed in the minors, coached in the majors, but failed always to get a big-league managing job because he was considered too outspoken.

In 1980 he was back in baseball with the California Angels after having spent the intervening years on his huge cattle ranch in Hartshorne, Oklahoma.

The hawk-nosed left-hander, winner of 363 games, was now teaching other youngsters how to throw that screwball and set up hitters for the fast ball under the chin. He was never overpoweringly fast. All Warren Spahn could do was win and win and win.

Hank Greenberg

(1930–1947)

On the last day of the 1938 season Hank Greenberg had 58 homers for the Detroit Tigers. Eleven years earlier Babe Ruth had hit 60 for the record. Greenberg, if he was to tie the record, had to do it against the best pitcher in the game, Bob Feller.

Feller was simply brilliant that gloomy Sunday afternoon with an astounding strikeout game, 18 K's, while Greenberg was held hitless. But left-hander Harry Eisenstat pitched Detroit to a victory with soft stuff and control, beating Feller's best.

It was probably the only big game in which Greenberg failed to make a significant contribution for his team.

The big, husky first baseman and outfielder for the Tigers was one of the game's greatest sluggers with 331 homers in thirteen seasons, including one of the most dramatic ever, a grand slam against the Browns on the final day of the 1945 season to win the pennant for Detroit.

"That had to be my most satisfying hit ever," said Greenberg. "It seems to be the one I'm most remembered for."

A bright, handsome, articulate man, Greenberg starred for the Tigers through the 1930s and 1940s, won four home-run titles and tied for another, led the league in RBIs four times, and batted over .300 in nine of his twelve full years in the big leagues.

Greenberg had developed into a smooth-fielding first baseman with huge hands and a good arm when Rudy York joined the team. The big Indian could play nowhere but first base.

"We needed his bat in the lineup so I agreed to move," Greenberg said. "I wasn't happy about it but I knew it would help our club."

The Tigers won the pennant four times in Greenberg's time and he batted .318 in the World Series with five homers and 22 RBIs.

Henry Benjamin Greenberg, born in New York, January 1, 1911, was the son of Rumanian Jewish immigrants. His father worked on New York's Seventh avenue in the clothing business and soon was doing well enough to move the family into a pleasant home in The Bronx.

Young Hank was soon an excellent baseball and basketball player (many of his school records were later broken by Ed Kranepool of the Mets), and scouts began coming around. His parents were more interested in their son gaining an education than in his playing baseball.

The hometown Yankees were interested in him but with Lou Gehrig in the midst of his incredible consecutive-game playing streak, Greenberg saw no future there. When the Tigers offered to pay for his education and delay his career until after college, Greenberg signed with them.

After one semester at NYU he decided he wanted to try baseball full time and reported to the Hartford club in the Eastern League. He was overmatched and batted only .214, but after being transferred to Raleigh, he batted .314 with 19 homers and 93 RBIs.

He joined the Tigers for one at-bat in 1930, played another couple of years in the minors, and became Detroit's regular first baseman in 1933. In 1934 he helped the Tigers win the pennant with a .339 average, 139 RBIs, and 26 homers.

In 1936 he suffered a broken wrist and played in only twelve games. He returned to action in 1937 to find a young center fielder on the Yankees by the name of Joe DiMaggio getting much attention as the game's best right-handed hitter.

"I always considered Joe my major rival," Greenberg says. "I used to read his statistics every day and try to stay ahead. We especially competed in RBIs. That was the most important item to me. When I won the RBI title twice in the next four years I was a very happy man."

Greenberg had 183 RBIs in 1937, only one behind Gehrig's league record of 184 (Hack Wilson had 190 for the Cubs) and had 150 in 1940.

In 1941 he was drafted into the Army, was released December 5, 1941, and reenlisted two days later after the attack on Pearl Harbor. He served with distinction in the China-Burma-India theater, attained the rank of captain in the Army Air Corps, and was discharged in time to help the Tigers win the 1945 pennant.

He led the league in home runs and RBIs in 1946 but batted only .277. The Tigers thought Greenberg was on his way down and didn't want to be stuck for a huge salary raise for 1947.

Greenberg was traded to Pittsburgh. The Pirates shortened their left-field wall to accomodate him and he smashed 25 homers with the help of Greenberg Gardens. He also met and helped a young handsome Pittsburgh slugger by the name of Ralph Kiner and that leftfield spot was soon renamed Kiner's Korner.

Hank retired after the 1947 season and joined the Cleveland Indians front office under Billy Veeck. He was soon the club's general manager and stayed there with another pennant winner in 1954. He then moved with Veeck to Chicago, where they fashioned a new championship team.

Greenberg and Veeck tried to get a franchise in Los Angeles in 1960 but the league expanded without them and Gene Autry was given the new team in Los Angeles, now the California Angels of Anaheim.

Still in marvelous condition and a tall, handsome, dignified retired investment executive, Greenberg finds time to play tennis daily at his Beverly Hills, California, home, almost always wins the Las Vegas celebrity tennis tournament at Caesars Palace, and looks as fit at seventy years of age as he did at thirty.

Yogi Berra

(1946–1965)

Casey Stengel called him his assistant manager. Players made fun of his face, but when Yogi Berra hit one over the wall he reminded his teammates, "You don't hit with your face." Not quite a master of elocution, Berra was famous for saying on Yogi Berra day, "Thanks for making this day necessary," and for saying of one of his managerial seasons, "It ain't over till it's over."

His old pal from the St. Louis Dago Hill section, Joe Garagiola, had a lot to do with promoting the dumpy left-handed-hitting Yankee catcher into a major celebrity. It also helped Garagiola become a star.

Yogi's face was his fortune, but he still would have made a fine living in baseball being called Larry Berra if he hit the way he did for the Yankees for nearly two decades. He could hit anything off anybody and make the other team like it.

Berra was a very tough man to pitch to because he was known as a bad-ball hitter. The pitcher might be thinking he was wasting one when Berra would suddenly lunge after the pitch and drive it over the wall in right field or into the gap in left. Most importantly, he hit most when it counted; he was the best clutch hitter of his time and had five seasons with 100 or more RBIs, quite a feat for a catcher.

Lawrence Peter Berra was born in St. Louis on May 12, 1925. His father worked in a shoe factory and young Lawdie—as he was called by his pals—did all he could to duck that kind of work. He took up sports as a way of

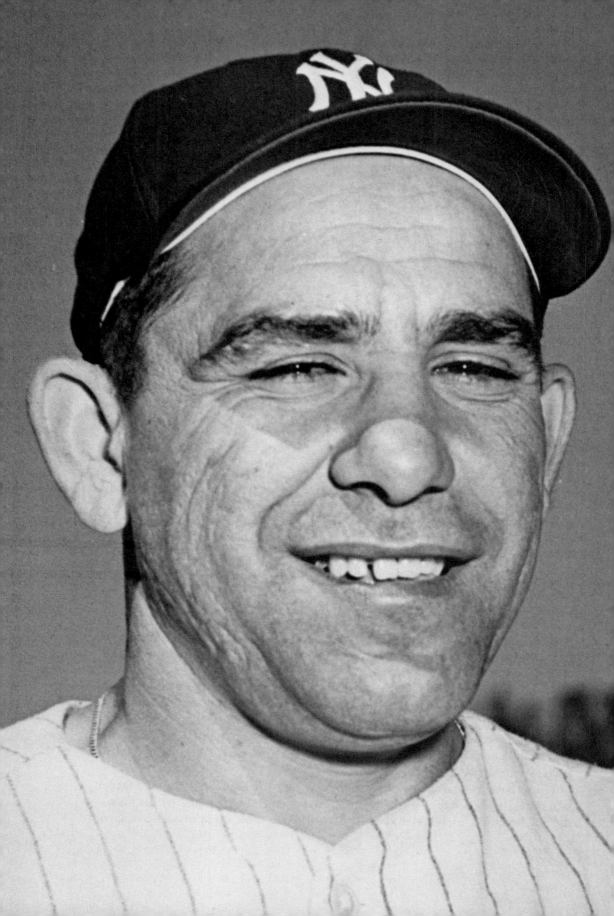

ducking work and a little school, and soon found he was as good as anybody in the neighborhood in baseball, football, basketball, and soccer.

One day young Lawdie and his pals went to a movie about India. They saw this old swami who was called a Yoga and soon began calling Lawdie a Yoga for no reason. The Yoga became Yogi and Lawrence Peter was hardly ever heard any more. Even his own wife, Carmen, and their three sons call him Yogi.

When Yogi's young pal, Joe Garagiola, received five hundred dollars to sign with the Cardinals, Berra expected the same if he, too, was to sign. One five-hundred-dollar bonus kid was enough, and the Cardinals wouldn't offer the funny-shaped catcher that kind of big bonus. So the Yankees, tipped off by Yogi's coach, heard about the left-handed-hitting, right-handed-throwing youngster, came up with the five hundred dollars, and signed him in 1943.

He played for Norfolk in 1943, entered the Navy, and served on a rocket launcher during the Normandy invasion. Upon his separation from service he reported to the Yankees in his Navy uniform, was looked upon by staid old Yankees as some sort of clown, and was soon playing at Newark. When he returned from that season and rejoined the Yankees at the end of 1946, he swung a bat quickly to prove he belonged.

In 1947 he was a catcher and outfielder under manager Bucky Harris. The Yankees won the pennant and Berra was embarrassed in the Series when the Jackie Robinson-led Dodgers ran him wild. The Yankees and Berra had the last laugh because they won.

Berra was soon a fixture behind the plate, starting in 1949 after Casey Stengel had become the Yankee manager, and catcher-coach Bill Dickey had worked with him. Yogi became a fine defensive catcher, a strong thrower, and a knowledgeable pitch caller.

But it was his bat, ever present in big games, that made him so popular with Yankee fans. He never won a home run, batting, or RBI title but he always was among the leaders. His best season was 1954 when he hit 22 homers, knocked in 125 runs, and batted .307. His career average was .285 and he hit 358 homers. He played in fourteen World Series, totaling a record 75 games, and had more World Series at bats, hits, and doubles than any other player. He also hit 12 Series homers.

In 1964 he managed the Yankees to a pennant, was fired because he supposedly couldn't control his team, went over to the Mets under Stengel, and was hired as the manager there in 1972 after Gil Hodges died. He won again in 1973 and was fired again in 1975 because he supposedly couldn't control his players again.

He soon joined the Yankees as a coach and regularly takes his swings in the batting cage as he nears fifty-six. He still hits a lot of bad balls into the Stadium seats.

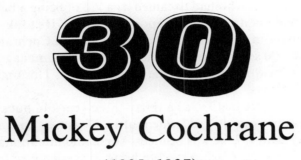

Mickey Cochrane

(1925–1937)

A late professional start because he was attending Boston University and an early retirement because he was beaned as the thirty-four-year-old player-manager of the Tigers, kept Mickey Cochrane from adding to his accumulated statistics.

Though Cochrane's career was relatively short, only twelve full seasons, he was one of the finest receivers ever, a tremendous line-driver hitter, a speedy runner, and a smart player. He ranks behind Yogi Berra in the list of Baseball's 100 because Berra's career was longer, his offensive work was more productive, and his defensive work was only a shade behind Cochrane's.

Cochrane was a heads-up ballplayer who was a natural leader on the fine Philadelphia and Detroit teams of the 1920s and 1930s. He played with Connie Mack's A's during their heyday when they won pennants in 1929, 1930, and 1931, and came back to help lead the Tigers to pennants in 1934 and 1935. Five pennants in little more than a dozen big-league seasons was certainly an indication of Cochrane's contributions.

His career was relatively short but his play was so smooth, so effortless, so stylish, that he was one of the most popular players of his time. He made catching into an artistic position with his graceful handling of pitchers, his smooth style, and his seemingly effortless performance.

He was a .320 lifetime hitter as well as the best defensive catcher of his time. He had nine seasons over .300 and batted an incredible .357 in 1930 for the A's while catching 130 games.

Gordon Stanley "Mickey" Cochrane was born in Bridgewater, Massachusetts, on April 6, 1903. His school work was as impressive as his athletic work and he enrolled at Boston University after graduation from high school.

He signed a professional contract in 1923, played another minor-league season in 1924, and was soon on his way to Philadelphia to play under Mr. Mack for the next nine seasons. The Tigers wanted him in 1934 as a player and manager and for one hundred thousand dollars they got him.

Mickey Cochrane, who had dreamed as a kid of being a big-league player and manager, had not dreamed an impossible dream. He took over the Tigers and won a pennant in 1934. His catcher, a guy named Cochrane, contributed mightily with a .320 season in 129 games. Showing his managerial skills were no fluke, Cochrane won again with the Tigers in 1935. This time he hit .319 as a player in 115 games.

He slumped to .270 in 1936 as a thirty-three-year-old but seemed to have regained his batting eye by 1937 when, after 27 games, he was hitting .306.

But on May 25, 1937, he was beaned—some said intentionally—by Bump Hadley of the Yankees. Cochrane's life hung in the balance for several days before he recovered from the fractured skull. He was soon well enough to manage the club again and even considered playing. But wiser heads prevailed and Cochrane accepted the word of owner Spike Briggs and stayed off the field. He ended his managerial career the following season.

He scouted and coached for several years afterwards before retiring from baseball. He returned briefly to work in a supervisory position for the Detroit organization until his death at Lake Forest, Illinois, on June 28, 1962.

Mickey Cochrane was as stylish a catcher as ever lived, a wonderful hitter, a great team player, a smart all-around man. He played thirteen seasons in all and had a lifetime .320 average, but his overall career was a shade under Yogi's. Mickey Cochrane deserves the recognition of finishing in the top thirty of Baseball's 100, but he also has to be rated a split hair behind Yogi.

Whitey Ford

(1950–1967)

Elston Howard, his catcher for many years, called him "The Chairman of the Board." Casey Stengel, his manager, once said, "If you had one game to win and your life depended on it, you'd want him to pitch it."

The man who won those accolades was a blond, stocky left-handed pitcher named Whitey Ford who won almost seven out of every ten times he took the mound for the Yankees.

Ford was 236–106 with a percentage of .690 in his sixteen years of pitching. His percentage, his victories, and his rank within Baseball's 100 might have even been higher if arm trouble and a circulatory problem hadn't cut short his career in 1967.

Ford won 20 games only twice in his career, 25–4 in 1961 and 24–7 in 1963, but he was such a consistent winner and infrequent loser that the Yankees counted on him as the key man in their marvelous staff.

An affable, witty, self-controlled man, who liked a good time but could handle a bad one, Ford was a mainstay of Casey Stengel's dynasty Yankees from 1950 through 1960 and slipped easily into the same roll for new manager Ralph Houk. He helped win a pennant in 1964 for old pal Yogi Berra, had one strong season for new manager Johnny Keane in 1965, but saw his effectiveness diminish in 1966 and 1967 when he came down with arm trouble.

Ford's greatest assets were his fine fast ball, excellent control, and pin-point breaking ball. He was one of the few pitchers who could slice a curve across the outside corner of the plate against a tough left-handed hitter. He

also had a few other pitches in his repertoire which helped him win. He threw the illegal spitter on occasion, only when necessary, and he was also helped by catcher Howard's trick of rubbing the ball against his shin guards. This gave Ford a better grip on the ball and allowed him to do more tricks with it.

Ford was as smart a pitcher as there was and was recognized as one of the best clutch pitchers of all time, a stopper for the Yankees and sort of a Yogi Berra with a toeplate. No hitter was too tough.

Edward Charles Ford, called Whitey because of his tousled head of blond hair, was born in New York City on October 21, 1928. His family moved to Astoria, Queens, where Ford attended an aviation high school hoping to become a plane mechanic. He played first base and pitched a little in high school and for amateur teams in Queens. His batting was unimpressive and he ended up concentrating on the mound chores.

The Yankees spotted him at a sandlot game, liked his fast ball and control, signed him, and sent him to Butler, Pennsylvania. His manager was Lefty Gomez, a former Yankee great who recalls Ford then with much glee.

"I once gave a guy five bucks to keep him up on a roller coaster in an amusement park because he would miss curfew. I wanted to know how he would react. When he came into the hotel breathlessly," says Gomez, "he began by saying 'Skipper, you won't believe why I'm late.' And I made out like I didn't and took his five bucks. Then I wanted to farm him out, to show you how smart I was."

Ford joined the Yankees from the Kansas City farm club in 1950, posted a 9–1 mark after getting shelled in his first big-league game as a relief pitcher in Boston, and won the fourth game of the World Series against Philadelphia.

The cocky New Yorker gave Stengel a snootful when the old manager came out to relieve him with two out in the last game of the 1950 Series after left fielder Gene Woodling dropped a fly ball.

Ford, Mickey Mantle, and Billy Martin were close friends and tore up a lot of hotel rooms in those days.

Ford missed the 1951 and 1952 seasons in service, but when he returned heavier and older in 1953, he won 18 games and lost only 6.

Stengel kept Ford, who never more than 180 pounds, fresh all year by spotting him and skipping starts, especially in Boston's famed Fenway Park with its short left-field wall and its army of right-handed sluggers.

Ford led the league in wins three times, in percentage three times, and in ERA twice. He also led in innings pitched twice, both under Houk.

Whitey pitched in eleven World Series and won 10 games, the most of any pitcher, but also lost eight, also the most. He didn't know the NL hitters as well as he knew those in his own league.

He coached and scouted for the Yankees, worked in various businesses, and kept people laughing and their beer cups filled at old-timers' days. Whitey Ford was the chairman of board but he was never bored and he never bored us. Baseball was too much fun for this grand guy among Baseball's 100.

Jimmie Foxx

(1925–1945)

Old Double X was long considered the only home-run hitter in the Babe's class. Jimmie Foxx could simply overpower a baseball with one of the largest frames and lustiest swings the game had ever seen.

He won three home-run titles, tied for another, won three RBI titles, won one batting title to prove he was not just a home-run or no-count guy, made a couple of token pitching performances, and played in three World Series.

Foxx hit 534 home runs, which hardly sounds like a lot compared to Hank Aaron's 755 or Babe Ruth's 714, but he did it before the ball was livened up and he did it with some poor clubs in Philadelphia and Boston with not much hitting ahead or behind him.

Aaron had Eddie Mathews and Ruth had Lou Gehrig to help him. Foxx had to help himself.

For twelve seasons he hit 30 or more homers with a high of 58 in 1932, another 50 in 1938, and a low during that period of 30 in 1931. He managed 120 RBIs and a .291 average in that "off" year.

"I never saw anyone hit a baseball harder," said Ted Williams, who played with Foxx in Boston from 1939 through 1942.

James Emory Foxx was born at Sudlersville, Maryland, on October 22, 1907. His father was a farmer and young James grew strong working in the fields, lifting bales, and loading grain on wagons.

He was soon playing baseball for his high school team and booming balls all over the local areas. He was almost fully grown by the time he was sixteen, a burly, heavy-chested kid weighing nearly two hundred pounds on a frame nearly six feet tall. He was right-handed all the way.

He was signed by the local Easton, Maryland, team and sold to the Philadelphia A's. Connie Mack brought him to the big club in 1925 when he was just past seventeen and kept the youngster on the bench near him.

He sent Foxx out to the minors in 1925 and brought him back to Philadelphia in 1926 where he rarely played. The same thing was true in 1927 when he mostly sat, a part-time player, and watched intently as the league's other sluggers awed him. The most awesome in 1927 was the Great Bambino himself, on his way to 60 homers, and who reminded young Foxx of himself. Even though the Babe was left-handed he had a quick, huge swing, feet whirling, body pivoting, eyes stuck on that baseball—the sort of swing young Foxx had.

By 1928 he was a regular with 13 homers, 79 RBIs, and a .328 average. He had started out as a catcher but was now playing first base and some third, and took an occasional turn in the outfield. He was an average fielder but his stroke was so awesome at the plate that few noticed his fielding deficiencies.

In 1929 he had 33 homers, knocked in 118 runs, hit .354, and began a streak that would make him the league's most feared hitter over the next decade. Ruth was gone after the 1934 season and Foxx was the league's biggest home-run attraction.

After the 1935 season the financially troubled A's had to unload him to Boston. There he hit 41 homers, had 143 RBIs, and hit .338. He immediately became a Beantown favorite. He had his best RBI season with 175 in 1938 and hit 50 homers and batted .349. He got up to .360 in 1939, Williams's rookie year, and dropped 63 points in 1940. He was now thirty-two years old.

Foxx had always been a late-night man even before late-night games. He drank heavily, caroused, got little sleep, and seemed to fade rapidly as a player in his final few seasons.

He finished his career as manager and player for the St. Petersburg club in Florida in 1947 and soon dropped out of the game.

His drinking habits, ill health, and financial problems filled the papers in his last years. Jimmie Foxx, Old Double X, died in Miami on July 21, 1967.

Anyone who ever saw Double X crush a baseball over that wall in Fenway knows he belongs here. Any man who can hit 534 homers with a .325 average certainly rates attention. He never hit a cheap one, either.

Al Kaline

(1953–1974)

Smooth as silk, the ultimate team player, a dedicated and proud man, soft spoken, a gentleman, and one of the finest all-around players the game has ever seen, Al Kaline had to be seen to be believed.

Oh, his numbers are impressive enough, twenty-three seasons, lifetime mark of .297, 3007 hits, 399 homers, 1,583 RBIs, and over 100 games played in each of twenty years.

But the true worth of Kaline's play came in the small things, the way he moved a runner with a ground ball, the way he took an extra base, the way he hit hard late in the game, the way he helped all his managers in the clubhouse and related to the fans. Kaline was a credit to his town and his team for more than two decades and it is no accident that one of the streets outside of Tiger Stadium is named Kaline Drive.

Kaline was at his best in a tough pennant race, especially against the Yankees, winning games with hits, runs, and catches.

"I never really appreciated how good he was," said Yankee, Detroit and Boston manager Ralph Houk, "until he played for me. He did those kinds of things that win games but don't get into the box scores. He was a pleasure to watch."

Kaline won a batting title at the age of twenty in 1955 when he hit .340. He never won another, but he almost always stayed in the race, with nine seasons over .300. His lifetime mark dropped under .300 in his final two seasons when he hit .255 and .262 while driving for his 3,000 hits. He also

103

missed by one homer the distinction being the first American Leaguer to collect 3,000 hits and 400 homers. Carl Yastrzemski did it in 1979.

"I did not know that was a unique statistic until I was out of the game five years and Yaz started going for it," Kaline said.

Kaline was never a pop-off player, never a hot dog, never a rabble-rouser around his club. He was a professional, a man who went to work every day and gave his employers a full day or night's work for a full day's pay.

"I never wanted to do anything that I was not proud of. I never wanted to do anything that would not reflect positively on myself, my family, the Detroit ball club, or baseball," Kaline said at his 1980 Hall of Fame induction.

A handsome, dark-haired, well-built man, Kaline was never considered a home-run hitter despite the fact that he accumulated 399 homers and only some three dozen players ever hit more.

"I went for a homer when I thought that might win us a game," he said. "The rest of the time I just tried to hit a ball hard somewhere."

Albert William Kaline was born in Baltimore on December 19, 1934. His parents were German immigrants and wanted young Al to get an education and make a good life for himself in America.

Soon he was making a good life by playing baseball in high school and with local amateur teams. The Detroit Tigers chased Kaline and signed him in 1953 with a thirty-five-thousand-dollar bonus. That meant he had to stay on the big club for two years.

After his free ride was over it seemed the Tigers would farm him out in 1955. He had batted .250 and .276 and many Tiger officials thought a year in Triple-A would make him a better player.

He fouled up their plans by getting off hot, leading the league from June on, and winning the title with a .340 mark. He would never spend a day in the minors.

A hard-hitting right-handed batter and fielder, Kaline soon became the league's best right fielder. He had a strong arm, great running speed, and marvelous reflexes.

He had 27 homers and 128 RBIs in 1956 with a .314 mark. The Tigers pushed him toward more homers at the cost of his average. He would hit 29 in two separate seasons but could never break the 30 mark.

His consistency as a hitter and everyday player was his main strength. In 1968 the Tigers finally won a pennant in Kaline's time as Denny McLain won 31 games and Mickey Lolich won 17, and 3 in the World Series. Kaline batted .379 in the Series, and the nation came to recognize what Detroit had always known, that this special man was one wonderful player.

Kaline hit .313 in 1972, had two poor seasons afterward, but got his 3,000th hit and retired to a broadcasting job after the 1974 season. He was elected to the Hall of Fame in his first eligible year of 1980.

Al Kaline never made waves when he played. He just did his job with dignity. He quietly earns his spot as number thirty-three among Baseball's 100.

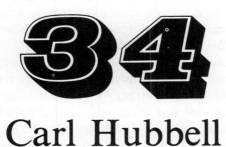

Carl Hubbell

(1928-1943)

Lefty Gomez, the delightful old Yankee pitcher, loves to tell the story of how he missed hitters' immortality because of a single by Bill Dickey.

"It was the nineteen thirty-four All-Star Game at the Polo Grounds in New York," Gomez begins. "Carl Hubbell was pitching and he struck out Babe Ruth, Lou Gehrig, and Jimmie Foxx in a row. Then he got three strikeouts on three great hitters in the next inning, Al Simmons, Joe Cronin, and old Lefty."

Before Hubbell could strike out Gomez, Bill Dickey singled and the streak of five straight strikeouts against five of the greatest hitters in the game—all now Hall of Famers—was ended.

"If Dickey didn't single everybody would have said Hubbell struck out the seven greatest hitters ever," Gomez says, "and I'd be with them."

King Carl Hubbell, the skinny left-hander for the New York Giants, was known as the Meal Ticket for manager Bill Terry's marvelous team.

Hubbell, who never weighed more than 175 pounds, was a dour-faced type who made his fame, his fortune, and his reputation among hitters on one pitch: a twisting, devastating, almost-impossible-to-hit screwball.

The reverse curve, which broke into the hands of left-handed hitters and floated away from right-handers, was the pitch that made Hubbell into a big-league star after six years of living on the fringes of success.

Once he mastered the pitch and mastered the hitters with it, Hubbell recorded 253 wins against 154 losses, had five 20-game seasons in a row between 1933 and 1937 (the Giants won three pennants in those five years), led the league in ERA three times, and led in strikeouts once.

His career was surprisingly successful for a pitcher who was given up by the Detroit Tigers and told by no less an authority than the great Ty Cobb that a crazy pitch like a screwball was useless in the big leagues and would ruin Hubbell's arm. Hubbell disregarded Cobb's advice, became a Hall of Fame pitcher, and lasted sixteen seasons in the big leagues.

Carl Owen Hubbell was born June 22, 1903, at Carthage, Missouri. His family afterwards moved to Oklahoma, where he was raised on a pecan farm.

The tall, thin youngster found farming boring and was soon playing in neighborhood baseball games as his major source of recreation.

He signed a professional contract with the Cushing, Oklahoma club as a nineteen-year-old and soon was fooling with his screwball. The Detroit Tigers purchased his contract and when Cobb first saw the lanky youngster throwing that reverse curve, he told him to forget it. Carl, an amiable youngster, obeyed his boss and was a journeyman pitcher for the next five years.

The Giants had watched him pitch in the Texas League at Beaumont. They saw nothing wrong with the screwball if he could win with it, and Giants manager John McGraw encouraged Carl in the use of the pitch.

He won 10 games as a rookie and 18 in his second season in 1929. From 1933 through 1937 under new manager Bill Terry, he was as dominating a pitching force as the league had seen.

After pitching a 1929 no-hitter, he compiled some incredible marks. He pitched 46 scoreless innings with 10 shutouts in 1933. He won an 18-inning route-going game that season without a walk. He registered 24 straight victories, including 16 in a row in 1933.

He did begin wearing down with that stress and strain on his left arm by the late 1930s. He won 13 games in 1938 and then won 11 games four seasons in a row before ending his career with a 4-4 mark in 1943 at the age of forty.

King Carl immediately was put to work with the Giants as a farm director and there he remains still, more than fifty-five years after he first tried that screwball in Oklahoma.

There are a lot of screwball pitchers in baseball. Only one, King Carl Hubbell, made a living at it.

Tom Seaver

(1967–present)

General William D. "Spike" Eckert was elected as Commissioner of Baseball because somebody got him mixed up with another Air Force General named Zuckert. When Spike got the job and the news flashed across America, Willie Mays innocently asked, "Who he?"

After that he was labeled the Unknown Soldier. But not around Shea he wasn't. Eckert was credited with one of the greatest pulls of all time when he pulled the name Mets from a hat and awarded that team with rights to a handsome right-handed pitcher who had been signed illegally by the Atlanta Braves.

The youngster's name was Tom Seaver and he was soon to make the Mets a serious team, a World Series winner by 1969, and a pennant winner again in 1973.

Seaver's absence would just about ruin the Mets in 1977, cause the team to disintegrate and deteriorate to such a point that a sale was necessary, and convince the fans at Shea to stay home by the hundreds of thousands.

Few players in baseball history have had that kind of impact on a franchise.

Seaver—known as The Franchise—was a 20-game winner five times, won three Cy Young awards, was the strikeout leader five times and ERA leader three times.

More importantly, he stabilized the Mets pitching staff, gave it credibility, and started no fewer than 32 games in any of his first thirteen seasons in the

big leagues. Arm trouble slowed him down in 1980, when he was only a 10–8 pitcher, but he still remained a viable starter at the age of thirty-five.

George Thomas Seaver was born November 17, 1944. His father had been a Walker Cup amateur golfer and had started a successful raisin-packing business in Fresno, that is where young George—called Tom to distinguish him from his father George—started playing ball.

"I always was emotional about pitching," he says. "I loved it so. I remember when I pitched a perfect game in Little League and when the last fly ball popped into the air I ran off the mound and buried my head in my mother's lap, I was so nervous about the whole thing."

He starred in baseball and basketball at Fresno High, entered Fresno City College, and transferred to the University of Southern California. He played under famed coach Rod Dedeaux.

"I remember hitting a homer against Seaver in an alumni game," says ex-big leaguer Ron Fairly. "I was batting and when the ball left Seaver's hand, I said, 'Prominent alumni,' a code word for 'Help,' and the kid catcher shouted, 'Fast ball.' I just timed it and whacked it four hundred feet. I didn't do as well against Seaver in the bigs. No catcher there would give me the pitch."

Seaver, now grown to six one and 195 pounds, a handsome youngster who believed mystically in the idea that he was the reincarnation of Christy Mathewson, was soon drafted by the Dodgers. He refused to sign and went back into the free-agent pool. Atlanta signed him for fifty-thousand dollars and that deal was voided because he had already started his next college season. His name was offered to all clubs for the same amount and only three bid—the Phillies, Indians, and Mets. Eckert pulled the Mets out of a hat—bless him—and New York baseball fortunes were on the way up.

Seaver was only 12–12 in his first pro year at Jacksonville, but was established himself as a big-league pitcher with a 16–13 year in his rookie season with the last-place Mets. He was the NL Rookie of the Year and was soon a club leader with 16–12 mark in his second season under new manager Gil Hodges. He was 25–7 as the league leader in 1969, won the Cy Young Award, won a game in the championship series and another in the World Series as the Mets took everything and became the darlings of all baseball.

Teamed with left-hander Jerry Koosman, Seaver was one half of a dynamic pitching duo which was to carry the Mets to some marvelous seasons in the next half-dozen years.

Seaver won 18, 20, 21, and 19 in the next four seasons. A back injury caused him to slump to 11–11, but he came back in the next season with a 22–9 mark. He was 14–11 in 1976 as the Mets began slipping down and was carrying the staff with an 8–2 mark when he was involved in a bitter contract hassle and traded on June 15, 1977. Slugger Dave Kingman, also unhappy with his contract, was traded at the same time in an event which became known as the Wednesday Night Massacre.

Mets fans wrote letters, tore up tickets, maligned the ball club and its chairman, M. Donald Grant, in their anger over the loss of Seaver.

The club was sold in 1980 almost as a direct result of the loss of faith in ownership triggered by the Seaver trade.

Tom went to Cincinnati, finished out another 20-game season there with a 21-6 mark, was 16-14 and 16-6 in his next two Cincinnati seasons. The Reds won the division title in 1979 with Seaver as a key ingredient, giving him three division titles, two pennants, and one World Series championship in his career.

At thirty-six and recovered from a severe elbow and shoulder problem, Seaver could win another 55 games or so to hit the coveted 300 mark.

Whether he makes it or not, he will always be regarded as the player who made the Mets a serious team. His loss also made them a tragic team.

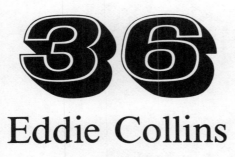

Eddie Collins

(1906–1930)

Lou Gehrig holds the one supposedly uncatchable record in baseball, 2,130 straight games played over fourteen seasons. Eddie Collin's mark won't be all that easy to catch, either.

He hit .235 as a nineteen-year-old for the Philadelphia A's in 1906 and .500 in three games for those same A's as a forty-three-year-old in 1930, a span of twenty-five big-league seasons, the longest continuous-service mark in American League history.

Collins also recorded eighteen seasons of over .300 with a high of .369 in 1920. The most ironic statistic about this aggressive, stylish-fielding second baseman is that he never won a batting title despite totaling 3,311 hits, third in the league and seventh overall behind Ty Cobb, Hank Aaron, Stan Musial, Tris Speaker, Pete Rose, and Honus Wagner.

Even though he never won a batting title, he did lead the league in runs scored three times, won three stolen-base titles, and stole six bases in two separate games eleven days apart. He also stole 81 bases in 1910 and 14 bases in the World Series.

A slashing line-drive hitter who could spray the ball to all fields, Collins did not have much power, accumulating only 47 homers in those twenty-five seasons. He never hit more than six homers in any one season.

Collins believed in contact hitting, using the entire field, driving the ball through the infield for a hit and then stealing second base. He was an aggressive hitter with a crouching style at the plate and would explode out of his left-handed stance for any pitch that was close.

113

Collins was a tough player, but unlike Cobb, his hitting nemesis who was winning all the batting titles during Collins's peak years, Eddie also had a gentle and intelligent side. He was a graduate of Columbia University in New York, read avidly, was interested in world politics, and had a good relationship with young players. As a Boston vice-president he was instrumental in scouting and signing a youngster by the name of Ted Williams.

Edward Trowbridge "Cocky" Collins was born May 2, 1887, in the small town of Millerton, New York. He was raised in Tarrytown, one of New York's oldest and most historic communities, where his father practiced law and encouraged Eddie as an athlete.

Collins was aiming for a law degree when he entered Columbia as a precocious sixteen-year-old in 1903. He played football as a flashy quarterback and played some semiprofessional baseball as a sideline in the summer to help with tuition costs.

Connie Mack, the A's owner and manager, was touted on Collins and soon made him a professional offer. Collins played under the name of Ed Sullivan—a different man by that name later became a famous television personality—to retain his college eligibility.

After playing six games for the A's in 1906 and 14 in 1907, he joined the A's as a full-time second baseman in 1908. He batted .273 and the next season hit .346 to start a streak of eight straight seasons over .300.

When Mack broke up his A's to raise money in 1914, Collins was shipped to the Chicago White Sox for fifty-thousand dollars. He played a dozen years with the White Sox and they released him in 1926 assuming that, at the age of thirty-nine, he was finished. He hit .338 at the age of forty and .303 at the age of forty-one in thirty-six games back with the A's. For the next two seasons he served as a player-coach for Connie Mack, and afterwards moved to Boston as vice-president and business manager.

Eddie Collins died in Boston on March 25, 1951, but his fielding, hitting, running, and all-around team play made him one of the most memorable players in the game in the first half of the century.

Frankie Frisch

(1919–1937)

"Ohh, those bases on balls," moaned the Fordham Flash, Frankie Frisch, when he was broadcasting the New York Giants baseball games.

Frisch knew how important walks were to the game ("A walk is as good as a hit," said some anonymous manager). He himself collected 728 in his nineteen-year playing career and was angry at every one his pitchers gave up in his managerial career.

"I hate walks," Frisch said, "except when my team is getting them."

Frisch was one of the most colorful, flamboyant, glibbest, angriest personalities the game has ever seen. He would argue with umpires, scream at his teammates, fight with his opponents, battle with his bosses. He was always moving on the field or off, an exciting, dramatic, marvelous player for nearly two decades and a baseball figure after that for another twenty years or so.

A very funny man, with a gravely voice and a way of talking physically by moving his hands nonstop, Frisch was as much enjoyed as an afterdinner talker in his retirement years as he had been as a second baseman in his playing years.

Frisch was probably the first power-hitting switch-hitter, with 105 homers in his career, including 12 in 1923, not a bad number for a player during a time when people were winning home-run crowns with numbers under 30.

"The Old Flash never went for a home run," Frisch, who was fond of discussing himself in the third person, once said, "when a single would win the game. If you shoot for home runs you are going to strike out a lot. As much as I hate bases on balls, I hate called third strikes even worse."

Frisch never saw a called third strike he liked and would stomp and scream and dance after one was called on him when he was a player or on one of his players when he was a manager.

The Fordham Flash—he graduated from that fine New York institution in 1919—was born September 9, 1898, of a German father and an Irish mother. He inherited his father's solid good sense and his mother's fire, using both to quickly excel in school and athletics as a New York City youngster.

Frisch was an excellent all-around athlete and student at Fordham Prep and at Fordham University, playing basketball and football and running track as well as playing baseball. John McGraw, who ran the New York Giants, was soon made aware of the youngster. When he offered him a minor-league contract, Frisch told him he wasn't interested in playing pro baseball. When the deal was changed to a big-league pact, Frisch was off and running to a happy, successful, emotional career.

Frisch joined the Giants in 1919, was the regular second baseman in 1920, and played on four straight New York pennant-winning teams under McGraw. He batted .341, .327, .348, and .328 in those four seasons. He would hit .316 lifetime with eleven straight seasons over .300 and thirteen overall.

Beside his rambunctiousness, Frisch's main area of attraction was his switch-hitting, a relatively unusual aspect of any player's game.

He was naturally right-handed and batted left-handed during his school days. He began fooling around right-handed and McGraw encouraged him to continue.

At five ten and 185 pounds, Frisch was not a graceful fielder but made up for lack of range and good hands with an aggressive style and an essentially unlimited capacity for hustle. He was simply the Pete Rose of his day.

On December 20, 1926, in one of baseball's most shocking deals, Frisch was traded even-up for the league's greatest player, Rogers Hornsby, then at the peak of his career. McGraw and Hornsby couldn't get along—few could get along with the Rajah—and he was soon shipped to Boston.

Frisch became the heart and soul of the Gashouse Gang, winning four pennants with them and becoming, in 1933, the team's manager as well as their second baseman. He later managed bad ball clubs at Pittsburgh and Chicago. He was Ralph Kiner's first manager at Pittsburgh.

Frisch was as colorful a skipper as he had been a player, and a great bench jockey and baiter of rabbit-eared umpires.

He spent the rest of his years broadcasting, doing banquets, and moaning about the lack of hustle modern players showed. He died after an auto accident on March 12, 1973, still feisty at seventy-five.

He could hit both ways, run, throw, and field, but as Frisch said and as many people have said after him, "Ohh, those bases on balls."

Gaylord Perry

(1962–present)

Called in to an extra-inning game for the Giants in 1964—a game that was to go twenty-three innings—Gaylord Perry decided to try out his favorite pitch, something he had been working on for years.

"It was use it or get out of baseball," says Perry. "That's how bad I was going."

The pitch was a spitball, an illegal pitch but still occasionally thrown by some of the more tricky performers in the game. It was to make Perry a big winner, probably baseball's next 300-game winner and an honoree among Baseball's 100.

Never denying that he threw the illegal pitch—he bragged about in his autobiography called *Me and the Spitter*—Perry challenged baseball umpires and officials to find it. They could search him, film him, strip him, or harass him but they never could find where he hid the greasy kid stuff which helped his fast ball sink in some mad ways.

He became an intriguing pitcher to watch, with his hands moving back and forth around his body, his cap, his shirt, and his mouth. Hitters spent so much time studying his body movements to determine where he got that wet one, that they forgot to hit the baseball.

Perry was the only pitcher to win the Cy Young award for pitching excellence in both leagues, winning it in 1972 with the Indians and 1978 with the Padres. He won 24 games for Cleveland in 1972 and 21 for San Diego in 1978.

Perry has won 20 games five different times, pitched over three hundred

119

innings six times, had a career ERA through 1980 of 2.93, and was still growing as a pitcher at forty-two years of age.

Gaylord Jackson Perry was born September 15, 1938, in Williamston, North Carolina, where he was raised on a farm and still resided after nearly a quarter of a century of traveling around the country as a professional baseball player.

He was soon playing in the fields behind the farmhouse with his dad and his older brother, Jim. They would take turns as the pitcher and catcher on local amateur and semipro teams.

Jim signed with Cleveland and Gaylord was signed by the Giants in 1958. He made it to the big club in 1962, was an in-and-out performer, and was struggling for survival in 1964.

A friendly, soft-spoken man with thinning hair and a drawling style of speech, Perry was ticketed for a return to the minors when he relieved against the Mets in that 1964 marathon. He began throwing that spitter and after nine innings of relief got the victory when Jim Davenport tripled home a run.

By the end of the 1966 season he had won 21 games for the Giants and anchored their pitching staff. He helped them to their only Western Division title in 1971 and was traded to Cleveland after the season for left-handed Sam McDowell.

The Giants believed the old adage about trading players a year too soon rather than a year too late. They thought Perry was going downhill at thirty-three. He was 24–16 with Cleveland and won the Cy Young award.

For the next four seasons he led that staff and caused opposing managers and players more gray hairs as they searched for the source of his spitter.

"If they want to strip me they can," he once drawled. "I like it. It makes my other pitches tougher to find."

When Billy Martin managed Detroit he ordered his pitchers to throw spitters to mock Perry and the umpires. It caused him to be fined and eventually fired for insulting baseball.

Perry moved to Texas, San Diego, and finally the Yankees where he beat Baltimore in a big game in his first start to help the Yankees win.

After signing as a free agent with the Atlanta Braves, Perry should get number 300 in 1981. Then he can tell us all where the wet one comes from. After he tells us, we still won't be able to stop it. The man is a pitching magician, well worthy of an exalted spot among Baseball's 100, and has proven again that the pitching hand is quicker than the batting eye.

Al Simmons

(*1924–1944*)

As long as the game of baseball has been played, managers have yelled at young hitters, "Get your foot out of the bucket."

It is an expression which simply indicated that the hitter is moving away from the pitch—into some imaginary bucket—instead of leaning into the pitch in the proven style.

That was good advice for everybody except Al Simmons, who hit .334 over twenty seasons with his left, front foot pointing toward third base instead of toward the pitcher, earning him the handle Bucketfoot.

Bucketfoot or not, Al Simmons was a slashing right-handed hitter with power who hit 307 homers and collected 2,927 hits, just 73 short of the magic 3,000-hit mark—an exclusive baseball club with only fifteen members—before ending his marvelous career.

He won two straight batting titles with a .381 mark in 1930 and an improved .391 in 1931 as he recorded eleven straight .300 seasons and fourteen overall. From 1925 through 1934 Simmons never hit less than .322.

He had five straight seasons with 200 or more hits and six overall with a high of 253 hits in 1925. He hit .384. Harry Heilmann won the batting title with a .393 mark.

Aloysius Harry Szymanski—later shortened to Simmons—was born May 22, 1902 of Polish immigrants in the famed beer-drinking town of Milwaukee. A big kid with large hands and feet, Simmons soon was playing baseball with much older kids in his Milwaukee neighborhood. By the time he was fifteen he was full grown at six feet and nearly two hundred pounds. He was not much of a student in school and concentrated on playing baseball, though his father urged him on toward an education because "that's how the young get ahead in America."

As a young player he swung so violently at the ball that his left foot turned toward third instead of pointing straight ahead. Some hitters do that because they are afraid of being hit by the ball. Simmons did it because he was opening up his stance faster to attack the ball.

Some coaches and opposing players kidded him about his style but after he hit .365, .360, and .398 for three different minor-league clubs, his style became accepted and respected.

Connie Mack brought him to Philadelphia, where he hit .308 as a rookie in 1924. Mack was building his second A's dynasty and Simmons would be one of the leaders on the club through its great seasons and triumphs in 1929, 1930, and 1931. He also played on a National League pennant winner with the Cincinnati Reds in 1939. He was obtained in August of that season and released at the end of the year.

Simmons had played nine seasons for the A's when he was traded to the White Sox. He then played for the Tigers, Senators, Braves, Reds, A's again, Red Sox and A's again before quitting after the 1944 season.

He coached for the A's and Indians, was elected to the Hall of Fame in 1953, and drifted out of baseball and into heavy drinking. He died on May 26, 1956, shortly after his fifty-fourth birthday, back in his hometown of Milwaukee.

Simmons had a long baseball career and a relatively short life but his place in the game was solidly established with his .334 lifetime mark and his foot in the bucket.

Paul Waner

(1926–1945)

One of the game's most notorious drunks, Paul Waner was always being annoyed by managers, preachers, and wives (he had a pair of them) to stop drinking.

He batted .354 in 1937, stopped drinking in 1938, and batted .328 in 1939. In 1938, when he was riding the wagon, his average fell under .300 for the first time in his big-league career. He said it was not his advanced age of thirty-five that did it but his abstinence from drink.

"When I was drinking," he once said, "I used to see two balls. I always hit the top one."

"When I had him," Casey Stengel once said, "he used to take a drink or ten but he could hit. I told my players to listen to him whether he was drinking or not and he could teach you how to hit a line."

Paul Waner—Big Poison in contrast with brother Lloyd Waner, who was known as Little Poison—was one of the finest line-drive hitters in the game's history. He used the entire field to place his hits and would often get three or four hits with a double against the right-field foul line, a double against the left-field foul line, and a single or two in between.

Waner had one of the smoothest, easiest strokes in the game; he held the bat loosely and could wait on a pitch before swinging until it was almost in the catcher's glove. He had eight seasons with 200 or more hits, won three batting titles, hit over .350 six times, and hit .325 at the age of forty-three in his final professional season in the minors at Miami in 1946.

A small man at five eight and 153 pounds, Waner realized he didn't have

much power; so he decided to hit the ball where it was pitched. He collected 3,152 hits in his twenty years in the bigs and was the seventh man to collect 3,000 hits. Little Poison played eighteen years—he and Paul were Pittsburgh teammates from 1927 through 1940—and collected 2,459 hits.

Paul Glee Waner was born April 16, 1903, in Harrah, Oklahoma, the second of three sons of a local farmer. Paul was an easygoing kid who quickly jumped into baseball and out of school. He wasn't much of a talker but had a droll sense of humor and was not above treating his baby brother as a baby brother when they both had long been starring in the big leagues.

Paul started out as a left-handed pitcher, hurt his arm, and switched to the outfield with his first professional team, the San Francisco Seals. He hit .369, .356, and .401 for the Seals before being sold to Pittsburgh. He batted .336 as a rookie in 1926 and played first base and the outfield for the 1927 league champions. The Pirates met the Yankees in that Series and the Series was over before it began as awed Pirate players sat on the top step of their dugout watching Babe Ruth, Lou Gehrig, Tony Lazzeri, and company, considered baseball's finest team ever, pop dozens of balls over the outfield fences in batting practice.

The display of power destroyed the Pirates' confidence and they went down easily in four straight games.

Waner was not awed by the Yankees; he collected five hits in fifteen at bat.

Waner won his first batting title in 1927 with his .380 mark, his second in 1934, and his third in 1936.

He was released by the Pirates in 1940, signed with the Dodgers, went to Boston, came back to Brooklyn, and pinch-hit for the Yankees late in 1944 and early in 1945 during the war years.

Waner managed for a time after that in the minors and served as a batting instructor for the Braves, Cardinals, and Phillies. In his last years he was considered one of the great authorities on hitting in the game, authored a widely circulated book on baseball hitting, and enjoyed talking baseball with young hitters and sportswriters until his death on August 29, 1965.

His book stressed that hitters should face the pitcher with both eyes instead of hitting against him with one eye hidden behind the shoulder. That way, presumably, a batter could hit the top baseball of the two he saw.

Joe Morgan

(1963–present)

Probably the smallest man in the history of the game to receive so many large honors, Joe Morgan was one of only seven players ever to win back-to-back Most Valuable Player Awards.

Ernie Banks, the home-run slugger of the Chicago Cubs, was the only other National Leaguer and Jimmie Foxx, Hal Newhouser, Yogi Berra, Mickey Mantle, and Roger Maris were the only American Leaguers.

Morgan weighed less than 155 pounds and stood five seven as he anchored the Cincinnati Reds in the middle 1970s, a team considered the best in baseball in its time and one of the best of all time with future Hall of Famers Johnny Bench, Pete Rose, and Tom Seaver helping them to five championship seasons.

A devastating line-drive hitter, a guy with exceptional power for a man his size (he hit 26 homers in 1973 and that had to be, pound for pound, the most impressive power performance in the history of the game), a marvelous, aggressive fielder and an excellent base stealer and runner, Morgan was the guy who made the Reds go.

"He won the games in little ways," says his manager then, Sparky Anderson. "If something had to be done, Morgan did it."

Morgan hit the bloop single in the ninth inning of the seventh game of the 1975 Series to beat Boston in what many baseball people consider the greatest Series ever played.

His lifetime average was only .277 going into the 1980 season but his contributions offensively, defensively, and intangibly were so dramatic for the fine Cincinnati teams that he clearly deserves high recognition among Baseball's 100.

Morgan clearly proved that a player need not be of superhuman strength or exceptional size to excel in baseball. For those reasons alone he should be considered among baseball's élite.

He hit .327 in 1975 and .320 in 1976, led the league in fielding in 1975, had 111 RBI's in 1976, and played on five championship teams, three pennant winners, and two World Championship teams in eight Cincinnati seasons.

Clearly a winning player, Morgan played out his option in 1980 and moved over to help the Houston Astros in their quest for their first title. He hit only .243 in 141 games for the Astros but was especially effective at the end of the season when they won the West title.

Joe Leonard Morgan was born in Bonham, Texas, on September 19, 1943. His family, soon operating without a father, moved to Oakland, California. He played baseball and football there as a youngster and signed with the new Houston Colts in 1963.

A talkative youngster with a high voice, Morgan had opinions on almost everything from baseball to ballet and irritated many of his older teammates who expected young players—especially black players in Texas—to remain hidden. Except on the field.

Morgan was labeled a troublemaker in Houston despite hitting .271, .285, and .275 in his first three seasons as a regular.

He fractured a kneecap in 1968 on a slide and was hampered as a base runner for the next couple of seasons. He still stole 49, 42, and 40 bases before being traded to Cincinnati in 1971 in an eight-player deal.

Encouraged and pushed in Cincinnati, he was soon becoming one of the best all-around players in the game. He batted as high as .327 but never lower than .288 through his next six Cincinnati seasons. Then he slowed down, couldn't agree on a contract, and was granted free agency. He signed with Houston for the 1980 season.

With a lifetime .277 mark, 213 homers, and the best glove of his time, and as a man who helped make the stolen base a forceful offensive weapon, Joe Morgan deserves high ranking among Baseball's 100.

130

Charlie Gehringer

(1924–1942)

This was at the annual Hall of Fame installation in Cooperstown, New York, on a brilliant summer afternoon in 1980.

The kids were gathered outside a huge room where the Hall of Famers assembled to autograph baseballs, sign programs, and be advised of the festivities planned this night after the installation of new members Al Kaline and Duke Snider.

Ted Williams came to the door of the room and small kids screamed. Then old-timer Burleigh Grimes, the last legal spitballer, and Whitey Ford and Bob Lemon and Cool Papa Bell and Sandy Koufax and a dozen more Hall of Famers, all recognizable, were screamed at and mauled for autographs.

In the midst of this furor, a distinguished-looking man walked toward the door wearing a gray pinstriped suit, a dark tie, a white shirt, and polished shoes. No one looked at him as he gracefully and quietly walked in with the Hall of Famers.

"Was that anybody?" a kid asked.

"Nah," another said, "probably just an executive."

The tall, thin, well-dressed man, now a sprightly seventy-seven years old and looking middle aged, was the smoothest, calmest fielding star and one of the best hitters of his generation.

Charlie Gehringer was still doing his chores without being noticed.

Gehringer, the anchor of the Detroit Tigers infield for nearly two decades, batted .320 lifetime, won the batting title in 1937 with a .371 mark, hit over .300 thirteen times—every year from 1927 through 1939 excepting a .298 in

1932—collected 2,839 hits, and played every game in four seasons. He did all this with such a lack of flair, self-promotion, or excitement that his work was always overlooked in favor of other, more flamboyant teammates. He was known as the Mechanical Man because it was believed he was run out there opening day and pulled in the last day with a certain .300 season and guaranteed fielding excellence. He tied or led in fielding percentages in nine separate seasons.

A strong left-handed hitter who socked 184 career homers, Gehringer played on three pennant winners in Detroit in 1934, 1935, and 1940. His consistency was evidenced by the fact that his World Series average of .321 tops his career average of .320.

Charles Leonard Gehringer was born May 11, 1903, at Fowlerville, Michigan. His father was a chicken farmer and young Charles was busy with his chores, often in the hen house. He tired of farming and took up baseball, starring for school and local teams and winning a baseball scholarship at the University of Michigan. He left college to sign with the Tigers in 1924.

A laconic man with modest habits and a thin, dour face, Gehringer was easily overlooked by his teammates and opponents. It often shocked many of them when the season was over and his average would be in the high .300's.

"I had my best year in nineteen thirty-seven," says Hank Greenberg, a Detroit teammate for a dozen years, "with forty homers and a hundred eighty-three RBIs. The newsmen always wrote about me in every town we went to. Then the year ended, I looked up, and Charlie had hit .371 and was the league's MVP."

Gehringer had three seasons over .350 and always was considered the finest fielder of his time. He quit after the 1942 season when he entered the Navy at the age of thirty-nine.

After the war he was a coach, vice-president, and general manager of his beloved Tigers. His last active baseball year was 1959.

He worked on his golf game after that, dabbled in the automobile business, and makes the annual pilgrimmage to Cooperstown to be ignored by the modern generation. He is a member of the old-timers' committee picking previously ignored players, a perfect job for this effortless player who was always being ignored in his playing days.

Why doesn't Gehringer rate higher among Baseball's 100? Because there aren't enough old yellowed newspaper clippings around extolling his performance.

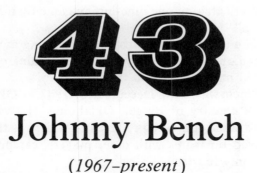

Johnny Bench

(1967–present)

This is one of the selections that caused me sleepless nights. Where does Johnny Bench belong in the list? Is he the best catcher ever or just a guy lucky enough to play with the best team of his time? Is he better than Yogi Berra, Mickey Cochrane, Bill Dickey, and Roy Campanella, all Hall of Famers?

A slugger of reknown, a two-time home-run leader, a three-time RBI leader, a two-time MVP, a solid figure in the Cincinnati Reds structure for fourteen seasons, Johnny Bench misses a higher rating, after I missed much sleep, for one simple reason. He could never hit .300. All the other catchers in consideration for best ever did, with Cochrane and Dickey, equal to Bench as a receiver, having lifetime batting averages of over .300.

In the 1976 World Series, Cincinnati manager Sparky Anderson was asked to compare the play of his catcher, who had just batted .533, to the play of Yankee catcher Thurman Munson, who had led the Yankees with a .529 mark.

"I don't want to embarrass any other catcher by comparing him with Johnny Bench," Anderson said.

It made the hair stand up on the back of Munson's head. The late catcher of the Yankees could not understand that Anderson was simply being loyal to his own man and refusing to get into a discussion over their relative merits. Bench was best. Period.

Better than Berra, Dickey, Cochrane? I think not, but certainly the best of his time, an incredible hitter, a marvelous defensive catcher, a most dramatic player with that special élan which separates him from the crowd. More times than the statisticians can count, Johnny Bench has won games for the Reds with late-inning home runs or saved others with late-inning defensive maneuvers.

"The thing about catching is that it is so mentally wearisome that it breaks you down after a while," Bench says. "The concentration is so intense. I feel more tired after catching one nine-inning game than I feel after playing a week at first base."

Bench would like to lengthen his career by moving away from catching, but the Reds depend on him so heavily they can not think of playing a season without this on-field manager behind the plate.

Johnny Lee Bench was born December 7, 1947 in Oklahoma City and raised in the ranch country of Binger, Oklahoma. He was an outstanding amateur player and was soon being referred to widely as the Binger Banger. Bench always played on teams with older players, catching against grown men when he was only fourteen.

A sturdy, moon-faced six one and 197 pounds, this part Choctaw Indian was signed out of high school in 1965 and sent to the Reds' Tampa club, and two years later was with the Reds.

He was the NL Rookie of the Year in 1968 and National League MVP in 1970. Mature, poised, and older than his years would indicate, Bench was an immediate leader on a club that was to win six championships, four pennants, and two World Series in the next ten years.

He batted .293 and won the home-run title with 45 and the RBI title with 148 in 1970. A right-handed hitter, he hit 40 homers two years later and has six seasons with over a hundred RBIs.

Perhaps it is Bench's throwing that is the most significant part of his game. He has a rifle arm that has intimidated almost every base runner during his time. His quick release from the crouch and the accuracy of his throws have made him the envy of all catchers.

At thirty-three Bench still seems capable of several more seasons of excellent play. If he moves away from catching, his newfound stamina might carry him to a season above .300. If that happens, we might have to move Bench up on the list of Baseball's 100.

Lou Brock

(1961–1979)

In the summer of 1962, in the first season of the New York Mets, manager Casey Stengel of the New Yorkers, who had seen every player in the game for fifty years, watched a lithe, five eleven, 168-pounder drive a ball left-handed into the center-field bleachers in the Polo Grounds some 505 feet away from the home plate.

"Amazin', amazin'," shouted the ebullient Stengel, "I gotta have that player."

Stengel never did get that fellow, but the National League fans had the joy of watching the antics of Lou Brock for nearly two decades.

Hitting long home runs was not really his thing, though he could occasionally surprise. What made Brock such an incredible performer is that he was a marvelous hitter, a man who collected 3,023 hits to join that exclusive club and established his own club in stealing bases with 118 steals in 1974 and a career total of 938. He led the league in stolen bases eight times and was one of only three players in baseball history to steal over 50 bases and hit 20 homers in the same season.

Brock had eight seasons over .300, collected more than 200 hits in four seasons, led in runs scored once and tied once, led once in doubles, once in triples, and hit 149 homers while not ever being considered a long-ball threat.

"I always wanted to be a complete player," Brock says. "I wanted to do everything well in the game."

Brock played on three pennant-winning St. Louis teams in 1964, 1967, and 1968, but probably his performance in a half season in 1964 after being traded

over from the Cubs was his most significant. He triggered a lethargic team into the championship with his flair and style.

Brock was an incredible World Series performer with a lifetime .391 average. He batted .464 and 1968 and stole a total of 14 Series bases.

Louis Clark Brock was born June 18, 1939, at El Dorado, Arkansas. He was a track man and basketball player in school and an occasional baseball player. He entered Southern University and taught high school mathematics after his graduation with playing some semi pro baseball. He starred in a Pan American baseball tournament in 1961 and was soon signed by the Chicago Cubs. They gambled a thirty-thousand-dollar bonus on the youngster because of his speed.

Soon Brock was playing in Chicago, a left-handed hitter in a park where the wind blew to the left field. He batted .263 and .258 in his two Chicago seasons and was traded to St. Louis on June 15, 1964, because the Cubs wanted a right-handed pitcher named Ernie Broglio.

Brock was placed in left field by Cardinal manager Johnny Keane and was a dramatic player from the start. Left field was the pressure position on the Cardinals that season because it had only recently been vacated by the great Stan Musial.

After the Cardinals won the 1964 pennant, Musial wired Brock, "If I didn't quit, the Cardinals never would have won. Congratulations."

Brock hit .315 that season and had .300 years in 1970, 1971, 1972, 1974, 1975, 1976, and his final season of 1979. His best year was 1971 when he batted .313, knocked in 61 runs as the leadoff hitter, and led the league in scoring with 126.

Brock also made the stolen base a viable offensive weapon, using it regardless of the score of the game.

"A hitter doesn't stop at second if he thinks he can hit a triple in a ten-to-nothing game," Brock said. "Why should I refuse to steal if we are way ahead or way behind? It's part of my game."

A straight-in slider with explosive speed, Brock made his stolen-base marks with his intelligence. He studied pitchers the way a Wall Street broker studies the market. He knew when to go and, more importantly, when not to go.

He had great speed in the outfield but not great hands. He was fast and could outrun his mistakes, but he did drop balls and led or tied in outfield errors seven times. No matter. He also caught fly balls other outfielders could only stare at.

Lou Brock made a ground-ball single and a stolen base as exciting as a line drive off the wall. He makes Baseball's 100 on speed, 3,000 hits, a lifetime .293 average, and an abundance of class.

Carl Yastrzemski

(1961–present)

The city of Boston thought it might never recover from the retirement of Ted Williams at the end of the 1960 season. Ted was a hero and villain all in one, but he was their hero-villain.

Along came a tall, thin, twenty-one-year-old ex-shortstop out of Southhampton, Long Island, and the University of Notre Dame to take the place of the great Williams.

He has been everything the Boston faithful could have wanted, a great hitter with more hits than Williams, a three-time batting champion, a guy who constantly seemed to disappoint the fans because he wasn't perfect, and one of the best clutch hitters of all time.

Captain Carl Yastrzemski of the Boston Red Sox, the left fielder who replaced Williams, has had a career that is probably just a shade behind that of his predecessor in Fenway Park.

In 1979 Yastrzemski became the first American Leaguer to collect 3,000 hits and smash 400 homers. Al Kaline had missed by one homer.

As a model of consistency over two decades, Yastrzemski has batted .300 six times, has played fewer than 144 games only twice in his career, was the last man to win the Triple Crown, and won the American League batting title with the lowest average ever at .301 in 1968.

Carl Michael Yastrzemski was born August 22, 1939, in Southhampton, Long Island, a community then surrounded by potato farms. His father was a poor but proud farmer who spent a lot of his off time playing baseball. By the time he was sixteen young Carl was playing shortstop on the same neighborhood team led by his father, who was the center fielder.

Yastrzemski's father wanted his son to get an education and avoid the backbreaking work of playing baseball as a sideline while he farmed. Yastrzemski attended Notre Dame, starred on the baseball team, and signed a hundred-thousand-dollar bonus when the Red Sox beckoned in 1958. He also promised his father he would get his school degree and completed his bachelor of science degree at Merrimack near his Boston home.

In 1960 Williams retired and Yastrzemski, who had batted .377 and .339 in two minor-league seasons, was ticketed to replace him. He had been converted from a shortstop to a left fielder.

Yastrzemski started slowly with a great deal of pressure on him and the Boston fans howling at him because he wasn't Williams. A left-handed hitter like Ted, Yaz was a line-drive hitter who didn't really pull the ball until 1967 when he hit 44 homers. He was content to hit for average and most of the Boston press resented him for that. Williams had belted 521 homers and Red Sox fans wanted the same from Yastrzemski. Sometimes thinking he might have chosen the wrong game if not the wrong town, Yastrzemski won over the fans in 1967, one of the greatest years any player has ever had.

Carl won the Triple Crown with a .326 average, 121 RBIs and 44 homers. He played the left-field wall at Fenway Park the way Heifetz plays the violin. He threw out runners from the base of the wall, he hustled madly for extra bases, he made diving catches, and he won games with long balls in the ninth inning.

"For that one season," says Dick Williams, who was the rookie manager of the Red Sox that year, "there could not have been a better baseball player."

He beat the Minnesota Twins almost single-handedly in the final two-game series for the pennant with seven hits in nine tries, marvelous defensive work, and incredible base running.

He won the batting title the next year and was before long being recognized as one of the game's great players. He helped the Red Sox to their second pennant in his time in 1975 and batted .310 in the Series. He was now playing first base as well as left field and playing first as well as any natural-born first baseman.

At the age of forty-one Yastrzemski was still a regular in the Boston lineup and was adding to his home-run and 3,000-hit totals as his career moved steadily onward.

Carl Yastrzemski may have proven that he was not Ted Williams and can't be rated in the baseball's top five. But 3,000 hits over twenty years, with two pennants, certainly allows him to be compared favorably with most other players of his time and makes him an easy winner of the number 45 position among Baseball's 100.

Ralph Kiner

(1946–1955)

One of baseball's most incredible sights was watching the mass exodus of fans from Forbes Field in the seventh inning of a meaningless game after Ralph Kiner had taken his turn at bat.

Kiner was the only player they had paid to see and when he was finished with his day's work they went home. They could hardly wait to read about him in the next day's papers and buy a ticket for the next game.

Kiner always put on an impressive show, smashing home runs into Kiner's Korner in left field, missing with a flair, or playing left field with less than the grace of a ballerina. Kiner isn't here because he was a graceful fielder. He is here because he may have been one of the top three or four home-run hitters of all time, an electrifying right-handed slugger, a dynamic player who threatened home-run records every season he put on a uniform.

He played in the big leagues only ten seasons, so his total numbers are not all that overwhelming. He got started late because of the war and he had to quit early because of a bad back, but for most of the years he played between 1946 and 1955 Kiner was as pure a home-run hitter as the game had ever seen. He hit 369 homers, an average of 36 a year.

Kiner led or tied for the lead in homers his first seven seasons; he hit 54 homers in 1949, 51 in 1947, and 47 in 1950. He hit 369 homers and his frequency of home runs per one hundred times at bat is 7.1, highest in the history of the game. Babe Ruth's was 8.5 and he is credited as the official leader because of so many more at bats.

Kiner averaged over 100 RBIs per season, was the leader once, and never

hit fewer than 18 homers in any season. He had a .279 lifetime average with three seasons over .300.

Ralph McPherran Kiner was born October 27, 1922, at Santa Rita, New Mexico. His family moved west to California and Kiner was playing baseball with a team called the Yankeee Juniors outside of his Los Angeles home when he was fifteen. He knew Joe DiMaggio still had a lot of years to go when he was being scouted in the early 1940s, so he signed with the Pittsburgh Pirates, figuring that team would move him up quickly.

After three minor-league seasons and 27 homers, he was drafted into the Navy and returned in 1946. His six-two frame had now filled out to 195 pounds, and he was a dashingly handsome figure with a wide smile and long black hair.

As a Pittsburgh rookie in 1946 he belted 23 homers to win the title. He was helped immeasurably as a hitter in 1947 by the arrival in Pittsburgh of veteran right-handed slugger Hank Greenberg.

"Ralph was willing to work and we would go out there early and take batting practice. He would work on getting his hands to move quicker. He was strong, so all he needed was some better mechanics," Greenberg says.

The left-field wall was shortened and named Greenberg Gardens (soon to be Kiner's Korner) in honor of the ex-Detroit slugger. Greenberg, going downhill, hit 25 homers while the second-year slugger, Kiner, hit 51. So did Johnny Mize of the Giants, who tied Kiner two years in a row.

The home runs made Kiner a national hero, and his handsome face was on the cover of many magazines. He was dating young actress Elizabeth Taylor, was romancing actress Janet Leigh, and later dated and married tennis star Nancy Chaffee.

Kiner continued to win the home-run title through 1952. In 1953 he was suddenly traded to the Cubs at the age of thirty-one because of a contract dispute and declining production. He was baseball's highest paid player at a hundred thousand dollars.

He spent two years with the Cubs and then finished out his active career with the Indians in 1955. He hit 18 homers and batted .243 while bothered by a bad back.

Kiner then moved to San Diego as that minor-league team's general manager, went into broadcasting, returned to Chicago, and came to New York in 1962 to broadcast the Mets games. He has been in New York ever since, a popular local figure, still handsome, a fine golfer and tennis player, a Hall of Famer, and the greatest right-handed home-run hitter over one decade baseball has ever seen.

Ralph Kiner was a Pittsburgh institution, a notable example of a career burning out too soon, but significant enough in his time to merit a place with Baseball's 100 in the top fifty.

Steve Garvey

(1969–present)

One of the most consistent hitters in the game's history, a marvelous fielder, a steady performer under all kinds of stress, Steve Garvey earns his rating among the top fifty players of all time.

He is the Lou Gehrig of this generation. He has played almost every day for eight years, hit .300 almost every year, batted in over 100 runs five times, collected 200 hits in six seasons, and led the Dodgers to three championships, three pennants, and record-breaking attendance records.

The Los Angeles Dodgers have been one of the most successful teams in baseball history, with a better winning record and a far greater attendance record than any other team in the game over the last twenty years.

Garvey has been the heart of that era, a steady performer on the field, a spokesman for the team, a handsome young man who has exemplified and typified all the best in baseball. Steve Garvey's records alone may not be that incredible, but his reliability as an athlete, a Dodger, and a man are outstanding.

One of the most unique baseball situations has occurred in over the last half dozen years in Los Angeles.

The same half dozen players have dominated the Dodgers in that period, including four infielders, one pitcher, Don Sutton, and one catcher, Steve Yeager.

Ron Cey at third, Bill Russell at shortstop, Dave Lopes at second, and Garvey at first have played together more games than any four infielders in baseball history. Garvey has been the cornerstone of that inner defense with his wide-ranging moves at first, his sure glove, and his quick hands.

He's batted .300 or better in seven of the eight seasons he has been a regular, played in 160 or more games in the last six years, and led the league in putouts for five of six seasons.

If ever a man was born to be a Dodger it was Steve Garvey. Anything else would have been a surprise. Steven Patrick Garvey was born December 22, 1948, in Tampa, Florida. His father was a local bus driver and young Steve would accompany his father on long bus rides while his dad drove the Dodgers in spring training.

"My favorite player was Gil Hodges," says Garvey. "He was always kind to me and treated me like an equal. He was just such a good man."

Garvey was to fill the position Hodges had left vacant a decade before when he moved to the Mets. The late Mets manager was always an admirer of young Garvey as a player and a man.

Steve starred in high school basketball, football, and baseball and won a scholarship to Michigan State. As a high school graduate he was selected in the draft by the Minnesota Twins but refused to sign. When the Dodgers drafted him in 1968 the dream was realized.

Garvey had served as a batboy for the Dodgers under manager Walt Alston and now he was playing for him. He started out as an outfielder, switched to first, made the Dodgers in 1970, sat on the bench for two seasons, and took over first base in 1972.

The handsome, always-smiling five ten, 195-pounder hit .304 in his first full season and was soon established as one of the most consistent players in the game.

Garvey was often criticized by his teammates because of his all-American boy image—warm, honest, friendly, a good scout—but that is what he was. There were people who considered him too good to be true and a phony, but Garvey drove himself hard, played hard, and enjoyed baseball. He didn't need the off-field companionship, night life, and heavy drinking of many of his mates.

Garvey attended to business, and by the end of the 1970s was recognized as the steadiest hitter in the game, the true successor to Pete Rose as an incredible hit man.

At thirty-two Garvey still seems on top of his game, a certain bet for 2,000 hits with an outside chance at 2,500. He has come a long way from handing out sandwiches on the Dodger bus to Gil Hodges.

Jim Palmer

(1965–present)

To a lot of ladies across the country, he is just another pretty face and impressive body in Jockey shorts. The face and the form on the ads are a lot tougher to take when Jim Palmer is firing his fast ball or snaking his curve from the mound.

Hollywood handsome, tall, thin, articulate, Jim Palmer has been the dominant American pitcher for the last fifteen years.

A three-time Cy Young Award winner and an eight-time 20-game winner, Palmer has led the Baltimore Orioles to five pennants and two World Series titles in his fifteen years with the club.

At thirty-five he has an outside chance of recording 300 wins before he retires to become a full-time underwear model or television talk-show personality.

As good as Palmer looks in the Jockey shorts ads, he looks even better on the mound in Baltimore's Memorial Stadium. His pitching form is almost perfect, a classic coordination of arm, shoulders, body, and legs as he throws his right-handed fast ball in on right-handed hitters and curves left-handers at their fists. Palmer can throw as hard as he ever did if not as often, has a wicked curve ball, can change speeds with magical ability and has excellent control.

Palmer has had two separate careers, one as a hard-throwing, one-pitch twenty-year-old and the second career after recovering from serious shoulder trouble.

"They told me I would never pitch again," says Palmer. "That was back in

149

nineteen sixty-seven when I was twenty-one years old. I had trained to be a pitcher. What else could I do but work my way back?"

He came back to Baltimore two years later, won 20 games for the first time in 1970, and compiled the amazing streak of eight 20-game seasons in nine years. He missed only once, in 1974, when he was on the disabled list for nearly two months with new shoulder ailments.

James Alvin Palmer was born October 15, 1945, in New York City. His parents divorced and Palmer moved with his step father to Los Angeles, where he grew up the son of a minor show-business actor. He was not interested in a show-business career and was soon winning honors as an athlete in baseball and basketball.

He attended Arizona State University and was signed out of college by the Orioles on August 16, 1963. Baltimore had been collecting some fine young players and would bring them all together for a pennant in 1966 under manager Hank Bauer.

The twenty-year-old Palmer shut the Dodgers out in the 1966 Series after a 15–10 regular season as a starter with a 3.46 ERA.

The shoulder trouble began the following spring, and the World Series star was back in the minors with Rochester, Miami, and Elmira attempting to rebuild his arm.

Working alone for hours, Palmer relearned some of the things he had once known about pitching. His arm finally came back strong in 1969 as he recorded a 16–4 season for a dumpy little Baltimore manager named Earl Weaver. The two began a long-running feud.

"It's not that I don't like Earl," Palmer says, "it's that I never agree with anything he says."

Palmer once was taken out of a game and held the ball out in front of him for the small manager to take.

"Don't shove that ball in my face," Weaver screamed.

"When it left my hand," said the six-foot-three inch 195-pounder "it was chest high."

Palmer continued winning through the decade of the 1970s, establishing himself as the premier pitcher in the league and one of the two or three best in the game.

He has pitched one no-hitter, led the league in wins once, innings pitched three times, and ERA twice in a brilliant career.

At thirty-five, as handsome as ever, Jim Palmer still is a man most female baseball fans will long dream about even if his fast ball has lost a little. He certainly hasn't.

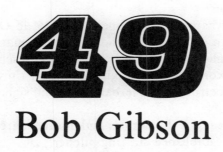

Bob Gibson

(1959–1975)

There wasn't anything subtle about Bob Gibson's pitching. He would just lean back, rock quickly as he generated forward motion, and explode that fast ball in a hitter's face.

Gibson was as intimidating a pitcher as ever toed a mound, a large, scowling black man of six feet one inch and 195 pounds, with intense eyes and a hard-driving pitching motion.

He was an exceptional competitor who would pitch often and early, taking his turn on the mound and taking someone else's turn when his manager thought he could win. When he pitched the seventh game of the 1964 World Series on two days' rest with other rested pitchers available, manager Johnny Keane was asked why he chose Gibson over the others.

"Because I had a commitment to his heart," the manager replied.

Gibson's fast ball was explosive, a rising, heavy ball that at the peak of his career was almost impossible to hit. His 1968 ERA of 1.12, barely one run a game over a stretch of 34 games and 305 innings, was astonishing. Only one pitcher ever did better, Dutch Leonard of Boston in 1914 with a 1.01.

Gibson, a handsome, intelligent man with a deep voice and brooding manner, was considered the toughest, meanest pitcher of his time. He asked no favors from hitters and gave none.

Roberto Clemente once broke his leg with a line drive and Gibson hobbled after the ball, picked it up, threw Clemente out, and collapsed.

Gibson seemed forever angry, upset that blacks were not totally accepted

153

as equals in baseball, angry when he didn't pitch or didn't win, and unhappy in the final days of his career as his skills deserted him.

While he was at the top of his game for the ten years between 1962 and 1972, few could match Gibson in performance. A two-time Cy Young award winner and a 20-game winner five times, Gibson was always at his best in big games. He was 7–2 in the World Series he started in and won the seventh game in 1964 and 1967.

Robert Gibson was born November 19, 1935, in Omaha, Nebraska. A large young man with exceptional hands and coordination, Gibson was one of Nebraska's finest all-around athletes. He played baseball, football, basketball, and ran track, won a scholarship to Creighton University, played a year with the Harlem Globetrotters basketball team, and signed with the Cardinals in 1957.

He spent three years in the minors and another three with the Cardinals before becoming an established starting pitcher.

He had his first winning season at 13–12 in 1961, won 15 the next year, and then won no fewer than 16 games in nine of the next ten seasons. In 1967, hit by Clemente's drive on July fifteenth, he stayed out six weeks before returning. The Cards won the pennant and Gibson won three games in the World Series.

He was 22–9 in 1968 with that unreal 1.12 ERA and was 20–13 in 1969 and 23–7 in 1970.

Gibson had a late start as a pitcher, not winning his first big-league game until he was twenty-four years old. He enjoyed major success for the next dozen years, but began to lose that hop on his high hard one in 1974. He was 11–13 that season and 3–10 at the age of thirty-nine in 1975.

The big right-hander retired after that year, did some television commercials, bought into an Omaha bank, purchased a controlling interest in a radio station, and stayed hidden from the baseball scene, unable to relate to the current crop of players or teams. He was finally talked back into baseball by old St. Louis teammate Joe Torre as a special pitching coach with the Mets. He was named to the Hall of Fame in 1981.

With a career record 251–174 Gibson certainly earns his position in the top fifty of Baseball's 100. As tough and intimidating a guy as he was, Gibson will probably lean me against the wall and argue for a higher rating. I guess the only reason he isn't rated higher is because I never faced him on the mound. A lot of hitters who did would say, "Bob Gibson was number one."

50

Brooks Robinson

(1955–1977)

He was the Picasso of his position, the greatest fielding third baseman the game has ever seen, a diving, daring, whirling figure in the dirt, quickly on his knees, firing the ball across the diamond to beat the runner by an eyelash.

Brooks Robinson made playing third base into one of the most thrilling spectacles in sports. Fans would sit and watch Baltimore games in hopes that Robinson would get a chance at a hard ground ball over the base.

In the 1970 World Series he put on such a magnificent exhibition of third-base play that Cincinnati's right-handed slugger Johnny Bench, victimized many times by Robinson's dives, vowed, "I will become a left-handed hitter to keep the ball away from that guy."

Unlike most excellent fielders, Robinson was a surprisingly slow runner. He had very little speed on the basepaths and not much speed in the field. He did have exceptional reflexes and an instinct for the ball which allowed him to catch grounders that other third basemen would not even consider trying for. He wore a thin glove with long fingers and seemed to be able to will a ball into a glove when its owner, the batter, wanted it otherwise.

Robinson, for all his magnificence in the field, was as dangerous a batter as the Orioles had for more than twenty years. He was only a .267 lifetime hitter but he was one of the best clutch hitters in the game with a league-leading 118 RBIs in 1964, 100 RBIs in 1966, the year the Orioles won their first pennant, and six more seasons with 80 RBIs or more. He was the

155

American League's MVP in 1964 with a .317 average, 118 RBIs, and 28 homers.

Those numbers would be impressive enough for a guy who had no glove. For a fielder the likes of Robinson, it probably meant two runs a game, one for his team and one he took away from the other team every day of the season.

A handsome, well-mannered soft-spoken gentleman from Little Rock, born in that Arkansas city on May 18, 1937, Robinson grew to be one of the most respected players in the game. Everybody liked Brooks and Brooks seemed to like everybody.

Robinson played 23 consecutive seasons with the Baltimore Orioles and became an institution in that town almost as famous as its luscious-tasting crabcakes.

Robinson started his baseball career as a slow-legged shortstop in high school, soon was moved to second, and then to third base. Baltimore manager Paul Richards took one look at Robinson's glove and lack of speed and planted him forevermore at third.

"It wasn't all that easy in the beginning," Robinson recalls. "I couldn't hit, I was nervous in the field, and I threw a lot of balls in the stands behind first base."

Robinson joined the O's in 1955, was up and down for a couple of seasons, and established himself as the regular in 1960.

That was the year the Orioles made a late run at the pennant against the Yankees. A pop-up was hit between third baseman Robinson and shortstop Ron Hansen in a key spot in the game. The two young infielders collided, the ball dropped, and the Yankees rallied to win.

"Yankee fans have always remembered me for that one," drawls Robinson with a smile.

Robinson played on five championship teams, four pennant winners, and two World Series Championship teams. He was the American League MVP in 1964 and the World Series MVP in 1970.

Robinson missed the 3,000-hit club (he has 2,848) but led the league in fielding eleven times. He was an excellent hitter, a tough out in a tough spot, but certainly the finest defensive player of his time.

One more thing about Brooks Robinson. If you had a son, Brooks Robinson is the kind of man you would like him to grow up to be.

Chuck Klein

(1928–1944)

While Babe Ruth was breaking down walls with his smashes in the American League, a husky redheaded six-footer was doing the same thing in the National League.

Chuck Klein dominated long-ball hitting in the National League from 1929, when he led the league with 43, until 1936, when he had his last big home-run year of 25 with 104 RBIs.

Like Ruth and unlike most of today's home-run hitters, Klein was also a man who could hit for average, could hit good pitching, and didn't care if the pitcher was a left-hander or a right-hander.

He hit as high as .386 in 1930 (Bill Terry hit .401 that year) and batted .368 in 1933. That year he held league-leading figures in RBIs with 120, homers with 28, doubles with 44, and hits with 223. He also managed seven triples; Arky Vaughan led in that department with 19.

Klein had a lifetime mark of .320 with 300 career homers and 2,076 hits. He had nine seasons over .300 in ten years and averaged better than .330 during that period.

Charles Herbert "Chuck" Klein was born October 7, 1905, in Indianapolis, Indiana. His father worked in a local steel mill and young Chuck, attempting to escape that grind, interested himself in sports. He was an outstanding football and baseball player and signed with the Evansville club in the Three-I league in 1927. He batted .327 as a twenty-one-year-old and was soon on his way to the Phillies.

The Philadelphia club then played in an old park called Baker Bowl with metal outfield fences. Klein would often rattle line drives off that fence to the cheers of the Philadelphia fans.

After six successful seasons with the Phillies he was traded to the Chicago Cubs for three journeymen players and sixty-five thousand dollars in cash. The Phillie bosses needed the cash to keep the franchise going.

Klein did not slow down in Chicago, hitting .301 in his first season in Wrigley Field with 20 homers and 80 RBIs. After another season with the Cubs he was traded back to Philadelphia in 1936, played with them until 1939, was released and signed by the Pirates, and then was released again and signed by the Phillies in 1940.

He was no longer a productive player but was kept around by the Phillies from 1940 through 1944 as major-league baseball was depleted by the loss of players during World War II.

In 1942 the Phillies named Klein a player-coach and he worked with some of the young hitters who were later to help the Phillies win a pennant in 1950, their first since 1915.

He retired after the 1945 season, in declining health, and lived out the rest of his life quietly back in his Indianapolis home.

Klein died in Indianapolis on March 28, 1958, and was remembered with extensive press coverage in Philadelphia for his home-run exploits. Out of kindness few mentioned the stocky outfielder's lack of fielding skills.

In 1980 the baseball old-timers committee elected Klein to the Hall of Fame and the slugging left-handed hitter was now enshrined in Cooperstown with the Babe and Lou Gehrig and other sluggers he was equal to for the big ten years of his career.

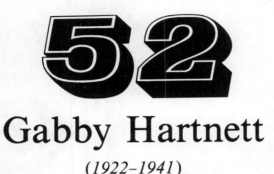

Gabby Hartnett

(1922–1941)

He was thirty-seven years old, the player-manager of the Chicago Cubs, up against Pittsburgh's tough relief pitcher, Mace Brown, in the growing darkness of Chicago's Wrigley Field. There were two out and none on as the jug-eared, affable Irishman stepped to the plate. Chicago was a half game behind first-place Pittsburgh.

With fans squinting through the fading light, Hartnett caught one of Brown's fast balls and rocketed it into the bleacher seats for the game winner and the deciding blow in the pennant race. It was one of the most dramatic home runs ever hit in the game, and for many old-timers it was equal to Bobby Thomson's famous 1951 Giants homer against the hated Dodgers.

Hartnett was probably the best all-around catcher the National League had seen up until that time. Johnny Bench and Roy Campanella may have impressive credentials but Hartnett was so good for so long that he still probably can lay just claim to his standing.

With Campanella's career cut short tragically after an automobile accident and Bench already complaining at thirty-three that catching every day is impossible, Hartnett's twenty years as the Man in the Iron Mask is an outstanding feat of durability, courage, and stamina. Maybe Hartnett is simply an example of why equipment used by catchers is called "the tools of ignorance."

Hartnett had a lifetime mark of .297, caught almost every day for thirteen seasons, had six seasons over .300, knocked in more than 80 runs in six seasons, and was one of the finest, headiest receivers of his day.

161

In 1930 he had one of the finest seasons any catcher ever had with a .339 average, 122 RBIs, and 37 homers. If that wasn't enough, he caught 141 games and led the league in putouts, assists, and fielding average.

Charles Leo "Gabby" Hartnett was born in Woonsocket, Rhode Island, on December 20, 1900, one of fourteen children of a local streetcar conductor.

While working in a steel mill, he played semipro baseball and was soon being scouted by big-league clubs. He was a tall kid, nearly six one, with a large pair of hands and wide shoulders. He would fill out later to over 215 pounds but was thin and rangy as a young catcher and right-handed hitter.

He signed a professional contract with the Worcester, Massachusetts, club and was purchased by the Chicago Cubs in 1922. He played on four World Series teams with the Cubs in 1929, 1932, 1935, and 1938.

He was an excellent receiver, a clutch hitter, a long-ball slugger with 236 round trippers, and a fast base-runner for a man his size.

Perhaps his most important quality was his durability, playing and catching more than 100 games for twelve seasons, including eight in a row.

An easygoing fellow with a friendly face and an easy smile, Hartnett was liked by all of his teammates and most of his opponents. He was chatty at the plate and was soon being called Gabby—a name tagged on him by a Chicago sportswriter—by most of the press and public. His teammates persisted in calling him Leo since he didn't like Charles, his first name.

Hartnett had a steady career except for the season of 1929. He injured his arm in spring training and could barely lift it all year. He caught only one game and pinch-hit in 24 others with only six hits. After a winter's rest the arm came back almost as mysteriously as it had gone. He then began his eight straight seasons of 100 or more caught games.

After being released by the Cubs in 1940, he signed on as a player-coach with the New York Giants. He had managed the Cubs for three seasons, including the pennant-winning one helped by his homer in 1938, and later managed and coached in the minors through 1966.

Hartnett died December 20, 1972. Chicago fans, who have not had a pennant in thirty-five years, like to remember Hartnett's homer fondly. It was one of the last times they could hold their heads up high with fans of other cities.

Ernie Banks

(1953–1971)

    With a twinkle in his eye, a smile on his face, a warm handshake, and
a high-pitched, warm voice, Ernie Banks would move close to a visiting sportswriter and laugh, "What a great day for baseball. Let's play two."
    The rain might be beating on the top of the dugout roof at Wrigley Field
or the clouds may be a dark, ominous gray or the world might be threatened
with a nuclear holocaust, but Ernie Banks would still offer in his cheery way:
Let's play two. Sometimes three.
    "I just love Wrigley Field and day baseball and the Chicago Cubs," he
would say, and he would make you believe it.
    What was there not to love if you were Ernie Banks, a lifetime .274 hitter
with 512 homers, a ridiculously high amount for a man who started out as a
skinny, right-handed-hitting shortstop.
    Banks style was easy, effortless; he was a line-drive snap hitter with
incredibly active wrists and arms, a man who never weighed more than 180
pounds on his lanky six-foot-one-inch frame.
    "It's all in here," he would explain, as he pointed to his wrists. "This is
how I turn the baseball from the pitcher's hand into a souvenir for Cubs fans
in the bleacher seats."
    Few players were as popular at home as well as on the road as Ernie
Banks was, a man millions loved and admired for the joys and skills he
brought to the game. Even at the end of his career when his skills diminished
and the party was over, Banks remained a cheery personality. His election to

the Hall of Fame on the first ballot was universally approved by baseball fans.

Banks was a tremendous home-run hitter who belted a total of 512 in his career including five seasons of 40 or more and thirteen of 20 or more. He won two home-run titles, two RBI titles, one slugging title, and two MVP awards, with back-to-back crowns in 1958 and 1959. He batted over .300 three times and defensively made the switch from shortstop to first base without any fuss.

Ernest Banks was born in Dallas, Texas, one of twelve children of a grocery clerk, on January 31, 1931. He played all sports in school and when he finished high school he signed to play in the old Negro Leagues as a seventeen-year-old. He had played more softball than real baseball in school but soon adjusted to the faster, tougher game.

After the Cubs purchased his contract from the Kansas City Monarchs, Banks never played a day in the minor leagues. His career lasted nineteen big-league seasons, and included a record-breaking 424 consecutive games over nearly four seasons as the Chicago shortstop.

The Cubs were rarely in contention, so the major point of interest for Chicago fans seemed to be whether or not Banks would win the home-run title. He hit 19 in his first full season of 1954 and then 44, 28, 43, 47, 45, 41, 29, and 37 before slowing down to 18.

At the age of thirty-eight, Banks was the regular first baseman on Leo Durocher's 1969 Cubs, the team that choked away a large first-place lead to the Mets. He played every game but seven that year as he pushed his body for that elusive pennant. The Cubs didn't win, Banks never played in a World Series, and Chicago may never see another pennant again.

Durocher was one of the few men the gentle, charming Banks would admit—even privately—that he didn't like very much. He said nothing publicly but was angry at Durocher's sniping at him. When asked publicly about Leo, he would wink, whistle, and say, "What a lovely day for a game."

What a lovely man—a wonderful shortstop, a fine first baseman, one of the game's greatest home-run hitters, and a Hall of Famer both on and off the field.

Ernie Banks makes me feel so good I want to award him two positions, number 53 among Baseball's 100 and number 44, in honor of his uniform.

Burleigh Grimes

(1916–1934)

He was approaching his eighty-seventh birthday, still a husky, hearty man, as he sat on the porch of the famed Otesaga Hotel in Cooperstown, New York, home of Baseball's Hall of Fame Museum.

Burleigh Grimes had been a great pitcher and successful manager, but now, as he sat in that huge hotel lobby, he was like an antique, a man from another time and place.

"How did you throw it?" a small boy asked.

"Just like this," said Grimes, as he put his fingers to his mouth and his fingers to a baseball.

And that's how he did throw it, his famed spitball, a rapid, sinking, impossible-to-hit pitch which helped Grimes win 270 big league games and made him a relic.

He was the last legal spitballer in the game, leaving the Yankees after the 1934 season, still plying his trade with the wet one fourteen years after the pitch was outlawed.

In one of the most curious moves ever made in baseball, the tricky pitch was outlawed in 1920 but the tricky pitchers were excused from the ruling. Grimes survived as the last legal spitballer, though Gaylord Perry, Don Drysdale, Don Sutton, and a handful of other pitchers of recent vintage have been accused of throwing the wet one.

Grimes pitched for nineteen years in the big leagues, and managed, coached, and scouted after that, but came into prominence for his spitball

pitching and his endless bitching. He hated umpires when he played and he hated them even more when he managed.

Burleigh Arland (Old Stubblebeard) Grimes was born August 18, 1893, at Emerald, Wisconsin, in the north lumber country of the state. His father was a lumberman and Burleigh soon gravitated to the trade. The work helped him build one of the strongest bodies any pitcher ever had, a shade over five feet ten inches tall, 195 pounds of solid muscle. He had a round face, a thick jaw and dark piercing eyes. He got his nickname from a sportswriter because he chose often to skip shaving, especially on pitching days when he wanted to frighten the hitters.

He signed his first pro contract in 1912, spent five years learning his trade—and picking up that spitter—before joining Pittsburgh in 1916. He was traded to the Brooklyn Dodgers in 1918 in a trade including Casey Stengel, who had joined Brooklyn in 1912. Grimes later played for New York, Pittsburgh again, Boston, St. Louis, Chicago, and the New York Yankees.

Grimes had a 19–9 season for the Dodgers in 1918, won 23, 22, 21, and 22 games in Brooklyn, and was traded to the hated Giants. He had fourteen seasons of ten or more wins with a high of 25 in 1928.

Grimes played on four pennant winners, one in Brooklyn, two in St. Louis, and one in Chicago. His spitter wasn't working well when he was slugged for seven runs in 2⅔ innings for the 1932 Series Cubs and came out of it with a 23.63 ERA.

Grimes succeeded Casey Stengel as the Dodger manager in 1937 and was succeeded by Leo Durocher after he was fired at the end of the 1938 season.

Tough looking with a gravely voice and a sun-baked face, Grimes was as combative a man as could be during his playing and managerial years.

That image softened in retirement back in Wisconsin and he is now a quiet, soft-spoken, pipe-smoking gentleman who has patience for kids, autograph hounds, and dogs.

"When you get my age," he says, "every day you get up is a good day. No use getting excited any more."

Burleigh Grimes was exciting, a 270-game winner, the last spitballer (legal type), and one of the National League's finest pitchers.

Best Wishes
Roy Campanella

Roy Campanella

(1948–1957)

He was twenty-five years old when Jackie Robinson became the first Negro allowed to enter baseball and he was thirty-six years old when he had a serious automobile accident which ended his career and nearly ended his life.

But for the color ban in baseball and that horrible accident, the statistics Roy Campanella could have compiled might have matched some registered by many of the game's greats. But couldas and wouldas don't mean much in baseball. What counts is what a man does and Roy Campanella did plenty in the ten years in the major leagues.

He was a three-time Most Valuable Player, a leader in RBIs—142 in 1953—a six-time leader in total putouts, for a catcher a four-time leader in catching averages. More importantly, Campanella was one of the leaders, along with Robinson, Pee Wee Reese, Gil Hodges, Duke Snider, and Carl Furillo, of the best baseball teams in the National League during the 1950s, the team immortalized in Roger Kahn's book *The Boys of Summer*.

Campanella was almost twenty-seven years old when he joined the Dodgers as a rookie in 1948. A good part of his early productive baseball career was used up in the Negro Leagues while the whites kept the game for themselves. There are no accurate records of Campanella's career from the age of fifteen until he was a professional at twenty-four, but Campanella would certainly have added 100 more homers to his total of 242 and maybe a thousand hits to his total of 1,161.

Campy was a squeaky-voiced, husky fellow with a great throwing arm, much batting power, and a desire to play and win. He loved the game of baseball and still is directly involved as a special representative of the Los Angeles Dodgers. He is a frequent visitor to baseball events in his wheelchair.

"I loved the game as a kid and I loved it as a professional," he says. "I still love it. I just wish I could have played it longer."

He played it long enough to earn a spot in the Hall of Fame and earn his number 55 rating among Baseball's 100.

Roy Campanella was born in the black section of Philadelphia known as Nicetown on November 19, 1921. His black mother and Italian father worked hard to give him good values, a proper home, and strong religious beliefs.

Campy was a husky, if not fat, youngster with an outgoing personality and a warm smile. He loved to play practical jokes on his parents and brothers and sisters and laughed delightedly when they realized he had tricked them again.

He was playing baseball with grown men when he was twelve and he quit school to play professional baseball in the Negro leagues when he was fifteen in 1936. No black dreamed of playing in the majors, a ritual followed ever since the time of the first advertised racist in baseball, Cap Anson.

Campy knew Josh Gibson, the black Babe Ruth, and he caught Satchel Paige as a teenager and he traveled through Mexico and South America playing with all the Latin stars.

Shortly after the Dodgers signed Jackie Robinson to a contract late in 1945, Campanella was contacted by Dodger boss Branch Rickey and offered a chance to be the second black in the big leagues. He grabbed the opportunity and was in Brooklyn by 1948. Dodger manager Leo Durocher moved catcher Gil Hodges to first base, catcher Bruce Edwards to third base, and put the rookie behind the plate. It was the making of the Dodgers, with a pennant to follow in 1949.

Campanella batted .287 that season, with 22 homers, as he earned the respect of all the players in the NL. Unlike Jackie, who carried a chip on his shoulder for the indignities heaped on him throughout his career, Campanella tried to take things lightly. He often chided Jackie for getting too excited over everything while Jackie attacked Campy as an Uncle Tom. They were never warm friends since Jackie was truly militant about race while Campy, half white, never quite felt the same pressures.

Campy won his first MVP in 1951 with a .325 average, 108 RBIs, and 33 homers. He slumped the next season with a hand injury, came back to win the award again in 1953, slumped again in 1954, and had his last big year in 1955 with a .318 average, 107 RBIs, and 32 homers. He was thirty-five in 1956 when he hit .219 and seemed finished after a .242 season in 1957.

Soon Campy heard the news that the Dodgers were moving to Los Angeles. He believed the warm weather and new environment would stimulate his career.

On the icy night of January 28, 1958, a couple of weeks before leaving for spring training, he missed a curve while driving early in the morning on a

Long Island highway, hit a utility pole, and fractured his spine. He was paralyzed from the waist down for the rest of his life.

In 1959, before 93,103 fans in the Los Angeles Coliseum, in an exhibition between the Dodgers and Yankees, the stands were darkened and candlelights lit up the California sky in Campy's honor, one of the most touching sports scenes ever. There was not a dry eye in the huge park.

Campanella stayed close to baseball, worked with kids, did radio work, helped the Dodgers in promotions, and continues to be a cheerful person, despite his handicap, as he approaches his sixtieth birthday.

Rube Marquard

(1908–1925)

He was a familiar figure at the annual Hall of Fame reunions each summer at Cooperstown, a weathered, slow-talking old man, worn down by age and illness but still quick of mind and capable of reminiscences.

I was writing a book about Casey Stengel, a Brooklyn Dodger teammate of his from 1915 through 1917, and when I asked Rube Marquard about Stengel before he was a teammate he said, "I didn't have much trouble with him. There weren't many I had much trouble with."

When Rube Marquard died in 1980 he was just short of his ninety-first birthday. It was difficult to imagine this old man as the finest left-handed pitcher of his time and one of the most celebrated athletes of all time.

In 1911, 1912, and 1913, the New York Giants owned the two finest pitchers in the game, two men who each won 20 games in those three seasons, Marquard, the left-hander, Mathewson, the big right-hander, both handsome, intelligent, and respected gentlemen.

Marquard could throw as hard as any pitcher of his time and became a big winner in 1911 after developing his curve ball. "That was the pitch that made me," Marquard told me. "Without that curve ball I never would have hung around as long as I did and had as much fun as I did."

Unlike Mathewson, who was basically a homebody, Marquard liked a good time. He was a clean liver, a nondrinker and nonsmoker, but a man who enjoyed the theater, popular music of the day, and beautiful women. He was married to gorgeous actress Blossom Seely, a Broadway star, and together they performed on the vaudeville circuit.

A handsome man with slick black hair, a thick jaw, and luminous dark eyes, Marquard stood six three and weighed 185 pounds at his pitching prime. His fast ball was explosive and his curve ball, helped by Giants coach Wilbert Robinson, later to be his Brooklyn manager, was a large overhead break which slid across the plate.

Marquard registered a 204–179 record, had three 20-game seasons, pitched a no-hitter, and set a mark in 1912 which still exists today some seventy years later. The twenty-two-year-old lefty won 19 straight games from April 11 to July 3, 1912.

Richard W. Marquard, later known as Rube because he was compared to another pitcher of the day known as Rube Waddell, was born in Cleveland, Ohio, on October 9, 1889. His father was an engineer of the city of Cleveland and wanted young Richard to follow in his footsteps. When young Marquard showed he was more interested in baseball than engineering, his proud father was upset and horrified. They refused to talk for ten years.

Marquard signed his first professional contract in 1907 at the age of eighteen, pitched in Canton, won 23 games, moved up to Indianapolis, won 28 games, and joined the Giants in 1908 under John McGraw. Mathewson was 37–11 that season.

In 1908, 1909, and 1910, Marquard struggled to adjust to the big leagues. He finally found his form in 1911, won 24 games, and established himself as one of the best in the game. He was 26–11 and 23–10 in his next two seasons but never won 20 games again.

In 1915 he argued with McGraw about the pitching rotation as the Giants manager struggled to keep his aging favorite, Mathewson, in a steady course. The arguments and the personal animosity McGraw showed toward Marquard, along with some jealousy involving Mathewson, forced the Giants to trade the big left-hander to Brooklyn.

He helped pitch the Dodgers to pennants in 1916 and 1920, was later traded to Cincinnati and Boston, and retired from baseball in 1932 after pitching and managing in the minors.

Marquard moved to Baltimore, worked as a ticket seller at local race-tracks, and retired in 1970. The old-timers committee discovered him in 1971, elected him to the Hall of Fame, and brought great joy to the old man for the rest of his life.

"Just being here, just being considered with Matty and Walter Johnson and some of the others," Marquard said, "that's enough for me."

Rube Marquard—no Rube, he—was a decent man who got the roses while he could still smell them, a nice baseball gesture.

Richie Allen

(1963–1975)

A lot of people remember him as the guy who scribbled a huge word BOO in the dirt around first base in Philadelphia's new stadium.

A lot of people remember him as a guy who jumped a lot of teams, fought bitterly over contracts, hated everything about baseball except playing the game, and was labeled a troublemaker.

"Baseball is the only business where you don't get a summer vacation," Richie Allen once said, "so I take it whether they give it to me or not."

I remember Richie Allen for hitting some of the most incredible blows over walls in ball parks I have ever seen. To me Allen was the finest power hitter of his time, a man who went his own way, but was hassled into being much less a player than he should have been.

"I just put him out there and he played for me," said Chuck Tanner, the Chicago White Sox manager who got an MVP season out of the big slugger.

Allen won two home-run titles, led the league in RBIs once, hit over .300 seven times, and was the most feared hitter of his era.

Allen's nickname was Crash because he could hit a baseball harder and farther than any other player of his time. He may not have always showed up for work on time, he may have taken a few drinks in his day, he may have bet on horses, but he could hit a baseball huge distances, excite a crowd, and play the game with spirit.

Richie Allen—he didn't become Dick Allen until he realized the diminutive form of his name was a subtle baseball racist putdown—was as productive a hitter as baseball saw through the 1960s and 1970s.

177

He played on one Philadelphia championship team in 1976, played in six All-Star Games, and never played on a league winner. It was about the only thing he never did as a player.

Allen won the Rookie of the Year award in the National League with the Phillies in 1964, won the American League MVP in 1972, led the NL in total bases one year, and led the AL in slugging in two years.

Allen hit 351 homers, knocked in 119 runs, and batted .292 in fourteen big-league seasons with five clubs.

Richard Anthony Allen was born March 8, 1942, in the western Pennsylvania town of Wampum. He was the finest athlete ever produced there, starring in baseball, basketball, football, and track.

He turned down more than one hundred college scholarship offers to sign with the Phillies for a sixty-thousand-dollar bonus in 1960. He was upset when he found out the Phillies had paid lesser players much more.

"They always have had separate standards for white guys and black guys," Allen said. "The white guys got more money and the black guys got more harassment."

True or not, Allen always felt that discrimination. He was a handsome man with a wide smile, a powerful body, thick legs and heavy, sleepy eyelids. He wore thick glasses and often seemed to be squinting behind them. He had a deep, rich voice and could be charming when he wanted to be.

He could also be contrary when that suited him, as in 1967 when he told a story few people believed. He had suffered severe, deep cuts to his hand. When sportswriters suggested an illicit cause, a barroom fight perhaps, Allen insisted the accident had occurred when he was pushing his car by the headlights on a rainy night. He said the lights broke and he cut his hand. What an athlete making a hundred thousand dollars would be doing pushing his car was another story.

Through all these controversies, Allen always hit and played third base or first base quite well. He hit 40 homers in 1966 and when the Dodgers traded him to Chicago in 1972, suggesting he was finished at thirty because of his lack of discipline, he hit .308, knocked in 113 runs, and hit a league-leading 37 homers.

Crash was never quite a company man but he could hit a baseball with the excitement of a Ruth, a Kiner, a Williams, or a Mays. He deserves inclusion among Baseball's 100 even if he wouldn't get an A on his report card in conduct.

Maury Wills

(1959–1972)

He was a small man, less than 165 pounds at his heaviest, five ten, a light-skinned black man with a high-pitched voice. Anybody who saw him on the bases from 1959 with the Los Angeles Dodgers through 1972 in his second tour with Los Angeles can never forget Maurice Morning Wills.

Maury Wills simply revolutionized that old game of ours. He made the stolen base into as exciting a weapon as the grand-slam homer. He was the forerunner of the base stealers to follow, Lou Brock, who was to wipe out his one-season mark, and Willie Wilson, Ron LeFlore, Omar Moreno, and Frank Taveras, any of whom could make Brock the second-best single-season base stealer.

Maury Wills stole 104 bases in 1962, wiping out the old record of 96, the amount stolen by Ty Cobb, a record that had seemed inviolate.

Wills not only made the stolen base part of his program, he proved that a good little man could be as effective in the game as a good big man. Wills hit 20 homers in his fourteen-year career but he scored 1,067 runs, a feat made possible by his feet.

He had learned to switch-hit in 1958 under manager Bobby Bragan and used that skill to great advantage after he made it to the big leagues. He would bunt, slap down on the ball, use the hard artificial turf to get a hit, force his way on base in any manner—and then watch out.

Wills made the Dodgers go, and from 1959 through 1966 he was their most potent offensive weapon despite his lack of size and power. Wills got on, stole, and scored on a Tommy Davis or Ron Fairly or Willie Davis hit.

Maurice Morning Wills was born October 2, 1932, in Washington, D.C., one of eleven children.

"The family had an insurance man by the name of Morning and when he'd come by to pick up his quarter for the policy all the kids would line up and say, 'Good morning, Mr. Morning' and then giggle. Along about that time I was born and my mom named me Maurice Morning after Mr. Morning."

The Dodgers called him Mousey and the opposition called him every obscenity they could think of because Maury Wills was a pest. Pitchers don't have their macho self-image damaged by a four-hundred-foot homer. A walk, a stolen base, a dribbler, and a wild pitch drive them nuts.

"That used to be our attack," says Sandy Koufax. "Maury would get on, get around somehow, come to the dugout, and say, 'There's your run, Sandy.' I had to make it stand up."

Wills was an outstanding young high school baseball player, but his size was against him. The Dodgers took a chance and signed him as a free agent in 1951. Then he played eight more seasons in the minors but was never considered enough of a hitter to be thought of as a serious prospect.

When he learned to hit left-handed and batted .313 in early 1959 at Spokane, the Dodgers, looking for a replacement for Pee Wee Reese, tried Wills. With his base stealing, all-around solid offensive play, and clever work at shortstop, Wills helped the Dodgers to the 1959 pennant.

He hit .260 and .295 the next year. Then he really hit his stride with marks of .282, .299, .302, .275, .286, .273, and .302 again. His lifetime mark was .281. He was the National Leagues' MVP in 1962 when he played a record 165 games, batted .299, and stole his 104 bases. Brock would later steal 118 for the new mark.

Wills was traded to Pittsburgh after the 1966 season, went to Montreal in 1969 and back to L.A. in June of that year. He was released after the 1972 season.

Wills became a broadcaster, helped his son Bump along the trail to the big leagues, and always talked of managing. Finally, in the last weeks of the 1980 season, he got his chance when he was named skipper of the Seattle Mariners.

They would certainly be a hustling, running, aggressive team in the image of their boss man, one of the game's best little men ever.

Bob Lemon

(1946–1958)

"I never take my troubles home," Bob Lemon once said, "I leave them in some bar."

Lemon may have had a kidding way of looking at the game of baseball after it was over, but while he was on the mound, he was one of the toughest, roughest pitchers there ever was.

A converted infielder, Lemon didn't start pitching in the big leagues until well into his second season.

"I'll tell you how it all came about," he said. "I was playing third base and center field and hitting about .150. I figured that was an average that wouldn't embarrass a pitcher so I started pitching."

Once he'd started, it was a dozen years before he stopped, and he had recorded a record of 207–128, a percentage of .618, one of the finest pitching marks of his time.

Lemon won 20 games seven times, led the league in wins three times, and was a vital part of a four-man rotation with Bob Feller, Early Wynn, and Mike Garcia that was considered baseball's best staff in the 1950s.

Lemon was a hard thrower with a sinking fast ball and a sharp-breaking curve ball. He led the league in strikeouts in 1950 and had a career ERA of 3.23.

He was 20–14 for the pennant-winning Cleveland Indians in 1948 and 23–7 for the pennant-winning Indians of 1954.

Throughout his career he was an excellent fielding pitcher, a good hitter

183

(bad for a center fielder but excellent for a pitcher) and a wonderful guy with a droll sense of humor who added to the ambience of a team.

One of Lemon's best friends on the Indians was Al Rosen, the third baseman, who later became the president of the New York Yankees.

"Lem was a great team player, a great buddy, and a guy who never had a bad day on the mound. He may not always win but it wasn't because he didn't think he could," Rosen said.

Robert Granville Lemon was born September 22, 1920, in San Bernadino, California. His father was an iceman (a man who delivered ice chunks for iceboxes, for you young readers who know only refrigerators) and he was a jovial sort who helped Bob develop his breezy life-style.

Lemon signed a contract with the Cleveland Indians in 1938, where he played third and pitched occasionally for fun. He hit over .300 in three minor league seasons before entering the Navy in World War II.

He made the Cleveland club as a utility player in 1946 and opened the season in center field. His average was slipping against big-league pitching, and by mutual agreement with manager Lou Boudreau he was moved to the bullpen.

In 1947 he was 11–5, played a couple of games as an outfielder, but decided pitching was his thing. He also realized pitchers worked only once every four or five days, leaving much more time for fun in between starts.

He had his first 20-game season in 1948 as he led the league in innings pitched with 293. There was no getting him off the mound after that, though he continued to be used as a pinch hitter, hit 37 big-league homers, and batted as high as .286.

Lemon left the Indians after the 1958 season, pitched in San Diego, returned to Cleveland as a scout, and coached and scouted for several clubs after that.

He managed in Chicago, was fired in 1978, and became the Yankee manager that year after Billy Martin was fired. Lemon led the Yankees to victory after Bucky Dent hit his famous play-off homer against the Red Sox.

Lemon's Yankees won the play-off against Boston, beat Kansas City for the pennant, and won the World Series.

His youngest son, Jerry, twenty-six, was killed in a car crash that winter and Lemon was an unhappy man the next spring. An impetuous owner named George Steinbrenner fired him in June. Lemon continued working as a scout for the Yankees and can still be seen solving all his problems over a bottle of beer, his large red nose lit up like that of Rudolph, the famed reindeer with the cherry beak.

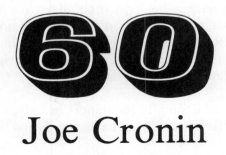

Joe Cronin

(1926–1945)

He is a round, moon-faced man of seventy-four now, ever present at annual baseball events, a glib storyteller, a hearty eater and drinker, a man who has spent his entire working life in the game of baseball.

It is difficult to imagine the rotund Joe Cronin as a skinny, undernourished-looking shortstop with a thin face and bony arms as he was more than fifty-five years ago when he first reported to the spring training camp of the Pittsburgh Pirates.

Cronin has been around the game so long that young fans might be shocked to hear he ever played at all. He has been a manager of two clubs, a general manager, a vice-president of the Red Sox, and a long-term president of the American League. The top position of Commissioner of Baseball is the only one to elude him, but that is probably for the best because Cronin has so many friends in the game it would be impossible for him to make decisions and enemies as a commissioner.

Some fifty years ago he was the smooth-fielding, line-drive-hitting short-stop of some excellent teams in Washington. He had eleven seasons of over .300, once hit .346 while playing all of his team's 154 games, and led all shortstops in fielding on two separate occasions.

Cronin was always one of the game's finest clutch hitters and an RBI man who had eight seasons with more than 100 RBIs. He also had considerable power, a rare commodity for a shortstop, and belted 170 homers in his long playing career of twenty years.

Joseph Edward Cronin was born October 12, 1906, in San Francisco, just a few months after the famed San Francisco earthquake. He was one of many major leaguers to come from the San Francisco area, including the three DiMaggio brothers, Lefty O'Doul, Frank Crosetti, Tony Lazzeri, Tug McGraw, and many more.

Cronin played semiprofessional baseball around the San Francisco area until he signed a pro contract with the Pirates in 1925. In 1926 and 1927 as a skinny, weak-hitting backup fielder, Cronin didn't see much action. He was with the pennant-winning Pirates all of 1927 but did not get into the World Series against Babe Ruth's Yankees. It doesn't mean he wasn't impressed.

"I was sitting on the bench when Ruth and Gehrig and some of those other big hitters began unloading in batting practice," Cronin said. "Anyone would be impressed."

Pittsburgh released Cronin to the minors in 1928, and Washington purchased his contract. He batted .242 in half a season and then improved to .281 in 1929.

From 1930 through 1934, now growing stronger and more experienced, the hard-hitting, right-handed-batting shortstop had four seasons over .300 and one at .284.

In 1933 he was named the manager of the Senators. He was twenty-six years old. He won the pennant and batted .318 in a losing Series effort against the New York Giants.

Boston owner Tom Yawkey, deciding to rebuild his team, purchased Cronin for the ungodly sum of $250,000 in 1935, the highest purchase price ever for a player until then, and installed Cronin as manager and shortstop.

Cronin hit .300 seven times for Boston, became a town favorite, but couldn't win a pennant in his playing time. He quit after breaking his right leg in 1945, and managed the Red Sox to a pennant in 1946 from the bench. His team, with Ted Williams batting a ridiculous .200, lost the Series to the Cardinals.

Cronin became the GM in 1948 and stayed there until he became the league president in 1959.

Now he is a near three-hundred-pounder who hardly looks like he could ever have played, but he is still a cigar-smoking, affable fellow, a fine raconteur and an interesting companion. In his day, which lasted twenty years, he was the best all-around shortstop in the game.

Bill Terry

(1923–1936)

The last man to hit .400 in the National League, Bill Terry batted .401 in 1930, the fourth year in his ten-year plan to hit over .300 in consecutive seasons. He was a marvelous left-handed hitter with good power, a stylish first baseman, and a playing manager.

Terry has a lifetime mark of .341, knocked in 1,078 runs, hit 154 homers, led the league in batting once, played 468 consecutive games, and hit six home runs in four straight games and five in three games.

He was a crusty guy, never smiling, with little regard for working sportswriters (who got even with him by making him wait eighteen years before naming him to the Hall of Fame), and little regard for opponents.

Terry was a vain and proud man who thought that he was the finest hitter in the game—at one point he wasn't far from wrong—and wasn't afraid to tell people. He seemed to rub many people the wrong way and even had feuds with his crusty manager John McGraw, whom he succeeded as Giants boss, and young Mel Ott, whom he always considered a threat to his own power on the Giants.

Terry played in three World Series, the first under McGraw in 1924, the second for himself in 1933, when the Giants beat the Senators, and the third in 1936 when the Yankees beat them. He batted .295 in the Series with two home runs.

William Harold Terry was born October 30, 1898, in Atlanta, Georgia. His parents were separated and young Terry started working on the railroads to help support himself and his mother.

He played some semiprofessional baseball, as a left-handed line-drive hitter and a left-hander pitcher with a good fast-ball and hard curve.

He moved to Memphis to play on an oil-company semipro team and signed a professional contract in 1922 with Toledo. He was a New York Giant under McGraw in 1923 but was ineligible for the Series. His first Giant Series was in 1924, when he was a part-time first baseman.

Terry batted .319 in 1925 and began a streak of ten straight over-.300 seasons in 1927. He was named manager of the Giants by McGraw in 1932 and lasted through 1941. Then his favorite outfielder, Mel Ott, got the job. He stayed on as farm director, then returned to Memphis to get rich in the oil business.

Terry later got into the automobile business with his son in Jacksonville, Florida, and lives there now as he approaches his eighty-third birthday, an avid golfer, fisherman, and occasional baseball watcher. He doesn't think much of the current crop of players. He wouldn't.

Three Finger Brown

(1903–1916)

Casey Stengel, my major source of information on players before 1920, once described Three Finger Brown to me.

"He had these three choppy fingers, see, with that one pointer finger missing, you know, and he could make that baseball do the damndest things. The first time I faced him, he threw me one of those three-finger jobs, whoosh, whoosh, whoosh and I was back on the bench before I could break a sweat. I asked my teammate, Zack Wheat, who'd seen him before me, if he was that good. Zack said, 'Imagine if he hadna lost those fingers.'"

"Three Finger" Mordecai Brown, lost his right index finger and mangled the other three on his right hand while fooling with a corn chopper on his uncle's farm. He was seven, so he never really knew how to throw a baseball except by choking it in those three remaining fingers and steering it homeward with that stump of a thumb.

He won 239 games, lost only 130, beat Christy Mathewson out of the pitching crown in 1909 with a 27–9 mark (Matty was 25–6), won 20 games six straight years, had 58 shutouts, and a 2.06 lifetime ERA.

Mordecai Peter Brown was born October 19, 1876, in Nyesville, Indiana. He worked on his family farm, worked in the mines, ran errands for local farmers, and dreamed of playing baseball.

In 1901 he signed a pro contract, was with the Cardinals in 1903 and in 1904 joined the Chicago Cubs.

His best pitch was a dancing, whirling curve ball that seemed to move differently every day. His fast ball was never more than mediocre because he couldn't squeeze the seams to get the vibrations needed to speed up the ball.

The Cubs won four pennants in five seasons when Brown was there and he won five World Series games for them. He played in the short-lived Federal League, returned to the National League in 1916, and ended his career after the 1920 season at Terre Haute.

He managed the Terre Haute club and then retired from baseball to operate a local gas station for many years. He died in Terre Haute February 14, 1948, known as much for his nickname as his pitching.

I never saw Brown. I don't know how good he was. Casey told me he was plenty good. More importantly, he did it all with less than ten fingers. That deserves recognition by itself and for that reason and a 239–130 record, Three Finger Brown is number 62 in Baseball's 100.

Frank Robinson

(1956–1976)

The only man to ever win the Most Valuable Player award in both leagues, Frank Robinson may even be more significant in baseball history as the game's first black manager.

Some thirty years after Jackie Robinson signed his first contract with the Brooklyn Dodger organization to break the color line, Frank Robinson, no relation, signed his first contract as manager of the Cleveland Indians.

Another unwritten barrier had fallen and Robinson was followed by Larry Doby and Maury Wills. It now seems that managers will be hired because of skills rather than skin color. Robinson returned as the manager of the San Francisco Giants in 1981.

Frank Robinson was a pacesetter in a lot of ways during his twenty-one-year career. He was one of the most aggressive players to ever play the game, a tough hitter, a tough competitor, a vicious slider, an outspoken individual. After ten brilliant years in Cincinnati he was traded over to Baltimore, changed the style of play in the American League dramatically by his presence, won the Triple Crown, and led Baltimore to its first pennant ever.

Robinson had a lifetime average of .294, had nine seasons over .300, hit 586 homers (only Hank Aaron, Babe Ruth, and Willie Mays hit more), ended his career only 57 hits short of the magical 3,000 mark, knocked in 1,812 runs, scored 1,829 runs, won one batting title, hit 49 homers for Baltimore in his Triple Crown season, and was an outstanding left fielder and first baseman.

Frank Robinson was born in Beaumont, Texas, on August 31, 1935, and grew up in Los Angeles. He was an outstanding high school athlete and was soon to be wooed and won by the Cincinnati Reds. He was signed to a

195

professional contract at the age of seventeen and sent to Ogden, Utah. He batted .348 there.

In 1956 he won a regular job as a rookie on the Cincinnati Reds, batted .290, led the league in runs scored, and was named the National League Rookie of the Year.

Robinson had a combative personality, stood up for his rights, played hard, and demanded respect. Some of his teammates resented his aggressiveness, but he took solace in his play and in his closeness to teammate Vada Pinson, another black Californian. The two outfielders were the heart of the Reds from 1959, when Pinson joined Robinson as a regular, through 1965, when Robinson was traded to Baltimore.

Rumors flew that Robinson was traded because he hadn't taken care of himself and was "an old thirty," had lost favor because of several racial incidents in Cincinnati, and no longer would casually accept the first contract offered him.

Quickly proving he was one of the "youngest thirty-year-olds" to play the game, Robinson had a Triple Crown season in Baltimore as the O's won their first pennant. Robinson had been the National League MVP in 1961 as he led the Reds to a pennant and now repeated with Baltimore.

More importantly he brought the toughness, competitiveness, and style of the black players over to the more quiet American League, known privately as "the brother-in-law" league since all players seemed friendly and eager to take care of each other on the diamond.

After six fine seasons in Baltimore, Robinson moved on to Los Angeles, the California Angels, and Cleveland. He had been managing in winter ball since 1970 and was well prepared to manage in the majors when the Indians named him their skipper in 1975. He continued playing for another two seasons; his club finished fourth two times and was on its way to last in 1977 when he became the first black manager to be fired.

At six one and 194 pounds, heavily muscled, trim and good looking with a violent swing and an aggressive style, Robinson made his mark on baseball for twenty years, a worthy member of Baseball's 100.

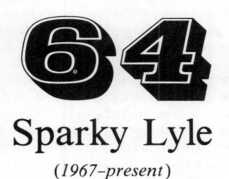

Sparky Lyle

(1967–present)

He has never started a game in the major leagues. He has never won more than 13 games in any season. He has never pitched more than 137 innings in any year.

Yet he is probably the dominant relief pitcher of all time, the only Cy Young Award winner among finishers instead of starters, a pitcher who made relief pitchers proud of their profession, and a colorful character who enjoys sitting nude on gooey birthday cakes as much as he enjoys snapping his slider past a hitter.

Sparky Lyle, twirling his mustache as he talks, laughing almost every minute he is in a clubhouse, pitching with more guts than any one man should have, has been for more than a dozen years the premier left-handed relief pitcher of his time.

Lyle, at thirty-seven, is driving on Hoyt Wilhelm's record for most games by a relief pitcher, and seems set for an extension of his career in a new league and with a new club in Philadelphia. During his career he has dramatically upgraded the role of the relief pitcher.

Before Lyle came along, few relief pitchers were trained as such. Most accidentally wound up in the bullpen when their stuff wasn't good enough to fool hitters for nine innings. Lyle, a cool, nervy, loose sort, was born to be a relief pitcher.

His out pitch has been his devastating slider. He learned it by practicing against a spring-training clubhouse wall.

"I was a kid pitcher starting out with the Red Sox," Lyle says. "I once asked

Ted Williams [then a Boston batting coach] what the toughest pitch for a hitter there was. He said it was the slider and suggested I learn it. So I started throwing it against a clubhouse wall before I was brave enough to ask a catcher to help me with it in a game."

Albert Walter "Sparky" Lyle was born in the coal country of western Pennsylvania at Reynoldsville on July 22, 1944. He was a talkative, bouncy kid and had soon won the nickname of Sparky—as in a sparky personality—from his parents. When he got a little pudgy during the early stages of his pro career he was sometimes called Fat Albert after a television character of the same name.

Lyle signed with the Orioles in 1964 and started his career at Bluefield, West Virginia, in the Appalachian League. He began as a starter but soon switched to relief work. Boston drafted him at the end of the season.

In 1967, with the Red Sox fighting for a pennant, he was called up to Boston, where he saved five games and won another for the American League champions. He came down with a sore arm just before the Series and did not get to play.

After the 1971 season he was traded to the Yankees for first baseman Danny Cater. He then began seven of the most productive relief pitching years any pitcher has ever recorded.

The six-foot-one-inch, 180-pounder with the nastiest slider in the game soon became a folk hero as he saved game after game for the Yankees. He had 35 saves in 1972, 23 in 1976, and 26 in 1977.

When the Yankees won their first pennant in a dozen years in 1976, Lyle had a 2.25 ERA, 23 saves, and 104 innings pitched. He was the man manager Billy Martin always turned to when the game was on the line.

"I loved those situations, two on, three on, two out, the game riding on every pitch. It was so damn exciting I couldn't wait to get in there to find out who won," he says.

After a contract dispute in 1978, Lyle was sent off to Texas, where he had 13 saves before being traded to the Phillies in September of 1980. Only Rollie Fingers had more career saves.

After winning the Cy Young award for pitching excellence in 1977, Lyle dedicated his trophy to all relief pitchers.

"I want to share this with all of the guys who come out of the bullpen," he said.

No man has come out of the bullpen with more excitement, more enthusiasm, more tenacity than Sparky Lyle. He's made relief pitching a noble profession and deserves a place here among Baseball's 100.

Willie McCovey

(1959–1980)

His graceful, fluid swing accounted for 521 homers in his four decades of play and no man was more intimidating at the bat than the loose, left-handed slugger of the San Francisco Giants, Willie McCovey.

McCovey had shattered some seats in the Polo Grounds when Casey Stengel decided it was time to visit the mound and discuss with his pitcher, Roger Craig, how to deal with him.

"Where do you want me to play the outfielders," asked Casey, "in the upper deck or the lower deck?"

Wherever the outfielders played, McCovey would usually hit over them anyway, driving some of the highest, hardest home runs ever seen off a bat. McCovey at six four and 225 pounds could be counted on to give the fans a thrill almost every day. He didn't always connect but he never cut down on his swing.

Wearing uniform number 44, McCovey was an awesome figure at the plate as he pumped that thirty-eight ounce bat, studied the pitch, and let fly with that wicked swing. He won three home-run titles, tied for a fourth, and, except for his final part season of 1980 and another season when he wasn't used much in San Diego, McCovey never hit fewer than a dozen homers for twenty-one years.

His best season was 1969, when he hit 45 homers, knocked in 126 runs, and batted .320. He won the National League's Most Valuable Player Award.

The Giants won only a single pennant in McCovey's time, so the nation

did not become aware of his prowess with the bat until late in his career as his home-run totals began to impress.

He had two seasons with over 40 homers and five more over 30. From 1963 through 1970 he hit fewer than 31 homers only once, with 18 in 1964. The other seasons in that span he smashed 44, 39, 36, 31, 36, 45, and 39. He hit 28 homers in 1977 at the age of thirty-nine. Babe Ruth hit 22 when he was thirty-nine.

Willie Lee McCovey was born and raised in Mobile, Alabama. Born January 10, 1938, his growth was rapid until he became a long, gangly teenager of some six feet four inches and two hundred pounds. His friends called him Stretch, but he had their respect thanks to his performance as a baseball and basketball player.

In 1955, as a seventeen-year-old, he signed with the New York Giants and joined the team in 1959 as a rookie after they had moved to San Francisco.

While Willie Mays was thought of by local San Francisco fans as a New York star from his Polo Grounds days, McCovey and Orlando Cepeda became the favorites of the San Francisco fans.

He joined the Giants in July of 1959, played only 52 games with 192 at bat, but batted .354 to win the rookie award. He got off to a slow start the following season and had to be shipped to Tacoma, but he came back strong.

He established himself as one of the biggest stars in the game in 1963 with 44 homers and 102 RBIs.

McCovey, a soft-spoken man with a self-controlled way of talking and acting, always seemed lost in the shadows of the gregarious, high-pitched singsong flamboyance of Mays. It did not bother him while he enjoyed the peace and quiet of the San Francisco hills.

The Giants won a divisional title in 1971 with McCovey hitting only 18 homers and his career seemed ended when he was traded to San Diego in October of 1973. He was thirty-five. He hit 52 homers for the Padres in a little less than three seasons and was sold to Oakland as the A's made a bid for a sixth straight divisional title. They just missed, and McCovey missed playing in an American League championship series. He had played for the Giants in the 1962 World Series and his wicked line-drive out ended the classic. Ralph Terry was the pitcher and manager Ralph Houk, eyeing McCovey with Mays up next, asked his right-hander what he wanted to do.

"Let's settle it here," said Terry.

McCovey hit a screecher to Bobby Richardson, ending the game.

It would be the way McCovey would always be remembered after he retired in 1980, hitting a screecher at an infielder who'd catch it to save his life, or hitting a huge homer to win another for the Giants.

Juan Marichal

(1960–1975)

That high kick, that blazing fast ball, that dipping curve ball, and that impeccable control marked the pitching of Juan Marichal for sixteen successful big-league seasons.

Marichal was as good a pitcher as there was in baseball during the 1960s when he was at his peak, and he was at his peak when another pitcher named Sandy Koufax was his major rival for pitching honors.

Marichal won 20 games six out of seven years, pitched one no-hitter, won 243 games against only 142 losses, and had a lifetime ERA of 2.89.

The Dodger-Giant games on those rare occasions when Marichal and Koufax matched up (both teams' managers tried to avoid that as much as possible) were classics of pitching excellence. The team that could squeeze out a run would usually win.

The right-hander was not an exceptionally big man, standing only five eleven and weighing less than 190 pounds, but he could generate enormous speed from his high kicking motion. Marichal's style was as close to Bob Feller's high kick as baseball had seen since the Cleveland right-hander retired.

Marichal was a workhorse pitcher who would rarely miss a turn. He pitched 3509 innings in his career, led the league twice in innings pitched, and went over the 300 mark in total innings in four separate seasons.

Marichal had nine separate seasons with an ERA under 3.00 and led the league with a 2.10 ERA in 1969 and a 21–11 record.

Juan Antonio Marichal Sanchez was born October 24, 1937, at Laguna

Verde in the Dominican Republic. Since the game was very popular in his country, he played a lot of baseball as a youngster. The Giants were regularly sending scouts to the Dominican once they had discovered Felipe Alou, and subsequently they signed his two brothers, Matty and Jesus.

Not speaking a word of English, Marichal was signed and delivered to the Giants farm at Michigan City, Indiana, in 1958. He ate a ham sandwich and apple pie every meal for a week because that was all he could order in a local diner. He had seen somebody next to him order that and pointed to that meal when the waitress asked what he wanted.

In 1960 he was with the Giants and by 1961 was a regular starter, ending the season with a 13–10 mark. He struck out 124 hitters and walked only 48. That performance stamped him as one of the best young control pitchers in the game.

He was 18–11 for the pennant-winning Giants in 1962 and 25–8 in 1963. Five 20-game seasons would follow in the next six years as Marichal worked hard on improving his craft.

He struck out more than 200 hitters in six seasons and never walked more than 90 hitters in any season in his career.

As his English improved, Marichal was generally regarded as a pleasant man, a little self-conscious with the language barrier, but a friendly, easygoing gentleman. He took defeats hard but lost so rarely in the middle of his career that he seemed a very controlled person.

He lost his self-control once when facing the hated Dodgers in a heated series. Marichal had been good at leaning back the Dodger hitters and had been especially tough on catcher John Roseboro. On Marichal's next at bat Roseboro returned the pitcher's throw past Marichal's ear. The right-hander whirled around, and knocked Roseboro down with a blow to his head with the bat. The catcher suffered a severe concussion.

Marichal was fined and suspended and for a time his career hung in the balance. After returning he seemed dramatically changed, more subdued as a person but was never involved in any new controversies.

In 1974 he was with Boston and in 1975 signed with the Dodgers. His arm was no longer sound and he was released after appearing in only two games for L.A.

Marichal returned to the Dominican Republic, worked with youngsters, and left behind a Giants legacy as one of the toughest pitchers the team ever had, in the winning tradition of Christy Mathewson, Carl Hubbell, and Sal Maglie.

Willie Stargell

(1962–present)

The strains of a rock number called "We Are Family" could be heard through the clubhouse of the Pittsburgh Pirates during their championship season of 1979. Every family has to start with a family founding father. On the Pirates it was Pops.

Pops is Willie Stargell, the huge first baseman who has led and typified the Pirates for nearly twenty years. He has been as influential a leader as any baseball team has ever had. Stargell leads not so much with rah rah speeches (only Knute Rockne really could lead that way) but with hustle, effort, pride, and determination.

"I don't have to go up to the guys and tell them to hustle," Stargell says. "They see the way I play. Leadership comes by example."

Stargell has set a magnificent example in leading the Pirates through some very successful seasons. His leadership qualities really came to the fore in 1973 after the tragic death of Roberto Clemente in a plane crash.

"Nobody could replace Clemente," says Stargell. "All I could do is show the guys how we must go on."

Stargell has been one of the game's most feared hitters ever since he joined the Pirates. He has won two home-run titles and has had fifteen seasons with 20 or more home runs, many of them of prodigious worth.

"There's no way to pitch to Willie Stargell," says relief pitcher Tug McGraw, "you just throw it up there, duck, and hope he hits it at someone else."

There have been some pitchers who could deal with that huge form at the plate. Sandy Koufax was one of them.

"Trying to hit Koufax," Stargell said, "was like trying to drink coffee with a fork."

Stargell had trouble with Koufax (who didn't?) but not with too many others for too long. He's had five seasons with over 100 RBIs and four more with over 90.

Wilver Dornel Stargell was born March 6, 1941, at Earlsboro, Oklahoma, and grew up in California. He was a basketball player of note and soon turned to baseball when he realized he was so good at the game.

He was signed by the Pirates in 1959 and joined the big club in 1962. He was a free swinger, a huge man at six three and 220 pounds who whirled his bat up and down in front of his face as he awaited the pitch. His swing was violent and he set the career strikeout record in 1979 when he passed the 1,850 mark. No matter. It was still a thrilling sight for fans to see him try.

He hit 48 homers with 125 RBIs and a .295 average in 1971 (Joe Torre won the MVP with a .363 mark and 137 RBIs) and hit 44 homers with 119 RBIs in 1973. That year Pete Rose won the MVP with a .338 average for the division-winning Reds.

In 1979, at the age of thirty-eight, he batted .281, hit 32 homers, and knocked in 82 runs. He won the MVP award this time in a tie with batting leader Keith Hernandez.

The Pirates won the World Series, and Stargell, with a .400 mark, was the MVP there. He had also been the championship series MVP.

A towering figure in Pittsburgh, Stargell conducts an annual bowling tournament to benefit sickle-cell anemia research and a great number of stars attend. He has worked for many charities and seems certain of a significant future in the game.

One of the great home-run hitters and great men of the game, Willie Stargell is easily one of Baseball's 100.

Mel Harder

(1928–1947)

He never pitched for a pennant winner and he never led his league in any pitching department. But for twenty years he was one of the steadiest, most dependable pitchers in the game.

Mel Harder, the curve-balling right-hander of the Cleveland Indians, won 20 games in 1934 and 1935 and then lost his number-one standing on the staff to a young right-hander from Van Meter, Iowa, by the name of Rapid Robert Feller.

Harder, a soft-spoken, low-key fellow, didn't fight for fame. He just continued going out on the mound every time the Indians asked him to and gave a good performance.

He was not an overpowering pitcher, so he had to use guile and smarts and guts in winning 223 games and losing only 186 from 1928 through 1947.

Harder spanned the eras from Babe Ruth to Joe DiMaggio and Ted Williams.

"I always had good luck against Williams but DiMaggio was very tough for me," Harder says. "He knew an awful lot about pitching and he could seem to guess right on so many pitches."

Harder had a big overhand curve ball that awed most right-handed hitters. Not DiMaggio.

"He just waited on that thing and smashed it to right center field or pulled it to left field," Harder says.

Not too many hitters handled Harder that way. He was a big winner with 15 or more victories for eight straight seasons. He had excellent control and was a team player who was willing to pitch out of turn to save a tired arm on the staff.

He had arm surgery in 1941, was released by the Indians, and came back to pitch six more years, winning 34 more games before his tired arm gave out.

Melvin Le Roy Harder was born on a farm near Beemer, Nebraska, on October 15, 1909. He was nearsighted as a youngster and didn't play a lot of sports. As he matured he got into baseball and was soon throwing his curve ball past schoolboy hitters throughout Nebraska.

The Indians signed him in 1927, sent him to Omaha, and brought him up in 1928. He was used mostly as a relief pitcher in 1928 and 1929, spent some few months working on his curve ball at Cleveland's farm at New Orleans, and came back to stay in the big leagues for the next seventeen seasons starting in 1930.

He was 20–12 in 1934 and 22–11 in 1935. He had five more winning seasons before arm trouble slowed him down to 12–11 in 1940, as the Indians almost won the pennant, and 5–4 in 1941. Then Cleveland released him, he underwent arm surgery, and came back to win a job in 1942.

He retired after 1947 to a coaching job, stayed with Cleveland until 1963, and then coached the New York Mets pitchers. He was a very well-liked gentleman—a courteous, dignified man who could often be seen sitting quietly in the hotel lobbies talking baseball with his pitchers or with Mets fans. He later coached the Chicago Cubs and Cincinnati Reds before retiring to the home he had purchased in Sun City, Arizona.

At seventy-one Mel Harder still knows more about pitching then most men who ever played the game. He probably has forgotten more than most pitchers of today know. Mel Harder won 223 games for a team that never won a pennant. He had to be using his head to do that.

212

Robin Roberts

(1949–1966)

They were classic duels, those battles of the early 1950s, between Don Newcombe, the big right-hander of the Brooklyn Dodgers, and the husky, handsome right-hander of the Phillies, Robin Roberts.

Roberts was an overpowering pitcher with a hard, rising fast ball, an excellent curve, and incredible control. It wasn't so much that he hardly walked anybody, it was that he seemed to own the corners of the plate at the batter's knees and shoulders.

He had a smooth, easy motion and never seemed to be throwing the ball very hard. Only the hitters could tell it was whizzing past their bats at speeds up to a hundred miles an hour.

Roberts was really two pitchers, one with a big lead and one in trouble. If he had a lead he would take a little off his fast ball and allow the hitters to take some good cuts at him with a league-leading 46 homers allowed in 1956. He seemed forever to be winning games 7–6, 6–5, 5–4. He wasn't concerned with pitching shutouts or having a low ERA—though his was under 3.00 six times. He was concerned only with winning.

"He might give you three or four good pitches to hit," says Ralph Kiner, "and you might even get a home run off him. Then it would be the eighth or ninth inning and you needed a single to win and he would throw that high fast ball and it was all over."

Roberts won 286 big-league games, lost 245, and had six 20-game seasons in a row. He was 28–7 in 1952 in 330 innings pitched with 30 complete games. He also led the league in strikeouts twice even though he was a pitcher who

seemed just as content getting a four-hundred-foot fly-ball out on the first pitch as a strikeout on the fifth.

Except for the 1950 Whiz Kid pennant-winning Phillies, he played with mostly bad ball clubs. His record was 19–18 in 1956 and 10–22 in 1957, as much because of his own pitching as because the Phillies didn't have much offense or much defense, either.

Robin Evan Roberts was born September 30, 1926, at Springfield, Illinois. His parents had come to the United States from England, where his father had worked as a miner.

Young Robin met retired pitching great Grover Cleveland Alexander at a high school banquet. Alexander had pitched for the last Philadelphia pennant winner in 1915. In 1950, thirty-five years later, Roberts would win 20 games for the next one.

The Phillies signed him as a bonus player out of Michigan State in 1948 and brought him to Philadelphia in June of that season. He was 7–9 as a rookie and 15–15 in 1949.

The Phillies had some marvelous young players—Richie Ashburn, Granny Hamner, Del Ennis, Mike Goliat, Eddie Waitkus, and Puddin' Head Jones—alongside a young staff anchored by Roberts and left-hander Curt Simmons. They won the pennant on the last day of the season when Dick Sisler homered off Don Newcombe.

Roberts was beaten 2–1 by Allie Reynolds and the Yankees in his only Series start.

Roberts was the dominant right-hander in the league for the next ten years. It was usually a question of Roberts or Warren Spahn winning pitching honors each year.

Roberts continued trying to throw hard as his fast ball slowed up, and he was 1–10 in 1961 with the Phillies. As manager Gene Mauch tried to get Roberts to use his curve and his change-up more, the right-hander seemed to be constantly struggling.

He was sold to the Yankees that fall, went to spring training with them, made the ball club, and, in a roster squeeze, was released when the Yankees decided to keep young pitcher Jim Bouton. Bouton would be a big winner in 1963 and 1964, come up with a sore arm, and later become an embarrassment to the Yankees when his iconoclastic book revealed baseball secrets.

Roberts made the pitching adjustment at Baltimore, was a winner for three seasons, and then was released again. This time he signed with the Houston Colt 45s, was released again, signed with the Cubs, and experienced his third release.

At the age of forty he pitched in the minor leagues at Reading trying for one more big-league chance, but elbow problems finally ended his active career.

Roberts was a leader among the early union organizers in baseball, was the most influential player in selecting Marvin Miller as the players' executive director, was outspoken about management's power, and never was hired for an on-field baseball job despite his marvelous pitching knowledge and skills.

Robby worked as an investment counselor, owner of a minor-league hockey team, a broadcaster, and finally a coach at a small college in Florida.

At fifty-five Robin Roberts, as handsome as ever, as bright and articulate, a Hall of Famer now, was still a popular visitor at baseball functions. No hitter who faced his high hard one could forget him.

Harmon Killebrew

(1954–1975)

Number five on the all-time home-run list with 573, Harmon Killebrew won four home-run titles, tied for two others, and hit 25 or more homers in thirteen of fourteen seasons.

He had 573 homers from 1954 through 1975, knocked in 1584 runs, and batted .256.

A husky, soft-spoken, bald-headed man with a quiet personality, Killebrew was one of those players who spent a good part of his career being overlooked.

He was never involved in controversy, was uncomfortable around newspaper reporters, and was modest to a fault.

Even when his team won the 1965 American League pennant with Hammerin' Harmon hitting 25 homers and knocking in 75 runs despite injuries, the attention focused on other players, the flamboyant shortstop Zoilo Versalles, the husky slugger Bob Allison, the tricky left-hander Jim Kaat, or the witty, winning right-hander Mudcat Grant.

Killebrew just seemed to roll along, quietly doing his job, knocking in over 100 runs in nine seasons and playing almost every day from 1959 through 1972.

Killebrew, who stood a shade over six feet and weighed between 210 and 215 most of his career, was an adequate third baseman, outfielder, and first baseman most of his career. He could never run well or field exceptionally well, but he was one of the strongest hitters to ever play the game, similar in style to Chuck Klein, the overpowering home-run slugger of the Phillies.

Killebrew won the Most Valuable Player award in 1969, when the Twins won their division title, with 49 homers and 140 RBIs. It was the second time he had 49 homers, duplicating his 1964 feat.

Harmon Clayton Killebrew, Jr., was born June 29, 1936, at Payette, Idaho. He loved the outdoors, hunting and fishing near his home, and got into baseball late as a teenager. His great strength helped him overcome his awkwardness and he was soon being talked about as the strongest player in the West.

His United States Senator, Herman Welker, wrote a note about him to Calvin Griffith, the owner of the Washington Senators.

Griffith sent a scout out to Idaho to see the boy with the lumberjack body and soon signed him. He kept him in Washington under the enforced bonus rules of the day and then sent him to Charlotte and Chattanooga for seasoning.

He hit 42 homers as a twenty-three-year-old for Washington in 1959. The Senators were thrilled because they had gone a long time without a hero or a team. They had given a bad name to the nation's capital, Washington, "first in war, first in peace, and last in the American League."

Killebrew's homers brought the congressmen out to Griffith Stadium in droves.

Soon Washington was moving to Minnesota and taking young Killebrew with them. He was an instant hero there as well, hitting 46, 48, 45, and 49 homers in his first four seasons in Minnesota.

The Twins won the pennant in 1965 and Killebrew hit a homer and batted .286 against the Los Angeles Dodgers.

Harmon played on championship division teams in 1969 and 1970, was released by Minnesota in 1975, played one season with Kansas City, and retired after the 1975 season.

He then went into broadcasting, commuting from his home in Idaho.

Harmon Killebrew and his 573 homers, all hit with quiet character, easily deserve a big spot among Baseball's 100.

Lou Boudreau

(1938–1952)

One of the few players to add his name to a defensive play, the Boudreau Shift—first used to clog up the right side of the infield against slugger Ted Williams—shortstop Lou Boudreau also had one of the finest single days in baseball history.

No man should make a list of Baseball's 100 for one afternoon's work, but a splendid career and an incredible day helped to push Boudreau into our select group.

The 1948 regular season ended in a tie between the Indians and the Boston Red Sox. Player-manager Lou Boudreau gambled on a left-handed knuckleballer named Gene Bearden, a crazy enough move in Fenway Park, and then went out and showed the boys how to do it. Boudreau and Bearden won the pennant for the Indians—their first since 1920—with stirring performances. Bearden made the Red Sox knuckle under (you knew that was coming) and Boudreau slapped two homers into the friendly Fenway screen and two singles to trigger an 8–3 win.

Boudreau's career was one of the most impressive in baseball for many reasons. First off, he managed the Indians at the age of twenty-four—youngest opening-day manager ever—in 1942 after only four seasons as a player. He led the club to a pennant and World Series in 1948 despite the fact that owner Bill Veeck tried to fire him before the season began. A fan rebellion saved his job.

Secondly, Boudreau proved that a great shortstop need not be fleet of foot if he is quick of brain. Knowing where to play the hitters was more important than great speed. Lou had lost most of his speed bouncing around hard basketball courts in his high school and college days.

Boudreau was also one of the game's best clutch hitters, one of the most intelligent and consistent players in the game in his time.

The handsome shortstop-manager of the Indians led the league in hitting with a .327 mark in 1944, batted over .300 with a high of .355 in four separate seasons, knocked in 106 runs in that marvelous year of 1948, and ended his career with a lifetime .295 mark—pretty impressive batting numbers for one of the game's greatest defensive players, one of the smartest, and one of the nicest.

Louis Boudreau was born in Harvey, Illinois, on July 17, 1917, of German and French parentage. His father was a machinest and a semipro baseball player. He took to sports early, equally comfortable as a baseball infielder, a football quarterback, and a basketball guard.

Basketball was the first sport to help make his name known. After an outstanding high school career, he won a scholarship at the University of Illinois, was an all-conference guard, and starred in an Illinois basketball win in Madison Square Garden in New York over New York University.

The next season he signed with the Indians, played two years in the minors, and soon was with Cleveland. He was called up to Cleveland with his second-base pal and partner, Ray Mack.

Lou hit his stride for the 1940 Indians with a .295 average. That club was torn by turmoil and earned the title of "Crybabies" after an attempted over-throw of manager Ossie Vitt. Boudreau stayed clear of most of that furor, which was led by pitcher Bob Feller.

Vitt's successor, Roger Peckinpaugh, resigned in 1942. Boudreau applied for the job and got it as the Indians responded to their young, tough leader.

Boudreau hit .300 in four of the five seasons between 1944 and 1948, played 140 games or more each year but one, led the club to the Series win, and became famous for his Williams shift, three infielders between first and second on Williams and other pull hitters, one between second and third.

General manager Hank Greenberg decided for the 1951 season that Cleveland needed a new young shortstop. Boudreau refused to quit. So he was fired as a player and manager, shipped to Boston, and finished his playing career there. He managed the Red Sox, Kansas City A's, and Cubs before leaving the field.

Boudreau now broadcasts Chicago Cub games, is still one of the best looking (if a lot chubbier than his five-foot-eleven, 185-pound playing body) men around baseball and a Hall of Famer. At sixty-three, Boudreau can still recite every play of the 1948 playoff game. Why not?

George Foster

(1969–present)

It took George Foster some seven years and two teams to find his level, but when he did, he proved to be one of the most awesome hitters the game has ever seen.

The tall, thin, laconic outfielder of the Cincinnati Reds knocked in an incredible 149 runs for the Reds in 1977 with 52 homers and a .320 average, missing the Triple Crown by 18 points with Dave Parker leading the league in hitting with a .338 average.

The six-foot-two-inch 195-pound Alabaman had four seasons in five over .300, led the league in RBIs three times in a row, hit 23 or more homers six times in a row, played on four championship teams, played on three Series teams and two winners, and earned the 1977 MVP award.

Foster has been one of the most feared hitters in the game for the last seven years, a fine outfielder with a strong arm, and a better-than-average base runner.

Foster hit three home runs in one game against Atlanta in 1977, hit 31 homers on the road in 1977 to set a record, and hit .333 in four All-Star Games.

George Arthur Foster was born December 1, 1948, at Tuscaloosa, Alabama. His family moved to California, where George excelled as a track and football star and baseball outfielder. He attended El Camino College in Torrance, California, and signed with the San Francisco Giants in 1968.

After two fine minor-league seasons he made it to the Giants in 1970. He had played nine games with San Francisco at the end of the 1969 season.

In 1971 he was traded to Cincinnati, struggled with the bat, was sent to Indianapolis for the 1973 season.

In 1974 he hit .264 as a platooned player under manager Sparky Anderson and became a regular in 1975, beginning five of the most productive seasons of any player of his time.

Foster was off to a slow start in 1980, rallied to finish strong, and shows no signs at the age of thirty-two of not being a powerful and productive hitter for a half a dozen more years.

He had some 225 homers at the end of 1980 and could easily join the exalted 400-homer club by the end of his career.

Babe Herman

(1926–1945)

It is only his image as a guy who got hit on the head with fly balls (false), a guy who doubled into a triple play (false), a guy who wasn't very smart (false) that has kept Babe Herman from the Hall of Fame.

The holder of six Dodge batting records, some fifty years after he set them, Herman was one of the most devastating sluggers the game has ever seen. He hit .393 with a .678 slugging mark in 1930 (Bill Terry hit .401 that year), he scored 143 runs, had 241 hits, and 94 extra bases, and had 416 total bases. His 1930 season was a career in itself for a lot of players.

He batted .300 eight different times and his lifetime mark of .324 has only been bettered by sixteen Hall of Famers in this century. Despite batting .340, .381, .393, .313, and .326 in five straight seasons, he never won a batting title, losing to Rogers Hornsby, Lefty O'Doul, Terry, Chick Hafey, and O'Doul again.

Herman specialized in extra-base hits. He had eleven straight seasons with over 25 doubles and ten straight seasons with five or more triples. He hit 181 career homers, with 35 in 1930.

A big, strapping left-handed slugger who stood six four and weighed 190 pounds at his peak, Herman was the big hitter for the Brooklyn Dodgers for half a dozen years and a tremendous fan favorite for his affability and slugging. He was a pleasant, talkative man who was willing to cooperate with newsmen who in turn thought nothing of making fun of the gangling slugger.

When a ball hit him on the shoulder they wrote that it hit him on the head. He laughed and went along with the gag. When he doubled with the bases loaded and a triple play ensued when runners were fooled about whether the ball would be caught or not, he took the blame for his teammates. When they wrote he was dumb, he simply laughed and proudly counted the money he made in oil investment, land, and stocks.

Floyd Caves Herman was born June 26, 1903, in Buffalo, New York. His family soon moved to Los Angeles and he grew up in Glendale, California. He was a close pal of baseball great Casey Stengel for more than sixty years.

Herman was signed originally by the Detroit Tigers, went to spring training under manager Ty Cobb, and was sold to Brooklyn in 1926. He hit .319 as a rookie.

After a .272 season, he hit .300 or better in seven of the next eight seasons with .393 in 1930.

"I was over .400 going into September," says Herman, "but I just wore out in the final weeks and went into a terrible batting slump. I not only didn't hit .400, I couldn't hold on to the batting lead."

Called the Babe—because he was a young player who was his manager's Babe in the Detroit system—he was called "Hoiman" by Dodger fans in Brooklyn. He was a fine outfielder who could run and throw, switched over to first base, and never was hit on the head by any fly ball or any pitched ball.

Herman held out in 1932 and was traded by the Dodgers to Cincinnati just before the season began. He batted .326 in his first Cincinnati season and became a popular player there.

He later played for Chicago, Pittsburgh, Cincinnati again, Detroit, and Brooklyn again in 1945 during World War II, accepting a call at his California avocado ranch to help out the Dodgers during the manpower shortage.

He retired after the 1945 season to a long scouting career for many clubs, raised avocados for years, grew prize-winning orchids, remained at his Glendale home, and continued to retain an avid interest in the game as he approached his eightieth birthday.

The Hall of Fame may have forgotten Babe Herman but Dodger fans—especially this Dodger fan of Brooklyn birth—have not, and he deserves ranking with Baseball's 100.

Marty Marion

(1940–1953)

OK, start those letters pouring in. What does a .263 hitter do to deserve inclusion among Baseball's 100? He fields better than almost anybody in the history of the game at shortstop.

I think it's time for defensive players to be honored for that aspect of the game alone, even if they only hit .263 and total 36 homers in thirteen big league seasons. Not that .263 is to be sneezed at when a player can contribute as much as Marty Marion did to the success of the St. Louis Cardinals for so many years.

A tall, skinny, loose-limbed shortstop who stood six feet two inches and never weighed more than 170 pounds, Marion anchored the great Cardinal teams of the early 1940s. They won four pennants from 1942 through 1946 and wouldn't have won any of them without Marty Marion.

Nicknamed Slats Marion for his lanky body, he was also called the Octopus because of his long legs, gangly arms, and incredible manner of covering ground between second and third. The Cardinals had some tremendous offensive players during his time—Stan Musial, Walker Cooper, Enos Slaughter, Harry Walker—and some fine pitchers, but they had to have that solid man in the infield to make them go. Marion was the one indispensable Cardinal during the height of that team's success.

It was almost impossible to get a ground ball through the left side of the Cardinal infield with Marion at shortstop.

Marion was no automatic out at bat, either, though his power was not much. He had a league-leading 38 doubles in 1942, managed 20 or more

doubles in seven separate seasons, and batted as high as .280. A guy fielding like Marion hitting .180 would be an asset to his club, a fact recognized in 1944 when he was the National League's Most Valuable Player with a .267 average as the Cardinals won their third straight pennant.

Martin Whiteford Marion was born December 1, 1917, in Richburg, South Carolina. He was a tall, skinny kid, rather weak as a youngster, and stayed away from sports until he was a teenager. His quick reflexes and strong arm made him an outstanding school shortstop and he was on his way to professional baseball.

In 1940 he joined the Cardinals, won the shortstop job, and batted .278 as a rookie in 125 games. The following season he played all 155 games, batted .252, and established himself as one of the league's best. With many of the stars gone off to service in 1942, Marion led the Cardinals to a pennant with a .276 average as St. Louis caught and passed the 1941 pennant-winning Dodgers in the final days of 1942. He played over 100 games at shortstop every year from 1940 through 1950.

Marion managed the Cardinals in 1951 and did not play. He returned to the field in 1952 and 1953 as a player and manager with the St. Louis Browns.

Marty Marion played 1,555 games as a shortstop for the Cardinals and Browns and none of them was a bad game for him. He was simply an artist at going into the hole, backhanding a ground ball, and throwing somebody out.

After he retired from the field, Marion worked at various jobs until the new stadium in St. Louis was built. Then he became the host at the private dining club in the ball park, a room with only a single picture of Marty Marion going deep into the hole for a grounder. What a shame. That's a better sight to see than a porterhouse steak.

Dave Parker

(1973–present)

A huge man with an earring in his left ear lobe, Dave Parker is considered one of the finest all-around players in baseball's history.

He won two batting titles back to back, hit .300 six straight seasons, won the Most Valuable Player award in 1978, has the strongest throwing arm in the game, and is one of the finest fielding defensive outfielders baseball has seen for years.

A complete ballplayer. That's what managers, teammates, and opposing players say about Parker. It is not enough for Parker to hit home runs or lead the league in batting or drive in 100 runs. He must run bases, catch the ball in the outfield, and throw out any runner who dares that big guy's arm.

While Willie Stargell became the emotional leader of the Pirates after the shocking 1972 death of Roberto Clemente, Dave Parker became the right fielder, the position Clemente had played for seventeen seasons. Talk about pressure.

The big kid from Cincinnati struggled for a couple of seasons to get his feet on the ground. Then he took off in 1975 with a .308 mark and hasn't slowed down since.

At six five and 225 pounds, Parker is an intimidator and pitchers try to think of ways of not facing him. He hits the ball so hard that no hurler can face him without some hidden fear of decapitation. He has hit line drives that have banged against outfield walls without getting higher than six feet off the ground.

Many regard him as the game's strongest player—a fierce competitor, a tenacious slider, and a team player. Parker wants to win and he will throw his body and push it against any object—runner or wall or baseball—to accomplish that end.

He hit .338 in 1977 and came back with a .334 mark in 1978. He had 117 RBIs and 30 homers and, with his fielding, running, and throwing, easily won the National League MVP.

There is no telling how many more titles this big left-handed slugger will win before he is through.

David Gene Parker was born June 9, 1951, at Jackson, Mississippi. His family moved to Cincinnati, where Parker grew up and starred in baseball, football, and basketball in high school.

He was drafted and signed by the Pirates in 1970 and batted .314 in his first pro year.

After three more minor-league seasons, Parker joined the Pirates in 1973. He batted .288 and .282 in his next seasons.

Then he began asserting himself and was soon establishing distance records for his homers and his throws.

"He's the finest all-around player in the game," Manager Chuck Tanner of the Pirates says. "He helps as much with his glove and speed as he does with his bat."

After his two batting titles, Parker was closely established as one of the finest sluggers, a tremendous outfielder, and a dedicated team player. He batted .345 as the Pirates made a memorable comeback against Baltimore in the 1979 World Series.

As he approached his thirtieth birthday, Parker seemed assured of being a threat for the batting title and a leader among the Pirates for another half a dozen seasons.

The man may be slightly unconventional in wearing an earring, but if you hit .300 five times in a row and stand six five, there are a lot of things you can get away with.

I'm not crazy. I wouldn't dare not include Parker among Baseball's 100.

234

Phil Rizzuto

(1941–1956)

Holy cow, what is this little guy doing here with these big fellows? He is here on merit, and as his old manager Casey Stengel would say, "You could look it up."

Phil Rizzuto was the finest fielding shortstop in the American League for nearly a dozen years, a fine bunter, an effective base stealer, and one of the games's most productive little players.

Only Bill Veeck's midget Eddie Gaedel and shortstop Fred Patek may have played smaller than Rizzuto's five six (maybe) and 150 pounds (maybe), but it never kept this hustling infielder from performing his tasks with some of the best Yankee teams ever.

Rizzuto had a lifetime .273 average, collected 1,588 hits, and made the bunt as significant an offensive weapon around the Yankees as a double down the line. A Rizzuto bunt, a steal, and a Joe DiMaggio hit, and the Yankees were on the scoreboard.

Rizzuto had two .300 seasons, batted .324 in 1950, won the Most Valuable Player award, and is remembered in Boston for one of the sweetest bunts ever made. The pitch was up and in, DiMaggio was coming in on a suicide squeeze, and Rizzuto laid it down as pretty as you please for a 1–0 win.

Philip Francis Rizzuto was born September 25, 1918, in New York City. He played high school baseball and tried out for the Brooklyn Dodgers in 1936. Stengel was the manager and sent him home, saying he was too small and advising him, "Get a shoebox, kid, you can't play."

The Giants also sent him home, but the Yankees, sensing something in that little fellow, signed him.

By 1941 he was the regular Yankee shortstop on a pennant-winning team in a year DiMaggio hit in 56 straight games.

"Then the streak ended and he borrowed money from me," Rizzuto said, "to stop off some place and be alone for a while with his thoughts."

Rizzuto hit .284 for the Yankee pennant winners of 1942 and then missed the next three years in service.

He returned in 1946 to hit .257 and field brilliantly. He hit his peak with a .324 mark in 1950, his MVP title, the best shortstop play in the league, and World Series heroics.

After hitting only .195 in 1954, Rizzuto knew he was in trouble. He was beginning to lose a step in the field as well, but thought he could make up for it with his experience.

He was a backup shortstop in 1955 and 1956 to Gil McDougald, and finally Stengel called him on old-timers' day in 1956 and released him.

"I was so angry I didn't know what to do," Rizzuto said. "It's a good thing I stayed hidden. I soon was offered a broadcasting job. I might have said the wrong thing."

He has said a lot of right things ever since, as he completes his twenty-fifth year as a broadcaster on the Yankees. He is well liked by the fans and his cry of "Holy cow" is imitated all over the country.

A handsome, gray-haired, dapper man of sixty-two, Rizzuto is an excellent golfer, a funny storyteller, and the finest fielding shortstop the Yankees ever had.

Holy cow. Phil Rizzuto is surrounded by Dave Parker and Fred Lynn, two pretty good hitters. He can bunt them over and play defense to save it for Baseball's 100.

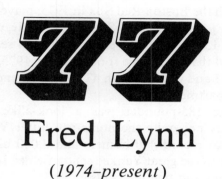

Fred Lynn

(1974–present)

Many ballplayers in the modern generation think the game begins or ends with a home run. Fred Lynn thinks it ends with a leaping, diving against-the-wall catch.

He has done that so many times he has almost patterned the play.

Four .300 seasons out of his five full seasons, a lifetime mark of .308, two seasons with over 100 RBIs, one batting title, and 124 homers certainly establish Lynn's offensive credentials.

This is a young player who plays defense as hard as he hits the ball, thinks nothing of making an impossible catch, and can run and throw with the game's finest defensive outfielders.

"I was a flanker back in college at USC," says the California center fielder. "It was routine to catch passes diving through the air. I am not concerned when I catch fly balls diving through the air."

Lynn's 1980 season ended with a .301 average, 12 homers, and 61 RBIs when he fouled a ball off his foot and broke his big toe.

"We had gotten within five games of first place when that happened," recalls manager Don Zimmer. "When we lost Lynn we were finished."

The handsome black-haired Californian had meant a great deal to the Red Sox offensively and defensively since joining them in the final days of the 1974 season.

Then he had one of the most incredible years any rookie ever had in 1975 with a .331 average, 105 RBIs, and 21 homers. That performance, as well as the miracles he performed daily on the field defensively, helped earn Lynn the

Most Valuable Player award and the rookie award in the same season, the only player so honored in the history of the game.

Except for a propensity toward injury, Lynn has probably been the most complete player in the American League for the last half dozen years.

Fredric Michael Lynn was born February 3, 1952, in Chicago, Illinois. He grew up in southern California and won a baseball scholarship to USC.

Lynn signed with the Boston Red Sox in 1973, played parts of two minor-league seasons, and joined the Red Sox in 1974. He was a regular in 1975 after hitting .419 in 15 games at the end of the 1974 season.

He then recorded that incredible rookie year in 1975, leading the league in runs scored with 103 and doubles with 47 while contending for leadership in all other batting departments.

The six-foot-one 185-pounder was a look-alike for teammate Carl Yastrzemski. He was not quite the home-run hitter Yastrzemski was (first American Leaguer to record 400 homers and 3,000 hits) but he was being favorably compared to the great Yankee center fielder Joe DiMaggio because of his batting prowess and fielding skills.

The left-handed hitter and thrower hit .314 in 1976 and slipped to .260 in 1977. He then bounced back with marks of .298, the .333 batting title, and then .301 in the injury-shortened season of 1980. He was traded to California early in 1981.

At twenty-nine, Lynn should just be hitting his peak, certain to contend for the batting title for the next few seasons and a man who can honestly be ~alled the most complete player in the American League today.

Pee Wee Reese

(1940–1958)

He was a marbles champion as a youth and earned the nickname of Pee Wee from the marble he used to win. He was often called the Little Colonel because of his small size and Kentucky background.

Mostly he was called the Captain, the leader of one of the best teams ever, the Brooklyn Dodgers of the late 1940s and early 1950s who seemed to have this habit of winning every year in the National League and losing every fall to the Yankees in the Series.

Roger Kahn wrote a book about those Dodgers after their playing days were over called *The Boys of Summer* and none of those talented players remained as fresh and boyish as did the Captain.

At five nine and 178 pounds, Pee Wee Reese still had that rich, pleasant voice of the South, those charming mannerisms, and that friendly greeting as he traveled the country at the age of sixty-one for the Louisville Slugger Bat Company.

When he played shortstop for the Brooklyn Dodgers, he was simply the best there was, an effortless fielder, a marvelous clutch hitter, a great lead-off batter, and an inspirational player.

Probably no greater example of Reese's leadership came than in the early days of Jackie Robinson's Dodger career. Robinson, baseball's first black, was undergoing enormous pressures when the man from Louisville walked over to him on the field, put his arm around Jackie's shoulder, and advertised for all the world to see that Jackie was a teammate and a pal.

Harold Henry "Pee Wee" Reese was born in a Louisville suburb of Ekron

on July 23, 1918. He was a successful high school baseball player despite his size and was signed by the Boston Red Sox.

The Red Sox were managed by Joe Cronin, who was still an active short-stop, and Cronin decided he would play awhile longer and didn't need this talented kid around as competition. The Red Sox sold Pee Wee to Brooklyn.

He joined the Dodgers in 1940, batted .272 before fracturing his heel in a slide and missing the rest of the season, and anchored the team at shortstop in 1941, the first pennant-winning season in Brooklyn since 1920. Reese batted only .229 that season but was such an effortless shortstop, and so clever with his bat control, that he was an asset to the team regardless of his average.

He batted .255 in 1942 and then missed three seasons with Navy service. He hit .284 in both 1946 and 1947. The Dodgers won again in 1947, starting a streak of six pennants in the next eleven years and three near misses.

Pee Wee hit .309 in 1954, his only .300 season. His career average was .269 and he hit 126 homers in sixteen years. He led the league in scoring one season and always finished high in hits and doubles. He recorded 2,170 hits in 2,166 games.

Reese went on to Los Angeles in 1958 with the Dodgers, soon became a coach, and then retired to work for the bat company.

His finest Dodger moment came in 1955 when Brooklyn, after seven tries (in five of which Reese played) finally won a Series, thereby beating the Yankees.

The last play of the Series was a grounder hit to Reese by Elston Howard. Reese fielded it and threw Howard out.

"You could see the grin on Pee Wee's face as soon as the ball was hit," said left-hander Johnny Podres, who pitched the victory.

No man deserved to smile more. Pee Wee Reese was one of the best players and nicest men I ever saw in baseball, a creditable candidate for inclusion among Baseball's 100.

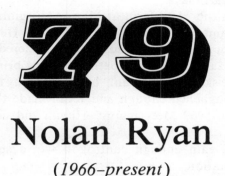

Nolan Ryan

(1966–present)

Only slightly better than a .500 pitcher, Nolan Ryan led the league in strikeouts seven times, holds the single-season mark with 383, has pitched four no-hitters, and may be the hardest thrower of all time.

A radar speed gun has timed Ryan as high as 101 miles per hour and there is no way, now, of measuring if that was faster than Walter Johnson, faster than Bob Feller, faster than Lefty Grove, the previous standards for pitching speed.

Ryan has had two 20-game seasons and two 19-game years, has led the league in innings pitched, has pitched over 300 innings twice, and is always capable of pitching a no-hitter and breaking that tie with Sandy Koufax as one of the only two pitchers with four each. Koufax had a perfect game among his four.

A perfect game for Ryan is impossible until he first pitches a nine-inning game without walking a man, a feat he has not yet been able to record in his long career.

"He is pleasantly wild," says Pittsburgh's Willie Stargell. "He can be wild enough just so that you don't take that little extra toehold against him."

Ryan has walked some 1,700 hitters in his career, but he has struck out over 3,000 and has a chance to pass Walter Johnson's 3,508 K's.

Lynn Nolan Ryan was born January 31, 1947, at Refugio, Texas. His father was a rancher and Ryan grew up outside the town of Alvin, Texas.

He was soon throwing baseballs against the barns and attracted attention with his pitching speed while he was still a gangling teenager.

245

In 1965 a New York Mets scout named Red Murff came to look at this local high school star. He noticed the big fast-ball and the skinny body. He liked the fast ball, but he wasn't sure of the body.

"I asked Nolan's daddy how big he was at the same age. He said he was just about like Nolan. That was good enough for me. He was now over two hundred pounds," Murff says.

Ryan began with the Mets farm at Marion, Virginia, and moved up to Greenville and Williamsport before joining the Mets. He was a quick attraction with his speed but also tended to suffer from blistered fingers. A cure was prescribed including salve and finger baths in pickle brine.

"It toughened the skin," says Ryan, "but it made my fingers smell awful."

Soon the skin toughened enough and Ryan made the Mets. He won a play-off game for the 1969 Mets against Atlanta and saved a World Series game.

He still couldn't gain enough control to win a spot in manager Gil Hodges's pitching rotation.

He was 6-9, 6-3, 7-11, and 10-14 in four inconsistent New York seasons. Then he was traded to California for third baseman Jim Fregosi.

He blossomed out West, winning 19 games his first year, 21 his next, and then 22. He led the league in strikeouts his first three AL seasons and established himself as the most feared pitcher in the game.

After a 16-14 season with California's winning 1979 team, Ryan played out his option and signed with Houston as a free agent. He agreed to a one-million-dollar-a-year contract for four seasons.

At Houston he had an inconsistent 11-10 season again, 200 strikeouts, struggled with control and injuries, but still managed to contribute mightily to the team's fine season.

Nolan Ryan may pitch a no-hitter any day he walks on the mound. A pitcher with that kind of skill deserves to be rated among Baseball's 100.

Jim Bunning

(1955–1971)

A winner of 100 games in each league, a pitcher with a perfect game to his credit, a 20-game winner in 1957 and a 19-game winner in four separate seasons, Jim Bunning was one of the toughest competitors the game has ever seen.

On June 21, 1964, Father's Day, this father of eight pitched a perfect no-hit, no-run game against the New York Mets.

When asked by a reporter why no Met hitter tried to break up his perfect game with a bunt, Bunning replied through a tightened jaw, "Would you like to try and bunt my fast ball?"

Bunning was a three-time strikeout leader with an intimidating pitching style. He would lean hard to his left side in his follow-through with his body nearly turned completely away from the batter.

Bunning was a hard-throwing right-hander with 2,855 career strikeouts against 1,000 walks. He was 224–184 in his career with some bad ball clubs. He never played on a pennant winner, which makes his career totals even more impressive.

He won 118 games in the American League and then won 106 in the National League, showing an almost perfect adjustment to his new opponents.

A tall, handsome man, Bunning was unsmiling and rarely saw anything amusing about his profession. He was not particularly well liked by press or public and even some teammates saw him as a hard, humorless man.

But he could throw hard, he was a fierce competitor, and he pitched professionally for more than twenty years.

James Paul David Bunning was born October 23, 1931, at Southgate, Kentucky. He pitched American Legion and high school baseball, attended Xavier University in Cincinnati, and signed his first professional contract with the Detroit Tigers in 1950.

Struggling with his control, Bunning did not make the Tigers until he had spent five years in the minors. He came to Detroit in 1955, slipped back to the minors in 1956, rejoined the Tigers that year, and was a winning pitcher for them in five of his next seven seasons including a 20–8 mark with a 2.69 ERA in 1957.

Detroit traded him to Philadelphia in 1963, where he won 19 games for three straight seasons, won 17, and finally slipped to a 4–14 mark.

Along the way he pitched the perfect game at New York's Shea Stadium, retiring the final batter, catcher John Stephenson, on strikes after seven straight foul balls on fast balls. He refused to offer Stephenson anything but his best as he labored for the perfect game.

When it was over he was still an unhappy man. "I didn't like the seats the Mets gave my family," Bunning said.

Bunning played for Pittsburgh and the Los Angeles Dodgers before being released by Los Angeles and signing again with the Phillies in 1969. He retired after a 5–12 season in 1971.

Bunning managed in the minors for the Phillies, did some coaching and scouting, but was always denied the opportunity to manage a big-league club, probably by owners who remembered his combative personality.

Always successful as a businessman in the off season, Bunning returned to his Kentucky home to work in the brokerage business. He later became an agent for baseball players.

One of the toughest pitchers to beat and one of the most intense competitors, Bunning belongs with Baseball's 100.

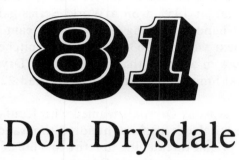

Don Drysdale

(1956–1969)

He may have thrown a spitter once in a while, but it was good old-fashioned blazing pitching smoke that made Don Drysdale the right-handed half of the Dodgers' dynamic pitching duo for half a dozen years in the early 1960s.

Teaming with Sandy Koufax, Drysdale won 20 games in two seasons and helped pitch the Dodgers to five pennants.

After Koufax retired following the 1966 season, the big handsome right-hander from California had one of the greatest years any pitcher ever had in 1968 when he recorded six consecutive shutouts and 58 scoreless innings.

He injured his shoulder accomplishing that feat, struggled through the rest of the season, and was forced to retire after a 5–4 season in 1969 and only 63 innings pitched. Drysdale had pitched 200 or more innings as the Dodger workhorse for twelve straight seasons. He was 209–166 lifetime.

Drysdale had a career ERA of 2.95 and led the league with a 25–9 mark in 1962. He also led the league with 314 innings pitched that year and 232 strikeouts. His strikeout high was 246 in 1960.

Always a shade behind Koufax in the esteem of opposing hitters, Drysdale was a much more difficult pitcher for hitters to face. He was wilder, was meaner, hit more batters, and thought nothing of throwing that spitter when he was in trouble. Koufax just threw an easy fast ball that nobody could hit, an occasional curve, and a once-in-a-while change.

Donald Scott Drysdale was born July 23, 1936, at Van Nuys, California.

A basketball and baseball player of note, he was signed out of high school by the Dodgers and sent to their Bakersfield, California, club in 1954.

Less than two years later he was with the Dodgers in Brooklyn, winning five games in 1956 and pitching regularly with a 17–9 mark in 1957.

All of the Dodgers slumped in 1958 under the glow of Hollywood's bright lights, and Drysdale was no exception. He was 12–13 but was 17–13 in the pennant-winning year of 1959, won a World Series game, and established himself as the right-handed pitching leader of the team.

The Dodgers next won in 1963 and Drysdale pitched a shutout against the vaunted Yankees in a Series that saw Koufax, Drysdale, John Podres, and Ron Perranoski limit the Yankees to 4 runs and 22 hits in a four-game sweep.

After two more seasons Drysdale teamed with Koufax in an off-the-field tandem that broke baseball's artificial hundred-thousand-dollar salary limit. Holding out together and threatening to retire to a life of sun and surfboards, Koufax won a $125,000 contract and Drysdale was paid $110,000. Salaries have continued escalating since with a 1980 top of one million a year for Nolan Ryan and a 1981 top of one and a half million for Dave Winfield of the Yankees per season for ten years.

Drysdale started having some arm problems after 1966 and was able to register his famed scoreless streak in 1968 before major arm problems slowed him down and finally forced him to quit at the age of thirty-three.

The big, easygoing (off the mound) six-foot-six 208-pounder immediately got into broadcasting, quickly took to that profession, and is now one of baseball's better announcers.

For one game against one right-handed hitter, Don Drysdale may have been up there with the best ever as a good bet, a big winner, a good guy, a fine pitcher with an honorable spot among Baseball's 100.

George Brett

(1973–present)

The excitement caused by George Brett in 1980 as he challenged the .400 mark is enough to include him among baseball's best hitters.

If that weren't enough, Brett appears at twenty-eight to be on the threshold of becoming the dominant hitter for the decade of the 1980s as Rod Carew was for the decade of the 1970s.

An old-fashioned hitter in the mold of Ty Cobb and Rod Carew, Brett uses the entire baseball field to spray singles, doubles, triples, and an occasional home run to every area of the field.

He has led the league in total hits three times in seven full seasons, won two batting titles, has hit over .300 five times, has never hit less than .282 for a full season, and also happens to be one of the finest fielding third basemen in the game.

The Kansas City Royals have won four divisional titles in Brett's seven seasons and his dramatic three-run homer tied the championship series against the Yankees in 1976 before Chris Chambliss untied it with a game-winning homer.

His huge three homer off Goose Gossage won the third game and the pennant in the 1980 championship series against the Yankees.

Brett may be the finest hitter in this decade and could easily win another three or four titles as his statistics accumulate.

George Howard Brett was born May 15, 1953, in Wheeling, West Virginia, into a family of four sons, all of whom became professional baseball players.

Older brother Ken was the youngest pitcher ever to pitch in a World

Series game when he pitched for Boston in 1967 at the age of nineteen years and twenty days.

It took George a little while longer to reach his maturity. After attending El Camino College in Torrance, California, George signed with the Kansas City Royals in 1971. He showed up in 1973 at Kansas City, started out in the minors in 1974, and won the third-base job on the big club by June of 1974.

Fielding smoothly, this good-looking blond six-footer, who weighed 195 pounds, also showed he was a hitter of note. Brett batted .282 in his rookie season of 1974, moved up to .308 in 1975, and won his first batting title in 1976 with a .333 mark. He beat teammate Hal McRae out by one point and opposing infielder Rod Carew of the Minnesota Twins by two points.

He hit over .300 in two of the next three seasons with much help from batting coach Charlie Lau of the Royals.

"I just helped him concentrate more on seeing the ball and hitting it where it was pitched," says Lau. "He always had all the ability in the world."

Brett shocked the baseball world in 1980 when he made a serious bid to be the first hitter to better the .400 mark since Ted Williams hit .406 in 1941. He ended the season hitting .390 and won his second batting title.

"I was glad to see him make that challenge," says Rod Carew. "There is too much emphasis in the game on hitting home runs. George just hits the ball where it is pitched and this might influence others to do the same."

Brett has 98 homers with a season high of 24, so he has more power than Carew, who has never hit more than 14 in any one year.

The handsome bachelor third baseman of the Royals is one of the finest young hitters to come along in years. A .400 season might still be in his future. His good try in 1980 and solid credentials earn him an honored spot among Baseball's 100.

Duke Snider

(1947–1964)

He could walk on walls chasing a fly ball at Ebbets Field. He could swing hard enough to wind himself up into a corkscrew. He could slam huge drives over the wall into Bedford Avenue.

Duke Snider hit 407 home runs in his career, collected 2,116 hits, knocked in 1,333 runs, and batted .295 from 1947 through 1964.

For all that he was probably best known as the left-handed hitter on an all-right-handed Dodger batting attack during the height of the Dodger years in Ebbets Field—as one of the famed Boys of Summer.

Snider was as intense a player as ever put on a uniform. His handsome face was covered by a thick head of gray hair before he was thirty.

Snider was also one of the most articulate baseball players of his time and felt unashamed to offer his opinions to any newsman who asked.

Once he was asked about the booing he was getting in his home park in Brooklyn from the angry Dodger fans.

"They are the worst fans in the world," Duke said, "they don't deserve a team."

The Dodger fans let Duke know what they thought about that the next day with the kind of sounds the Christians heard when the lions were chasing them.

Then Snider collected four hits and suddenly all Brooklyn was in love with the Duke of Flatbush.

Snider was a solid all-around player with tremendous power. He hit 40 or more homers five seasons in a row between 1953 and 1957 as the Dodgers won three pennants and one World Series, smashed 20 or more homers in ten of eleven years, hit over .300 seven times, led the league in runs scored twice, and tied once, led in homers once and RBIs once, and rated a shade behind Willie Mays in the judgment of New York fans in outfield defense.

Edwin Donald "Duke" Snider was born in Los Angeles September 19, 1926. He grew up on a fruit farm and was a noted high school pitcher and outfielder as well as a basketball player.

He was signed by the Dodgers in 1944, made it to Brooklyn in 1947, slipped back to the minors in 1948, and established himself as the Brooklyn center fielder in 1949. Snider hit .292 with 23 homers and 92 RBIs as the Dodgers won the pennant. He was overwhelmed by the Yankee pitchers in the World Series but came back in 1952 to hit .345 with four homers against those same Yankee pitchers.

Snider had his finest year in 1955 when he batted .309, knocked in 136 runs, and smashed 42 homers to help the Dodgers win the pennant again, and this time, miracle of miracles, they beat the Yankees in the World Series.

He was one of the few Dodgers to have a good year after the franchise shifted to Los Angeles in 1958, recording a .312 mark—though he lost much of his home-run potential with the odd-shaped Los Angeles Coliseum as a home field.

Slipping badly as a player, Snider was traded to the Mets under Casey Stengel in 1963 and finished out his career with the hated Giants in 1964.

He was the only Dodger to experience the loss of two pennant play-offs to the Giants—in 1951 and 1962. Snider remembered having said after the Bobby Thomson homer, "Thank God, I won't ever have to go through this again." Then he did eleven years later.

After retiring as a player he managed in the minors and scouted for the Dodgers before becoming a broadcaster with the Montreal Expos.

Snider was named to the Hall of Fame in 1980 and brought back sweet memories of the Ebbets Field Dodger days when he talked about Jackie and Campy and Pee Wee Reese and those other Boys of Summer.

He struck out a lot, he had some trouble with left-handers, but the Duke of Flatbush was a memorable player in the fabulous fifties, a well-respected member of Baseball's 100.

Red Ruffing

(1924–1947)

He played with the Babe and he played with Lou Gehrig and he played with Joe DiMaggio and he just missed playing with Mickey Mantle in a long and distinguished career with pieces of all of the Yankee dynasties.

Red Ruffing was a hard-throwing, competitive right-hander with a knack for putting a fast ball under a hitter's chin and a curve ball on the corner of the plate.

Just in case his pitching wasn't enough to ensure a Yankee win, Ruffing could belt the ball out of the park. He had a career batting average of .269 and belted 36 homers, many as a Yankee pinch hitter.

Ruffing won 20 games four years in a row for the Yankees from 1936 through 1939, the first team to win four World Series in a row. The only other team to record that feat was Casey Stengel's Yankees of 1949–53 with five in a row. Only Oakland with three in a row from 1972 through 1974 could come close to that mark.

Ruffing was 273–225 lifetime with a league-leading 21–7 in 1938. He also led the league in losses with 25 and 22 in two seasons with the Boston Red Sox.

The big, rawboned redhead stood six two and weighed 210 pounds at the height of his career. He had a blazing fast ball, a wicked curve, and excellent control.

He struggled early in his career with some bad Boston ball clubs, but when he came over to the Yankees in 1930, he really hit his stride.

Ruffing pitched on seven pennant winners with the Yankees and had a 7–2 mark in postseason play.

Charles Herbert "Red" Ruffing was born May 3, 1904 in Granville, Illinois. He wasn't much interested in school and soon left to work in the coal mines with his father and play on the local sandlot team. He suffered a serious accident and the loss of four toes when a coal car ran over his left foot.

Ruffing quit playing for a while. When he returned a year later and realized that his batting swing was affected by the accident, he subsequently switched to pitching.

He signed with Danville in the Three-I League in 1923, was bought by the Red Sox in 1924, and pitched regularly for them from 1925 through May of 1930.

Ruffing now became a winner with the Yankees as well as a hard worker who pitched over 200 innings thirteen years in a row. He won 19 games for the 1934 Yankees, fell to 16 in 1935, and then won 20 or more for the next four pennant winners.

He was 14–7 for the 1942 Yankees at the age of thirty-seven and surprisingly was drafted at the age of thirty-eight for three years during World War II.

Ruffing returned from service at forty to win seven games in 1945 and record a 5–1 record in 1946. He pitched with the White Sox in 1947 with a 3–5 record at the age of forty-two.

A burly man with dark eyes and thick hair, the square-jawed right-hander scouted and coached after his retirement, including a stint as the first pitching coach of the New York Mets under ex-Yankee manager Casey Stengel.

Ruffing retired after that season, was elected to the Hall of Fame in 1967 and shortly afterwards fell into declining health. He suffered a stroke that rendered him speechless but his loyal wife, Pauline, would accompany him to Hall of Fame reunions at Cooperstown.

"Charles understands everything you say," she would tell a visitor. "He appreciates your concern."

At seventy-five only the memories were left. They were quite substantial for a guy who could bust a hitter inside as well as anyone.

Luke Appling

(1930–1950)

Old Aches and Pains is what they called Luke Appling, the short-stop of the Chicago White Sox from 1930 through 1950. During those twenty years he played 2,422 games, 2,218 of them at shortstop.

This was a guy who couldn't seem to take the field without a bandage on his wrist, a tape on his arm, a headache or a bellyache from real or imagined ailments. Managers would listen to Luke complain, sympathize with him, appreciate his inability to make the game, and then put his name on the lineup card.

Complaining all game long, he would make every fielding play in the book, cover enormous amounts of ground, and rifle line drives all over Comiskey Park.

Appling hit .388 to win the 1936 batting title, the highest mark ever recorded by a shortstop, won the batting title again in 1943 with a .328 mark, and hit .300 in fifteen of his twenty big-league seasons.

His lifetime mark was .310 and his lowest mark as a regular was .262 in 1942. It was also the one year in his career that Appling hardly complained about any injury.

A shade under six feet and a sturdy two hundred pounder with black, curly hair, Appling was a friendly sort of guy who enjoyed the company of his teammates. He would often sit around hotel lobbies with them and talk baseball and in later years, as baldness gave him a new look, he often wore a hat in the lobby. When it was suggested he should take his hat off, Appling told his friends he was just getting ready to leave.

Appling was not a home-run hitter (45 career homers), so his true talents mainly went unappreciated during his playing years as he accumulated 2,749 hits and scored 1,319 runs. The White Sox never won anything in his time so he also missed out on a lot of national publicity. It did not stop voters from picking him for the Hall of Fame.

Lucius Benjamin "Luke" Appling was born in High Point, North Carolina, on April 2, 1909. He was raised in Atlanta, where he starred on his school baseball, football, and track teams. He was signed in 1930 by Atlanta, one of organized baseball's strongest independent franchises, and was sold to the White Sox at the end of that season.

Appling played in six games for Chicago in 1930 and won the regular shortstop post in 1931. He was not yet an accomplished infielder and not fully developed in height or weight at the age of twenty-one. He batted only .232 as a rookie and made 42 errors.

His hitting and fielding improved in 1932 and he had his first .300 season for the Southsiders in 1933. Cub fans had big stars and pennant races to cheer on while Appling soon became one of the few fan favorites of the White Sox.

His .388 batting title in 1936 quickly brought attention to Appling and his Aches and Pains image was locked into the minds of the fans as he started most interviews by saying, "I don't know how long I can talk to you because my [back, arm, shoulder, leg] hurts so much."

He continued to hit .300 regularly except for 1942. After another .300 season he was drafted into the Army and missed the 1944 and part of the 1945 season.

Appling, now balding, bent over, and complaining a mile a minute, hit .300 four more times before slipping to .234 in 1950 at the age of forty-one.

He retired as a player after the 1950 season, coached, scouted, and served as a hitting instructor for many years until he retired permanently to his Atlanta home.

At the age of seventy-two, Appling seemed to be more sprightly and to have fewer complaints than he had as a player. Old Aches and Pains proved that a career filled with ailments and injuries, real and imagined, could not keep a good man from Baseball's 100.

Eddie Mathews

(1952–1968)

The most devastating home-run punch in baseball history was not Babe Ruth and Lou Gehrig with a career total of 1,207 but the 1,267 compiled by a black Alabaman named Hank Aaron and a white Texan named Eddie Mathews.

Mathews hit 512 homers in his career for a ninth place tie on the all-time list with Ernie Banks. He won two home-run titles and he hit 20 or more homers for fourteen straight seasons.

Mathews had over 100 RBIs in five seasons and played over 100 games for sixteen seasons. His lifetime average was .271 but he had 2,315 hits and 1,509 runs scored in seventeen years.

Aaron and Mathews—the greatest home-run hitter ever was a right-hander and Mathews a left-hander—gave pitchers fits from 1953 through 1966 in Milwaukee and Atlanta.

They led the Braves to pennants in 1957 and 1958 and always seemed to be teamed as home-run and RBI leaders for many years.

"Playing with the Hammer definitely helped my career," Mathews said. "I usually batted behind Hank and if the pitcher got him out he was so tired from that effort he might make a mistake with me."

A powerful slugger with huge shoulders and arms, Mathews hit some of the longest homers ever seen in Milwaukee's County Stadium. Aaron was basically a line-drive home-run hitter with his effortless style while Mathews hit those huge, high drives.

Unlike many sluggers Mathews was also a marvelous fielder with a strong

throwing arm who could make the play from deep behind third base. He also played the outfield and first base adequately late in his career.

An extremely handsome guy with thick black hair—later thinning to a fringe—Mathews was a big hit with the fans and especially the ladies. He enjoyed a good time and could down a few drinks when the occasion presented itself, which was almost every day. It hardly seemed to bother his performance, as he was always ready to play.

Edwin Lee Mathews, Jr., was born October 13, 1931, in Texarkana, Texas. He was a high school pitcher and slugger and was signed by the Braves in 1949 after high school graduation.

He played in Atlanta for two seasons, played in Milwaukee, and joined the Braves in Boston in 1952. The franchise shifted to Milwaukee in 1953 and Mathews, who had batted .242 with 25 homers as a rookie, was joined by a skinny ex-second baseman by the name of Aaron. Soon placed in the outfield, Aaron and Mathews keyed the Braves attack for the next fifteen years.

Mathews batted .302 and hit 47 homers in his first Milwaukee season and was a hero everyplace he went.

"In those days we couldn't buy anything. You'd go into a store and they'd give you shoes and shirts and suits for free. You'd go into a grocery, fill up a bag and couldn't pay for it," he said.

Mathews had three seasons over .300, but he was basically a slugger who went for the long ball. He hit 40 or more homers four times.

Mathews moved again with the franchise in 1966 to Atlanta, where he had played as a minor leaguer, and was traded to Houston at the end of that season.

The personable, smiling, witty left-handed slugger then spent two seasons at Detroit, including the championship season of 1968, before hanging them up.

He was a batting coach and manager for the Atlanta Braves, was named to the Hall of Fame in 1978, and continued to be linked with Aaron as that great slugger's Hall of Fame time grew close.

A great home-run hitter, a fine third baseman, a good guy to have on a camping trip with you, Eddie Mathews deserves a place among Baseball's 100.

Pie Traynor

(1920–1937)

This will come as a terrible shock to all you granddads out there. Pie Traynor is number 87 of Baseball's 100 and Brooks Robinson is number 50. Bah, humbug. And bah, humbug to you, too, pops, because Brooks was better.

Pie Traynor was generally considered to be the best third baseman in the game's history, a fine fielder, a wonderful clutch hitter with seven seasons of over 100 RBIs, a lifetime .320 hitter, and the solid leader of the Pirates during the 1920s and early 1930s.

But Robinson was simply better. He was the best, the very best third baseman who ever lived, Pie or no Pie. He only had a .267 lifetime average but he had more hits than Pie, played six more seasons, led in fielding eleven times (Pie did it once), never committed more than 22 errors in one season (Pie led in errors five times) hit 268 homers to Pie's 58, played in four World Series to Pie's two.

Brooks was best, rates higher than Pie, but all this does not take away from Pie's own credentials for inclusion among Baseball's 100.

Pie Traynor was the dominant third baseman of his time, if not Brooks's time. A line-drive hitter with ability to hit to all fields, this moon-faced, pleasant six footer, who weighed 175 pounds, had ten seasons over .300 in accumulating his .320 lifetime average. He hit as high as .366 in 1930 (that was the year the ball was souped up and Bill Terry won the batting title with a .401 and Babe Herman didn't with a .393), never hit lower than .282 as a regular, and had five seasons over .330.

He hit .346 as the Pirates were beating the Washington Senators in the 1925 World Series and .200 as the Yankees were beating the Pirates in 1927.

Harold Joseph Traynor was born November 11, 1899, in Framingham, Massachusetts. His father was a printer and young Harold soon acquired the nickname of Pie as a regular eater of his mother's home-baked pies.

Like Yogi Berra and Babe Ruth, Pie Traynor got as much recognition because of his nickname as he did because of his hitting.

Traynor signed his first professional contract with the Portsmouth club of the Virginia league. His .270 average and fine fielding interested the Pirates, who purchased his contract and farmed him to Birmingham.

He came back in 1921 to establish himself as the regular Pirate third baseman for the next fifteen years and a favorite among the fans.

Traynor was a soft-spoken gentleman with intense dark eyes, a smiling open face, and a warm voice. He would often lean against the stands at Forbes Field and sign autographs for kids.

He was soon one of the most popular players on the team, especially in contrast to the famed Waner brothers, who were less patient with fans, especially Big Poison, Paul, who was often hung over before games and unavailable for small favors for fans.

In June of 1934 Traynor was named the manager of the Pirates, finished out that season as a player, played some in 1935, and stayed in the dugout all of 1936. He played five more games in 1937 and managed until 1939.

The Pirates kept him on as a scout and goodwill ambassador for the club for many years and he also did some local broadcasting.

He was elected to the Hall of Fame in 1948 and was a constant visitor at old-timers' days and Hall of Fame reunions until his death on March 16, 1972.

Old Pie Traynor was a fan favorite, a great third baseman, a tremendous player. He was not, I'm sorry, the best third baseman ever. See number 50 of Baseball's 100 for that fellow.

Dave Winfield

(1973-present)

He is so big, so strong, so awesome in appearance that Dave Winfield seems to be a better ballplayer than he really is. His numbers are impressive—not overwhelming—but the suspicion nevertheless is that he is approaching his peak at twenty-nine and could well compile some amazing numbers in the years to follow.

Winfield is capable of a Triple Crown season, capable of a home-run and RBI title (he led the league in RBIs with 118 in 1979) and so capable of some marvelous feats in the outfield that he deserves inclusion among Baseball's 100.

He has never won a major award yet but he has only played with the terrible San Diego Padres and that may have kept him down. He will certainly be more productive as a twenty million dollar Yankee.

"When you play for a club that is in last place or struggling to stay out of last place, you don't have much incentive," he says, "especially late in the season."

Winfield may have the strongest arm in the game today—only Dave Parker could argue with him about that—he may be the fastest runner in the game for a man his size, and he may be able to hit a ball right-handed as far as anybody who ever played the grand old game.

There are days when Winfield seems to be the greatest all-around player the game has ever seen. Unfortunately those days do not come often enough.

David Mark Winfield was born October 3, 1951. He was probably the finest all-around athlete ever seen in his hometown of St. Paul, Minnesota,

and won a scholarship to the University of Minnesota in three sports. He was drafted in the football, baseball, and basketball drafts in 1973 and chose baseball because it offered more security and longevity.

"I guess my favorite sport was football with basketball next and baseball third," he says. "I just felt I would last longer and go further in baseball."

The handsome, mustachioed six-foot-six-inch 220-pounder joined the San Diego Padres in 1973 directly off the campus of Minnesota. He was placed in their outfield and told to play.

With no professional experience he batted .277 and hit three homers in 56 games. Then he batted .265 and hit 20 homers in his second season.

In 1977 he hit his stride with 25 homers and a .275 mark. He then had two seasons over .300.

Winfield, an articulate, intelligent young man, also understood his impact on his fans. He saw a relationship between his team, his town, and himself, and was willing to contribute part of his salary for the use of kids who were invited to his games as his guest.

"I'm hoping to give back some of the things I've taken from the game," Winfield says.

As his peak years approached, Winfield could be on the threshold of some remarkable seasons. I think that will happen and I want to be the first to say I told you so.

For that reason Winfield is among Baseball's 100. Just because he is strong enough to crush a can with a pinky has no bearing on his selection. None, none, none.

He is also wealthy enough with his ten year twenty million dollar package from George Steinbrenner's Yankees to buy that team. It won't happen.

Winfield would rather give a lot of his money back to the kids of the Dave Winfield Foundation, a group he has organized to help underprivileged youngsters.

89

Phil Niekro

(1964–present)

Bob Uecker, the broadcaster, comedian, and former baseball player, was once asked if knuckle balls are difficult to catch. Uecker, because he couldn't hit, was always the catcher assigned to catch knuckleballers.

"A snap," said Uecker. "All you have to do is let them roll to the backstop and pick them up after they stop rolling."

Phil Niekro has made some catchers cry in his twenty-one seasons of professional baseball, but he has also made a lot of hitters cry and managers (his own) laugh.

Niekro has the most devastating knuckle ball in baseball today, a pitch which has kept him in the Braves pitching rotation for sixteen years.

"Early in my career managers wouldn't let me throw it," Niekro says. "They said it wasn't a good pitch and besides, they didn't have enough catchers willing to catch it."

The knuckle ball can dip and dance and dodge a batter or a catcher like a baseball with a will of its own.

"I don't usually know where it's going," Niekro says, "so the batters don't know where it's going."

Surprisingly, Niekro has registered 2,500 strikeouts to 1,200 walks, so his knuckle ball has been tougher on hitters than on catchers.

Niekro has three 20-game seasons, has led the league in innings pitched four times, and has a no-hitter over the San Diego Padres.

Philip Henry Niekro was born April 1, 1939, in Blaine, Ohio. He grew up on a farm and was soon playing baseball for the town teams with his brother, Joe, who was five years younger.

"Sometimes I would catch, sometimes Joe would catch, and all the time we would throw the knuckle ball," Phil says.

He was advised against the crazy pitch in high school because sixteen-year-old catchers simply can't handle knuckle balls. Not too many twenty-six-year-old catchers can, either.

In 1959 the Braves signed Niekro and sent him to Wellsville in the New York-Penn League. He was twenty years old, a sturdy six one and 180, and had a decent fast ball. They thought he could win with it. Niekro knew better.

Used mostly as a relief pitcher, Niekro failed to impress the Braves. He was not brought to the major leagues until 1964 and did not become a starter until 1967.

After he showed that his knuckler could be a potent weapon, Niekro was finally given the green light to use it. He won 14 games in 1968 and was 23–13 with the division-winning 1969 Braves. He would never win fewer than 12 games again. He would also lose 20 games twice, as much because he was hit as because his catchers couldn't catch.

Thin faced, laconic, a tough competitor, Niekro was still going strong in 1981 at the age of forty-two, and with the knuckle ball an easy pitch to throw with little arm strain, he might be a pitching grandfather.

He has accumulated 233 wins and a lot of people are in the Hall of Fame with less. For all his victories and for making the knuckle ball respectable in this generation, Phil Niekro deserves his spot among Baseball's 100.

Catfish Hunter

(1965-1979)

On a snowy New Year's Eve in 1974, a husky, handsome young man, wearing a sport jacket and slacks and a New York Yankee cap for the first time, signed a contract for $3.75 million for five years, the highest player contract ever signed.

Catfish Hunter was a Yankee and the era of huge salaries would be on in full force with dozens of players becoming instant millionaires after playing out their option year and selling their services to a new club.

Hunter was the first and the most expensive of the modern-era free agents, and that was fitting because he was also the first pitcher on the scale of active American Leaguers when he made that move across country from Oakland to New York.

Hunter was the anchor on the good ship Charles O. Finley, that craft that sailed the seasons smoothly as the best in the West and the best in baseball during the early 1970s.

He won 224 games, lost only 166, won the Cy Young award in 1974, had five 20-game seasons in a row, pitched 234 innings or more for ten straight seasons, won the ERA title once, led in percentages twice, and struck out 2,012 hitters while walking only 954.

The A's won three straight World Series titles—only the Yankees had ever done that and they did it twice—and Hunter was the key pitcher on the club each year.

Never the possessor of a blazing fast ball, Hunter could throw hard

enough to intimidate hitters but made control, change-ups, a good curve, and all-around pitching smarts as important a part of his arsenal as his fast ball.

He had that knack of seemingly being easy to hit while winning, but if he was tied or in a one-run late-inning game, he was suddenly impossible to hit. Hunter—like Robin Roberts before him—didn't mind winning 7–6 if he could win. It was a lot better than losing 1–0.

James Augustus Hunter was born on his daddy's peanut farm in Hertford, North Carolina, on April 18, 1946. A playful kid and lackluster student, Hunter soon took to sports and was an outstanding high school pitcher. The Kansas City A's came around to scout him one summer. That winter Hunter shot off the large toe on his right foot. Scout Clyde Kluttz reported to owner Charles O. Finley that Hunter was still able to pitch and was still worth the seventy-five-thousand-dollar bonus.

After signing with the A's, Hunter spent one season not pitching in Daytona Beach as Finley tried to hide the youngster from other clubs. In 1965 he joined the A's and was 8–8 as a nineteen-year-old rookie.

Hunter was called Jimmy by his friends but Finley wanted something more colorful. He asked him his hobby and when Hunter replied, "Fishing, mostly for catfish," Finley renamed him Catfish.

"Whenever anybody called Catfish from the stands," Hunter says, "I knew they didn't know me."

Finley also tried to get Vida Blue to change his first name to True Blue, but that didn't work.

Hunter was not a big winner until 1970 when he was 18–14 with the A's after the franchise shifted to Oakland.

His only pitching trouble seemed to be home runs (he gave up a record 374 in his career), but when he wanted to turn it on he could, as evidenced by a 1968 perfect game against the Minnesota Twins.

Oakland won the divisional title in 1971 with Catfish at 21–11 and won the World Series three seasons in a row after that with Hunter winning 20 games each year.

After the 1974 triumph it was discovered that his contract had a loophole and could be thrown out; so Hunter became a free agent. After all clubs made huge bids, he signed with New York, whose scout, Clyde Kluttz, had originally signed him.

"He was a good friend of mine," says Hunter of the late scout. "Anytime a man is a friend and you hunt with him, you learn to trust him. You can't go out in the woods with a man with a gun unless you trust him."

Hunter won 23 games for the Yankees in 1975 and was 17–15 with the first Yankee pennant winner in a dozen years in 1976.

He helped the Yankees to championships in 1977 and 1978, was bothered by arm trouble in 1979 with a 2–9 record, and retired.

He went home to Hertford, raised his peanuts, planted his soybeans, coached his son's Little League team, and showed up for spring training as an extra coach.

At thirty-five, still a husky 195-pounder with a six-foot frame, Catfish seemed capable of winning the close ones. First he would give up a couple of homers and strike out the key hitter just for fun.

A dominant pitcher in the 1970s, James Augustus Hunter, Charlie Finley's Catfish, is a solid citizen among Baseball's 100.

Jim Kaat

(1959–present)

One of the few players whose career spanned four decades, Jim Kaat won his first game in 1959 and might win his three hundredth around 1982. He is still going strong in 1981 at the age of forty-two.

"I take care of myself," says the lanky left-handed pitcher with the herky-jerk motion. "If you watch what you eat, watch your habits, get proper rest, do proper exercises, you can hang around this game a long time."

The six-foot-four-and-a-half-inch left-hander they call Kitty Kaat has won 20 games three times, had fifteen seasons in a row with ten or more wins, has struck out some 2,400 hitters while walking only a thousand, led the league in innings pitched once, and had more than a half a dozen comebacks after being written off as washed up.

Kaat was sort of the modern-day Walter Johnson, pitching well for a bad Washington-Minnesota team, sneaking into one World Series with them and losing as often as he won simply because he played with a bad ball club.

Kaat pitched over 200 innings in twelve of thirteen seasons and was in 25 or more games in nineteen seasons. If longevity were tossed out as a criterion, Kaat would still earn a spot among Baseball's 100 for his effortless pitching, his incredible control, and his all-around baseball skill.

One of the finest fielders at his position the game has ever seen, Kaat was also an excellent bunter and competitive hitter until the DH came into the American league. He continued his fine hitting ways after moving over to the National League.

Kaat's pitching trademark was a fast ball on the hands, excellent control,

and an ability to throw as few as eighty or ninety pitches in a nine-inning game. Regardless of the weather he always pitched without shirtsleeves, a tribute to his stamina and youth, regardless of his advancing years.

James Lee Kaat was born November 7, 1938, in Zeeland, Michigan. He was a basketball and baseball star in high school, won a scholarship to Hope College in Highland, Michigan, and signed with the Washington Senators in 1957. He made it to the big club in 1959 with an 8–8 season at Chattanooga.

He had his first big year after the franchise shifted to Minnesota in 1961 and was renamed the Minnesota Twins. He was 18–14 with a bad ball club. He was 18–11 with the pennant-winning Twins of 1965.

In 1966 Kaat won 25 games, lost 13, and led the league in innings pitched with 305. He was twenty-eight, but after a change of pitching coaches (Johnny Sain was his favorite) he did not win 20 games again for the Twins.

His next 20-game seasons came in 1974 and 1975 for the White Sox after they allowed him to pitch on a four-day rotation again.

The White Sox decided he was finished at thirty-eight and traded him to the Phillies. In his first National League season, 1976, Kaat was 12–14, then 6–11 as a spot pitcher and 8–5 as a relief pitcher in 1978.

The Phillies gave up on him in 1979 and he went to the Yankees.

In 1980, without a contract, he won a job with an impressive spring training, then was released after the Yankees ran into a roster problem.

He soon signed with the Cardinals, won his first game in his fourth decade, and was being counted on for 1981.

At forty-two Kitty Kaat still had the body of a younger man, the head of an older one, and the admiration of many fans who have been watching him finesse hitters since 1959.

Joe Gordon

(1938–1950)

A rare breed among baseball players, a second baseman with power, Joe Gordon could hit, run, field, and throw. He was the middle man in that smooth Yankee championship infield, first with Frank Crosetti as the shortstop and then with his little partner, Phil Rizzuto.

Gordon was the Most Valuable Player in the American League in 1942, batted .322 that season, had eleven seasons in a row with 10 or more homers, and smashed 253 homers in his career. Rogers Hornsby, the all-time second base leader, had only 302. Gordon had four seasons with over 100 RBIs, an incredible offensive figure for a second baseman.

After helping the Yankees win five pennants, Gordon was traded to Cleveland in one of the most celebrated deals of the time for pitcher Allie Reynolds.

The Yankees lost the pennant in 1946 to Boston and decided they could not win without another pitcher. They offered Gordon to the Indians and were given the choice of several Cleveland pitchers in return. General manager Larry MacPhail consulted Joe DiMaggio.

"Get Reynolds," DiMaggio said. "He has always given me the most trouble."

Gordon went to Cleveland in 1947, batted .272, and then batted .280 in 1948 in helping the Indians to their first pennant in twenty-eight years.

He teamed with manager-shortstop Lou Boudreau, the 1948 MVP, to give the Indians one of the most devastating offensive second-base combinations in baseball history.

Joseph Lowell Gordon was born February 18, 1915, in Los Angeles, California. In 1936 he was signed by the Oakland Oaks of the Pacific Coast League, hit .300, and was purchased by the Yankees. They sent him to Newark, where he batted .280 and hit 26 homers for the 1937 Bears, considered by many observers the greatest minor-league baseball team of all time.

In 1938 he was ready for the Yankees and was the steady guy in the infield for the next seven years on some great clubs led by Joe DiMaggio, Charlie Keller, Tommy Henrich, Bill Dickey, and Spud Chandler.

After finishing up in Cleveland, Gordon managed and played in the Pacific Coast League again, scouted, coached, and managed in the big leagues with Cleveland, Detroit, and Kansas City. He also worked as a batting coach before his retirement.

The slightly built five-foot-ten-inch 170-pounder could generate exceptional power and had fine form as a slugging right-handed hitter. In later years, under a hot spring sun, a bald-headed man now, Gordon was still working with young kids.

When he died in 1978, Joe Gordon was still considered the best all-around second baseman the Yankees had ever had and one of the best of Baseball's 100.

Ferguson Jenkins

(1965–present)

He was taken so matter-of-factly throughout his long and distinguished career that a drug charge, lodged against him in 1980, caused people to examine his records for the first time. What they found was one of the most consistent pitchers of the last two decades.

Ferguson Jenkins, a tall, soft-spoken Canadian, had his bags checked as they arrived on a flight into Toronto in 1980 after he had departed without them from the airport. The examiners found drugs and Jenkins was charged with possession. While the case was being investigated, Jenkins was suspended by Commissioner Bowie Kuhn, a ruling later overturned, and the right-hander lost several precious starts on his march toward 300 career wins. He pleaded guilty and was let off without punishment.

At thirty-seven, if the embarrassment over the drug charge does not block his path, Jenkins seems a good bet to record that exalted number.

He has had seven 20-game seasons, six in a row, and has had only one losing season since becoming a 20-game winner in 1967 with a 20–13 mark.

It was Jenkins's misfortune to spend most of his career with the Chicago Cubs, a team that has gone the longest in baseball history, thirty-five years, without winning a pennant.

Pitching most of his career with poor second-division clubs, Jenkins was a model of efficiency and consistency, winning 149 games and losing 109 in the National League and winning over 100 games in the American League, one of baseball's rarest feats.

Jenkins was 24–13 with a league-leading 325 innings pitched for the 1971

Cubs. He won the Cy Young award. He has never come close to a World Series, so his record does not indicate how good he could be in postseason play. It is enough to say he has been a consistent winner in both leagues going back some fifteen years.

Ferguson Arthur Jenkins was born in Chatham, Ontario, Canada, on December 13, 1943, son of the town's rarest of citizens, a black farmer.

Jenkins played ice hockey and baseball as a youngster and was signed by the Philadelphia Phillies in 1962. He had a good fast ball, excellent control, and a good changeup which encouraged the Phillies to give him a chance in 1965.

In 1966 he was traded from the Phillies to the Chicago Cubs, home of Wrigley Field, day baseball, and choke-up teams.

In 1969, under manager Leo Durocher, they choked under the stress of nine-and-a-half-game lead, blew the pennant to the Mets, and saw their last chance for a pennant fade into the Chicago sunlight.

"I think the day ball was a factor," Jenkins says. "The Cubs got tired in the heat of playing every day while other teams called off at night."

Jenkins continued to excel while the Cubs didn't. In 1973 he was traded to Texas, was 25–12 in his first American League season, and pitched in Boston in 1976 and 1977. He went back to Texas in 1978, finishing 18–8 and 16–14 in his next two seasons. He was 12–12 in 1980 to bring his career-record to 259–194.

Ferguson Jenkins should make that 300 mark and deserves a spot among Baseball's 100. Here's betting that he gets it.

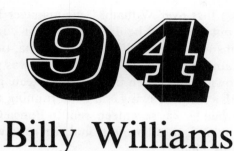

Billy Williams

(1959–1976)

From September 22, 1963, through September 2, 1970, Billy Williams was in the lineup of the Chicago Cubs for 1117 consecutive games, a league record. For most of those games Ernie Banks was also in the lineup.

Banks was the bouncy shortstop and later first baseman of the Cubs, one of the game's steadiest players, one of the most dramatic home-run hitters, and a personality of unlimited ebullience.

Williams was lost in the shadow of the bigger man on the North Side of Chicago, just playing and hitting and being unnoticed for nearly fifteen Chicago seasons.

When he was gone and you looked it up, Billy Williams turned out to be one of the most consistent hitters of his time, a 1972 batting champion, a five-time .300 hitter, a guy with 426 homers, a 200-hit man in three seasons, a 100 RBI man in three seasons, a man with thirteen seasons with 150 games or more. He batted .290 over eighteen seasons.

Williams was tall and thin at six foot one and a half and 170 pounds, but he had such quick wrists and timing that his line drives rocketed off the bat. He was a left-handed line-drive hitter who was dangerous against lefties as well as righties.

"I tried to pull a pitch when it was inside," he says, "but I would go with it if it was away. I took what they gave me."

Playing in Wrigley Field, playing day baseball, Williams was one of the few Cubs of his time not to complain about the rigors of fighting off the hot

291

Chicago sun. He was a southerner, used to heat, and just went out every day and did his job.

Unlike his flamboyant teammate, Banks, Williams was a soft-spoken man with a gentle voice and a slow, careful way of speaking. He was friendly and pleasant but never seemed to get the kind of attention from the press most of his teammates did.

"Nobody makes a fuss over Williams," his manager Leo Durocher said, "you just stick him out there and he does the job for you every day."

Billy Leo Williams was born in Whistler, Alabama, on June 15, 1938. He came from a large family, money was tight, and he was playing semiprofessional baseball on town teams when he was still a teenager.

Tall and thin with a whippet swing and good running speed, Williams was signed by the Cubs when he was seventeen, sent to Ponca City, Idaho, for two seasons (he hit .310 in his first full professional year) and was soon moving up the ladder of the Cubs' chain.

He arrived in Chicago in 1959, hit .323 with their Houston farm in 1960, hit .278 as a regular in 1961. Two years later he began his consecutive-game streak as the Chicago left fielder.

He hit .312 in 1964 and .315 in 1965. In 1972, at the age of thirty-four, he won his only batting title.

After the 1974 season he was traded to Oakland and helped the A's win their fifth straight division title in 1975 with 23 homers, 81 RBIs, and a .244 mark. His best homer season was 1970 with 42.

He was released by the A's in 1976, stayed out of baseball for a year, and returned as batting instructor and coach with the Cubs.

Quietly, efficiently, and steadily, Billy Williams hit line drives all over National League parks for more than a dozen years.

Quietly, efficiently, and steadily, he has earned his spot among Baseball's 100.

Tony Oliva

(1962–1975)

Tony Oliva had the most amazing talent I have ever seen in base-ball. He could throw his bat at baseballs and hit line drives. It used to drive Yankee manager Ralph Houk wild.

Houk would order his pitchers not to give Oliva, a famed Yankee-killer, a good ball to hit. Several times he would order Oliva walked or pitch out on him while he was up and a Minnesota teammate was running.

Oliva would send the bat flying in midair, watch it make contact with the ball, and see a line drive fall past the infield for a hit.

The tall, rangy left-handed hitter might have become one of the finest batters of all time if not for two weak knees which gave out on him early in his career and forced him to play in pain for many seasons.

In pain or not, he was a marvelous hitter with incredible bat control and an utter disregard for whether the pitcher was left-handed or right.

Oliva had a lifetime mark of .306, won three batting titles, hit .300 seven times, never batted lower than .291 in his first eleven seasons, hit 219 homers, and was the hit leader in five seasons. He had 217 hits as a rookie in 1964, won the batting title, and led the league in runs scored and doubles.

He was an average fielder but an excellent base runner. He played in one World Series and two championship series for the Twins, hitting .385 and .500 in his two championship tries.

Antonio Oliva Lopez was born July 20, 1940, in Pinar del Rio, Cuba. He came from a large family of sugar cane workers and games were played in the fields after work.

He was signed by the Twins in 1961 and was one of the last Cuban players allowed out of the country after Fidel Castro took over. His family remained behind in Cuba and he felt constantly alone as he couldn't rescue them.

He hit .410 in his first minor-league season and .350 in his next one. The Twins brought him to Minnesota in 1962, farmed him out for most of the 1963 season, and brought him up to play left field in 1964.

Oliva responded with one of the finest all-around seasons since Joe DiMaggio was a Yankee rookie in 1936. He was quickly recognized as one of the finest young hitters to come along in years.

He won two batting titles back to back in 1964 and 1965 and helped the Twins to their first pennant in the latter season. The Dodgers held him to five hits in the Series, one of the major reasons for Minnesota's defeat.

Oliva came back in 1966 to hit .307 but began having serious knee problems. He continued playing regularly through 1972, when his knees finally gave out following two operations. Oliva had been an excellent bunter and base stealer and those skills disappeared after the knee surgery.

Fortunately, the American League adopted the DH rule and Oliva was no longer forced to play the outfield on sore legs.

He batted .291, .285, and .270 on his bad knees before being forced to quit at the age of thirty-five.

When he was young and could run, Tony Oliva was one of the finest hitters ever seen in the game. He compiled a lifetime .306 mark and it is not extravagant to think it might have been 30 points higher if his knees had been sound.

Still, .306 for fourteen seasons is nothing to sneeze at. In fact, it's something to applaud in this day and age and recognize with a spot among Baseball's 100.

Johnny Mize

(1936–1953)

One batting title, four home-run titles, a lifetime average of .312, and a late career as one of the most potent pinch-hitters of all time still hasn't gotten Johnny Mize into the Hall of Fame.

The Big Cat was one of the most feared hitters of his time, a huge, dour, hulking man with a ferocious swing and a competitive nature that frightened teammates and opponents alike.

Mize played with some of the best baseball teams ever, the Cardinals in the 1930s and the Yankees in the 1950s.

He was part of Casey Stengel's early Yankee dynasty with five World Championships in five years, a never-equaled feat.

Mize was not a particularly likeable fellow among his teammates and the press, certainly a strong reason for his absence now from the Hall of Fame. He was a bit of a braggart, mean and overbearing at times, and a second-guesser.

"We were facing Carl Erskine in the World Series," teammate Billy Martin remembers, "and Erskine was setting a World Series strikeout mark. He was getting us out on that sinking curve ball and Mize got on us by telling us to lay off the low ones. Then he batted as a pinch hitter, struck out, and I screamed, 'Lay off those low ones.'"

Mize hit the low ones and the high ones a country mile with 51 homers in 1947 to tie Ralph Kiner for the league lead, 40 in 1948, 43 in 1940, and 28 in 1939. His career home-run total was 359.

He led the league in RBIs three times with a high of 138 in 1947 and also led the league in runs scored in 1947 with 137, a rare feat for a number-four hitter.

Despite his bulk, Mize was a smooth first baseman. He stood six two, weighed 215 pounds at his peak, and got over 240 pounds late in his career as a Yankee pinch hitter.

John Robert Mize was born January 7, 1913, in Demorest, Georgia. He was scouted in high school and signed by the St. Louis Cardinals. His rookie season of 1936 saw the Big Cat—a name hung on him by an admiring reporter early in John's career—bat .329 in 126 games. He played eight games in the outfield that season but never played anyplace but first base and hitter after that.

A strong left-handed hitter and right-handed thrower, Mize had a surprisingly tight swing with rapid bat movement and much grace as he went after his pitch. Unlike a lot of sluggers, he could hit the curve ball almost as well as he hit the fast ball.

He won the batting title in 1939 with a .349 mark, won the home-run title with 28, and failed to win the Triple Crown by 20 RBIs with 108 to Cincinnati first baseman Frank McCormack's 128.

Mize won the RBI and home-run titles the next season but this time hit only .314 to Debs Garms's winning .355.

Mize was traded to the Giants in 1942, reached his home-run peak of 51 in 1947 in the short porch of the Polo Grounds right field (the team hit 221 homers), and went over to the Yankees in 1949.

Casey Stengel used the big fellow as a pinch hitter, occasional relief first baseman, and extra coach on the bench for his knowledge of pitchers.

Johnny Mize was one of the best sluggers in the game. The Hall of Fame voters may have missed his act but I haven't. He still scares me even now in retirement at sixty-eight as he comes back for old-timers' days.

"You a sportswriter?" he asks. "The sportswriters kept me out of the Hall of Fame."

Not me, Big Jawn. I always voted for you. I vote for you again for Baseball's 100.

Mark Belanger

(1963–present)

His lifetime average is .228. He has 19 home runs in his career. He has batted under .200 in four separate seasons and he once batted .186 with 53 hits as the regular shortstop for the Baltimore Orioles.

What in the world is this Punch and Judy hitter doing with the big guys? Did you ever see him field a ground ball? That's what he's doing here.

Defense has long been the stepchild of baseball, an ignored skill that has been minimized at the expense of the more dramatic homer. This is an attempt to remedy that ridiculous attitude.

When the New York Mets were first formed in 1962 the first player they selected in the player draft was a catcher named Hobie Landrith. He wasn't much of a hitter, either. Why Landrith?

"Because if you don't have a catcher," Casey Stengel answered logically, "you have a lot of passed balls."

If the Orioles didn't have Belanger they would not have had six championships and two World Series titles in his time.

On a team that never had great offense, the Orioles won on pitching and defense in the late 1960s and 1970s. Jim Palmer provided much of the pitching. Mark Belanger provided much of the defense.

A tall, rangy, skinny guy with dark eyes and a sunken chest and skinny arms, Belanger made shortstop play an art form. He was smooth, easy to watch, and effortless as he chased ground balls behind the bag or deep in the hole, raced after pop-ups over the infield, or pulled his pitcher out of a jam with a good tag play on a steal.

The left side of the Baltimore infield for many years consisted of Mark Belanger and Brooks Robinson and hitters were shattered by their gloves time after time after time.

Mark Henry Belanger was born in Pittsfield, Massachusetts, on June 8, 1944. He started playing baseball in Little League as a pitcher and soon gravitated to shortstop with his strong arm. He attended Tampa University and was signed by the Orioles in 1965 out of school. He played his first professional season in Bluefield and batted .298. Even an .045 mark in eight games in a higher classification at Elmira didn't frighten the Birds. Belanger came to Baltimore in 1963.

By 1968 he was the regular shortstop and won three fielding titles, but his real value lay in the way he covered ground.

The Orioles won their first title under Earl Weaver in 1969 with Belanger playing 150 games and batting a resounding .287. He would never do anything like that again.

Soon he was settled in his pattern as the finest fielder in the game and one of the weakest hitters. He could still bunt, hit behind the runner, and rarely struck out.

He led the league in assists three times—an indication of how much ground he swallowed up—and was still playing well, if occasionally, for the 1980 Orioles.

Mark Belanger was the finest fielding shortstop of his time and that part of the game deserves to be recognized. He carries the banner for all the weak-hitting infielders who made pitchers look good.

Try winning a game without a shortstop. Not too many passed balls but a lot of hits. He has earned his spot among Baseball's 100.

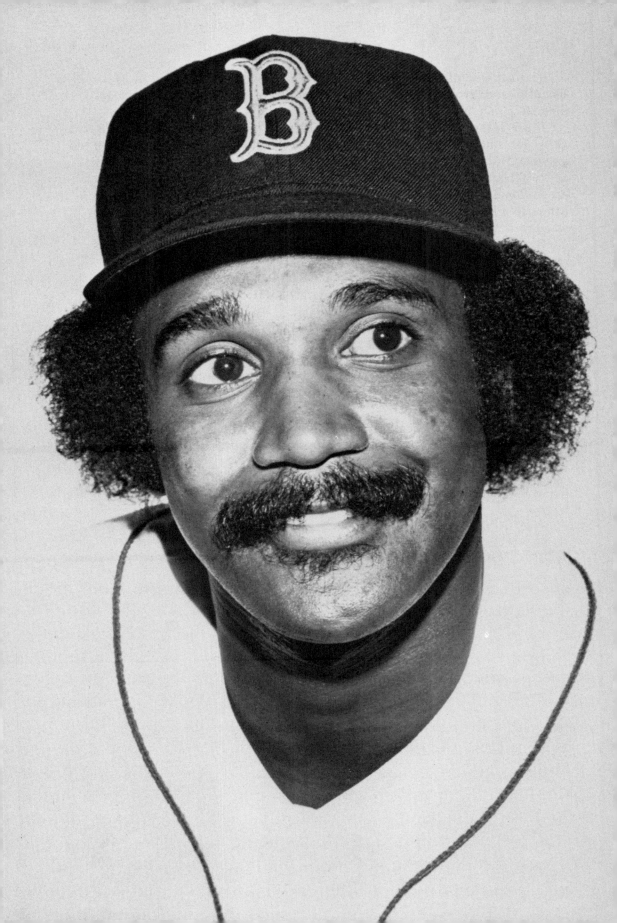

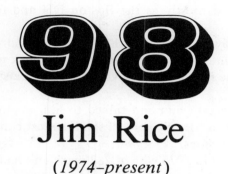

Jim Rice

(1974–present)

The Yankees won the pennant in 1978 after one of the most dramatic baseball seasons ever, including a play-off in Boston with Bucky Dent's famous homer, Carl Yastrzemski's famous pop-up, and Jim Rice's famous fly ball.

It was probably the only important time all that season that Rice didn't hit a ball off the wall or over it, didn't make a dent in the Fenway Park wall, and didn't thrill Boston fans.

The fly ball came just before Yaz's game-ending pop-up as the Yankees won the division title. It still could not keep Rice from the Most Valuable Player award in one of the most productive offensive seasons any player has ever had.

Rice won the home-run title with 46, won the RBI title with 139, batted .315, scored 121 runs, led the league with 213 hits, and played every one of his team's 163 games.

Rice has hit .300 in four of his six seasons with the Red Sox, has averaged more than 33 homers a year for six seasons, has accumulated over 1,000 hits faster than any player in his time, and is considered the most powerful slugger in the league.

Rice also was the first player to be paid nearly a million dollars a year when he signed a seven-year contract for more than five million dollars.

James Edward Rice was born in Anderson, South Carolina, on March 8, 1953. He was an outstanding baseball, football, and basketball star in high school and was soon being coveted by pro baseball coaches and college basketball and football coaches.

He chose baseball and signed with the Red Sox in 1971. He spent his first season at Williamsport, Pennsylvania, moved up through the Boston system, and made it to Fenway park in 1974. He batted .269 in 24 games.

In his rookie season of 1975 Rice hit .309 and knocked in 102 runs with 22 homers. He was used mostly as the Boston DH and found that cause for distress.

Rice is a perfectly coordinated athlete of two hundred pounds on a six-two frame. He is a intense, brooding man with a thick mustache and square jaw. Unless someone is a personal favorite, he can be silent and unpleasant with the press.

"I've become close to him and talked to him about that," says Boston coach Johnny Pesky, a friendly sort. "I think he just concentrates so hard he hasn't time for the niceties."

Rice slumped a bit in 1976 with a .282 mark and had another fine season in 1977 with a .320 average, 114 RBIs, and 39 homers.

As the Red Sox jumped off to a 14-game lead in 1978, Rice carried their offense. Then he slumped and they slumped, falling out of first in the final two weeks of the season and hanging onto tie the Yankees at the end. Then they lost the play-off on one of Boston's darkest days.

Rice had another big season in 1979 with a .325 mark but was slowed in 1980 by a bad wrist. He still hit .294 with 24 home runs.

At twenty-eight Rice could be on the threshold of half a dozen big seasons. As a right-handed hitter in Fenway Park, every time at bat is a potential homer.

This is one of the toughest hitters around. One of the toughest guys, too.

Don Sutton

(1966–present)

Never a spectacular strikeout pitcher, never an incredibly hard thrower, never even a winner of 20 games in more than one season, Don Sutton is still one of the steadiest pitchers.

Sutton was 21–10 in 1976, and has won 19 games twice and 18 games once. For fifteen seasons he has given the Los Angeles Dodgers a chance to win every four or five days when he is on the mound. Now he will try and do the same for the Houston Astros.

At thirty-six he has an outside shot at 300 wins and has pitched in three championship series, three World Series, and four All-Star Games.

Sutton started the 1977 All-Star Game at Yankee Stadium. It was the realization of a dream.

"When I was a kid growing up in Florida," he says, "I used to dream about playing for the Yankees. I used to see myself on the mound at Yankee Stadium and see myself striking out the best hitters in the game."

Sutton finally saw that dream come true as he stood on the Stadium mound. It was no less thrilling than he'd predicted it would be.

"It feels exactly as I imagined," he said. "It is just overwhelming to look out there at all those monuments of famous players and know I have played here."

Sutton was born April 2, 1945, in Clio, Alabama, and grew up in Florida. He had come from a religious family and played baseball on many church teams.

The Dodgers signed him in 1965 and brought him to Los Angeles in 1966

where he was a pitching teammate at twenty-one of Sandy Koufax and Don Drysdale.

He was 12–12 as a 1966 rookie, was 11–15 in 1967, slipped back to Spokane in 1968 before rejoining the Dodgers, and then had ten winning seasons in a row. Sutton has pitched over 200 innings for twelve straight seasons.

Steady, unspectacular, and a good guy, Don Sutton has earned his spot among Baseball's 100 as one of the most consistent pitchers of all time.

He turned down a huge Yankee offer as a free agent and signed with Houston for four million dollars for four years. He may just be the extra pitcher they need to beat the Phillies in the championship series this time around.

Roger Maris

(1957–1968)

The greatest single-season home-run hitter of all time. Period. Asterisk or no asterisk from Ford Frick. Babe Ruth never hit 61 homers in a year. Willie Mays didn't do it and Hank Aaron didn't do it.

Roger Maris did in 1961 under the most enormous pressure any ballplayer has ever been subjected to. That alone entitles him to recognition among Baseball's 100, but there is a lot more to Maris than that.

He was the league's MVP two years in a row, he hit 275 homers in twelve seasons, he twice led the league in RBIs, he led in homers once, and he was one of the best right fielders of his time. In 1964, when Mickey Mantle got hurt, he moved to center field and helped the Yankees win another pennant.

Maris never hit for high average—.283 was his career high—and he had a lifetime mark of .260.

A blond six-footer who weighed 205 pounds, Maris wore his short hair in a crew cut, was a quiet sort of fellow, and was always in the shadow of Mantle, that era's most popular Yankee.

In 1961 Maris held his head high and defied incredible pressures as he chased Ruth. Commissioner Frick decreed he had to hit 60 homers in 154 games rather than in the newly lengthened season of 162 games to earn the record.

"A season's a season," Maris said.

While old-timers attacked him and fans wrote hate mail because he was gaining on the lovable Babe's record, Maris continued hitting homers.

He got his fifty-ninth in game 154, just missing his sixtieth as he drove for the record.

Then he got Baltimore right hander Jack Fisher for number 60 on September 26 and Boston rookie Tracy Stallard on October 1, 1961, for the record-breaking sixty-first homer.

"I don't feel bad about it," said Stallard. "He got a lot of other pretty good pitchers before he got me."

He led the Yankees to a runaway pennant in the confusion and did the same thing the next year.

Roger Eugene Maris was born September 10, 1934, at Fargo, North Dakota. He was an outstanding football player and baseball star.

The Cleveland Indians signed him in 1953 and brought him to the big club in 1957. He batted only .235 with 14 homers and was traded the next season to Kansas City.

The Yankees brought him to New York in 1960 and he hit .283 with 39 homers and 112 RBIs.

He hit his first homer in game eleven of the 1961 season and continued hitting homers all year as he drove for the record.

After finishing off his record season, he hit 33 homers in 1962 ("Only 33," fans said) and had 100 RBIs for the third straight season.

He injured his hand in a slide the next season and the Yankees said he was malingering when he didn't play.

He lost heart with that kind of treatment and was never the same player again. He had taken so much press abuse and so much public abuse and was finally traded to the Cardinals in 1967. He helped them win two pennants and then retired.

Maybe there were better hitters than this lefty with the grooved swing and better outfielders and faster runners. But Roger was a complete player, modest to a fault and an honest if not particularly warm fellow.

Anyone who saw him perform under stress in 1961 remembers what a thrill it was. I'm not ashamed to include the greatest single-season home-run hitter of all time in Baseball's 100. Even if he is the bottom man.

10 Honorable Mentions

1. Shoeless Joe Jackson
2. Harry Heilmann
3. Early Wynn
4. Richie Ashburn
5. Hoyt Wilhelm
6. Joe Medwick
7. Lefty O'Doul
8. Orlando Cepeda
9. Gil Hodges
10. Luis Aparicio

They'd all belong if this were a book of Baseball's 110. Jackson, even though he was caught in the Black Sox scandal, was a .356 lifetime hitter before he was kicked out of baseball. Heilmann, O'Doul, Medwick, and Ashburn were all high-average hitters. Hodges and Cepeda were sluggers, Aparicio was the premier American League shortstop of his day, and Wilhelm, even though his head tilted sideways, was the best relief pitcher of his time with the meanest knuckle ball.

10 Best Left-handed Hitters

1. Babe Ruth
2. Ted Williams
3. Stan Musial
4. Ty Cobb
5. Lou Gehrig
6. Tris Speaker
7. Mel Ott
8. George Sisler
9. Rod Carew
10. Mickey Mantle

Sure, Mantle was a switch hitter, but left-handed he was better than right-handed because he saw more right-handed pitching. He probably was a better home-run hitter right-handed because he hit a high pitch and didn't do that left-handed. Casey Stengel used to say he was "blind up there."

How would you like to be a right-handed pitcher facing this bunch? Johnson, Mathewson, and Feller might have challenged them.

10 Best Left-handed Pitchers

1. Lefty Grove
2. Sandy Koufax
3. Babe Ruth
4. Warren Spahn
5. Whitey Ford
6. Rube Marquard
7. Sparky Lyle
8. Carl Hubbell
9. Herb Pennock
10. Tug McGraw

Fooled you on the Babe, didn't I? He was 94–46 as a pitcher with a 2.28 ERA and 17 shutouts. I still think Mays and Aaron were better all-around players. The other pitchers were all starters except for Lyle and McGraw. Pennock won 240 games. McGraw may not be the best relief pitcher of all time (then again he may be), but he is certainly the most dynamic, emotional and entertaining. Ya Gotta Believe he belongs here with these big left-handers and may move up if he keeps performing as he did in the 1980 World Series.

10 Best Right-handed Pitchers

1. Walter Johnson
2. Christy Mathewson
3. Grover Cleveland Alexander
4. Bob Feller
5. Dizzy Dean
6. Tom Seaver
7. Jim Palmer
8. Bob Gibson
9. Burleigh Grimes
10. Bob Lemon

Nobody could touch Johnson and Mathewson on a good day. The rest were almost as good. Nolan Ryan may have thrown harder than any of them, but he was not the complete pitcher the other guys were. If I had one game to win tomorrow, I'd have to pick Seaver. He is still at the top of his game. I'd hate to lose a game with any of them.

10 Best Right-handed Hitters

1. Rogers Hornsby
2. Hank Aaron
3. Willie Mays
4. Joe DiMaggio
5. Roberto Clemente
6. Jackie Robinson
7. Hank Greenberg
8. Al Kaline
9. Johnny Bench
10. Pete Rose

Hornsby was the best right-handed hitter ever. Aaron was the best long-ball hitter ever. Mays, best all-around player, is only third-best hitter. DiMaggio and Clemente earn high spots and Jackie is here because if there is anybody on with all these home-run guys, I want him up to knock them in. Wipe your hands dry, Jackie, and slap a double to left. Rose is here because he is a right-handed slap hitter of reknown.

10 Best Managers

1. Casey Stengel
2. Joe McCarthy
3. John McGraw
4. Walter Alston
5. Sparky Anderson
6. Leo Durocher
7. Billy Martin
8. Danny Murtaugh
9. Johnny Keane
10. Connie Mack

Casey was the best. He admitted once after a win, "I never coulda done it without my players," but he done it with flair and excitement. Billy Martin has to rate because he does it all over. Keane is here because he handled the Cardinals so beautifully in 1964, moved to the Yankees and lost with class. Losing isn't anything but it's nice when it's done with style. When Keane pitched Bob Gibson in the World Series on short rest when he had other rested pitchers, he was asked why and replied, "I had a commitment to his heart." A man like that belongs with the best. Mack proved you can be successful managing a ball club if you own it, if you have the players.

Murtaugh proved managing can be fun, and rarely has a manager enjoyed a win as much as Danny did in 1960. He smoked two cigars at one time to celebrate.

10 Best General Managers

1. Larry MacPhail
2. Bill Veeck
3. George Weiss
4. George Steinbrenner
5. Hank Peters
6. Bob Howsam
7. Branch Rickey
8. Al Campanis
9. Buzzie Bavasi
10. Connie Mack

MacPhail brought the Dodgers back from the dead. Veeck made baseball interesting in four places. Weiss won without spending money. Steinbrenner never had the title, just the power as he ran his Yankees back into a dynasty. Peters keeps Baltimore winning. Howsam built the Big Red Machine. Rickey built the farm system. Campanis has the Dodgers winning and drawing three million every year. Bavasi got the Brooklyn Dodgers a pennant and the California Angels a contender. Mack built his team over three different times.

10 Best Defensive Infielders

1. Brooks Robinson
2. Mark Belanger
3. Luis Aparicio
4. Marty Marion
5. Phil Rizzuto
6. Gil Hodges
7. Ferris Fain
8. Pee Wee Reese
9. Billy Cox
10. Nellie Fox

Robinson was the best ever at third. Belanger is the best ever at short. Aparicio, Marion, and Rizzuto were all terrific with the glove. Hodges could play first base like a shortstop. Ferris Fain did wonders on a bunt play. Pee

Wee Reese was incredibly steady at the position. Cox was a marvelous third baseman with a rocket arm. He could count the stitches on the baseball and still throw you out. Fox was a great fielder and double-play pivot man.

10 Best Defensive Outfielders

1. Willie Mays
2. Jimmy Piersall
3. Terry Moore
4. Joe DiMaggio
5. Roberto Clemente
6. Pete Reiser
7. Curt Flood
8. Tris Speaker
9. Carl Furillo
10. Al Kaline

Willie didn't invent center field. He just played it as if he did. Piersall was a great outfielder who could kick an obnoxious fan in the butt and catch a fly ball at the same time. Moore was as smooth an outfielder as ever played. DiMaggio's only weakness was a relatively short career (thirteen seasons) and a dead arm at the end. Clemente was incredible in right but center fielders are more important. Reiser might have been one of the greats in everything if he hadn't attacked walls with his head. Flood, famed for his challenge at baseball's reserve clause, was a marvelous center fielder. Never saw Speaker. They tell me he was Joe D. He wasn't Willie. Furillo, next to Clemente, was the best right fielder I ever saw. Oooh, that rifle arm. Kaline was not spectacular. Just near perfect.

10 Best Baseball Parks

1. Ebbets Field
2. Fenway Park
3. Veterans Stadium
4. Dodger Stadium
5. Crosley Field
6. Wrigley Field
7. Astrodome
8. Yankee Stadium
9. Anaheim Stadium
10. Milwaukee County Stadium

Ebbets Field was warm and wonderful, small and stylish. The fans were part of the game. I can still see those Old Goldies into Bedford Avenue. Ask your dad what that means. Fenway has the Green Monster and so much drama. Philadelphia's Vet is the best new park of all. And I love the Phillies Phanatic. Dodger Stadium is Hollywood, all gold and glitter and clean and antiseptic and has so many beautiful people. Crosley Field in Cincy was intimate and funny with that hill in left. Wrigley Field has great home runs and Bleacher Bums. The Astrodome is a wonder, a great place when its 110° outside. Yankee Stadium lost something in remodeling but still is awesome and impressive. Anaheim is clean and neat and I love the Angels' Big A. Milwaukee is fun, easy access, well kept, old fashioned.